Peace, Order and Good Government

TO MARY

PETER J. T. O HEARN, Q.C.

Peace, Order and Good Government

A NEW CONSTITUTION FOR CANADA

1964

THE MACMILLAN COMPANY OF CANADA LIMITED

TORONTO

© *Peter J. T. O Hearn 1964*

Printed in Canada

Contents

Acknowledgments

Many Canadians probably share the opinions expressed in this book but my views are not necessarily to be imputed to those who helped me with it. Some of them, in fact, were quite ignorant of what I was doing. To all, in the words of the noblest of prefaces, 'it is truly worthy and just, right and worthwhile, to give thanks'.

To my dear wife, especially for a peaceful and loving home, maintained with courage and patience in endless pain. To my brother Walter for his care, encouragement, and many valuable suggestions. To Mr. J. W. Bacque, of Macmillan's, particularly for reducing the text to readable size and shape. To Mrs. V. J. Pottier for gracious help in revising a French version of the Articles. To Dean W. A. MacKay of Dalhousie Law School and to my brother Donald for their encouraging response to the original text. To the reference room staff of the Halifax Memorial Library for digging out facts so cheerfully and to Mr. Dal Warrington of Canadian Press for lending me material distributed at the November 1963 Federal-Provincial Conference. To the late Mr. Justice V. C. MacDonald, whom I affectionately claim as kinsman, friend, and teacher of constitutional law. His interest in this book was real but his illness deprived me of the benefit of his comments.

It might embarrass some others to be thanked in a polemical

book such as this and so I will omit their names. It took many years to write it and memory is fallible. If, as is likely, I have omitted to mention others to whom I am indebted, I beg their indulgence and assure them of my gratitude.

Peace, Order and Good Government

Introduction

The purpose of this book is to propose certain changes in the Canadian constitution, chiefly in language, but also in matter and essential form. Here the word *form* is used in its ancient sense of individual essence or principle of structure and operation. Much of what follows is concerned with the mere shape of the constitution, how it is worded, what paragraphs it is divided into, what the sentences are called, and the like, but there is also a definite aim to bring about a number of desirable and indeed necessary changes in the way we Canadians govern ourselves. These changes go to the very nature of the constitution, and would amend not only the way it reads but the way it works.

To do an intelligible job it will be necessary to state what the constitution is, how it got to its present state, and why changes are to be desired. But this does not purport to be a scholarly restatement of Canadian constitutional law; it is propaganda in favour of certain specific reforms. Any apparatus of reference is designed to let the non-legal reader consult the sources if he wishes, and may also serve as some slight shield against the experts. The book should not be judged as a contribution to learning but to life and politics.

Canadian constitutional law is an extreme case of judicial lawmaking. It is more or less difficult to form an opinion of the outcome of any untried question in other fields of law, but in

1

this field it is virtually impossible. No doubt this is somewhat inevitable: no field is more political, more subject to change of current emphasis, and in consequence more needing to be adapted to the times. But in Canada, the language, the structure, and the political principles embodied in the chief law, the British North America Act, 1867, have imposed upon the courts an undue share of the navigation of our national course. The courts have tried to act with the best interests of the country in mind, but the result has lacked clarity and has failed to engender confidence. So this book first took shape, sixteen years ago, as a protest against the uncertainties of the law, and that protest continues to be a major objective.

A few years after it was first written there was a fresh outburst of constitutional interest among the people most concerned, that is, lawyers in and out of government. A Dominion-Provincial tax conference was proposed, and this proposal led to the idea of a re-allocation of taxing powers. This in turn would require a change in the B.N.A. Act. Naturally, this revived the discussions that had taken place in the '30s about how to achieve constitutional amendment by an all-Canadian process without recourse to the British parliament. Around the same time, Senator A. W. Roebuck proposed a bill of rights in the Senate, as an addition to the B.N.A. Act.[1] In such an atmosphere the present book took a definite shape and was completed, although not in its latest form. Things were looking up.

But the great tax conference got nowhere. Mr. St. Laurent, the prime minister, finding he could not get a collective agreement with the provinces, decided to negotiate individual tax settlements. Meanwhile, to strengthen his hand and to impose his own preference for what is called a 'flexible, organic type of constitution', he secured from the British parliament a very drastic amendment to the B.N.A. Act[2] which stripped that instrument to less than the bare essentials. This 1949 (No. 2) Amendment is very different from its predecessors: it permits the parliament of Canada to 'amend the Constitution of Canada' except for a small list of important matters. This is a power so wide and unrestricted that no lawyer would care to put any definite limit to its meaning. Indeed, it was Mr. St. Laurent's avowed intention to get in the field of federal government the same power that the provinces already have to alter their own constitutions: this the provinces can do, except as relating to the office of lieutenant-governor.[3]

It is an incidental purpose of this book to show that this federal power is not desirable except within straiter limits than the amendment provides. The amendment was probably necessary, as a measure of practical policy in order to bring the question to the fore, but the ultimate answer should be more stringent.

The bill of rights was not accepted by the government and was not enacted; indeed it has been said that some members of that administration considered the bill an occasion of mischief. As time passed it became apparent that there would be no need for some time for a Dominion-Provincial tax conference and hence no fulcrum on which to lever the reforms that had seemed so imminent so short a while before. We were again in the doldrums: short periods of activity punctuate long stretches of lethargy in the history of Canadian constitution-making.

After years of latent ferment culminating in many political changes, the constitutional brew again began to boil. The significant causes appear to be three:

Firstly, the prime minister, Mr. Diefenbaker, long a champion of the individual and of the underdog, introduced a bill of rights in the Canadian parliament in 1958 and again, in revised form, in 1960.[4] The subsequent act[5] is unique in that it is an interpretation act, that is, a guide to the courts on how to read and apply the laws. In thus approaching the subject, Mr. Diefenbaker adopted a course that the courts themselves took in the last few centuries – a quite successful course from which precedents of value yet remain. And the act is thus, to some extent, a code: that is, a restatement of the existing law. One possible course for the courts to pursue is to interpret it as only a code and so not intended to change the existing law.[6] This possibility is causing some alarm to those who look to the act for more fundamental effects; such a course is not inconsistent with its mode of expression, and there will certainly be a tendency to restrict the operation of the act to the scope of the stated freedoms as they have existed.

The bill was criticized because it did not deal with rights within provincial jurisdiction and because it was not proposed as a constitutional guarantee but as an ordinary statute which the parliament can amend or repeal at any time. It is not quite clear why Mr. Diefenbaker took the tack he did, knowing, as he would, the kind of objections that would be raised. Possibly he did not wish the bill, which was a very personal matter, to become too contentious. Perhaps he felt that constitutional entrenchment was premature or would prove too inflexible. Or possibly he cast his bread upon the waters, willing to let the bill grow into as mighty an instrument as parliament or the people should demand.

A second cause of increased interest in the problem of constitutional amendment was the activity of the Senate. When the government of Canada proposed a humble address to the British parliament to alter the B.N.A. Act so as to require superior court judges to retire at a fixed age, the Senate balked. The debates made much of the indignity of the process but there was much stress also on making amendment possible in Canada, from start to finish.

Again, in the 1961 session of parliament the Senate refused to pass a government bill to fire Mr. James Coyne, governor of the Bank of Canada, without giving him a hearing. This was the occasion of strong, if somewhat vague, threats of Senate reform, but one suspects that people on the whole supported the Senate on this occasion.

The third cause was the Dominion-Provincial Tax Conference, 1960, and in particular the proposal of Quebec Premier Jean Lesage that the allocation of tax sources should be redetermined by the constitution and that the process of amendment should be wholly Canadian.[7] This gave quite an impetus to the movement, as Quebec, under the Duplessis régime, was an adamant foe of any constitutional change.

It is also probable that another contemporary movement gave added force to the constitutional one. From 1960 to 1963, two N.D.P. members of parliament, Mr. Frank Howard (Skeena) and Mr. Arnold Peters (Timiskaming) waged very bitter filibusters in the Commons against the passage of divorce bills. The purpose was to unload divorces on some court as it was a manifest waste of the time of the Senate and House of Commons to act as a court of domestic relations. But since these divorces originate from Quebec and Newfoundland only, it has naturally occurred to a great many members and others that it is anomalous that Dominion jurisdiction over Marriage and Divorce[8] should exist merely to give dissident Québecois and Newfoundlanders an escape from the legal morality of those provinces. The evident and simple solution, as Senator J.-F. Pouliot has suggested,[9] is for the Dominion to vacate the field, but this would require a constitutional amendment.

Finally, a formula for constitutional amendment in Canada was drafted following on the proposal of Premier Lesage. This, the Fulton Formula, is the work of representatives of the various attorneys-general in Canada and at this writing it has not been subjected to any extensive public criticism or even consideration.

At first sight it is an appallingly complex formula and holds promise of being even more appallingly rigid in operation. It is certainly not the kind of thing that children can memorize, although it might be good exercise in mental agility for them to try to construe it. In short, it is meant for lawyers only, and in its present terms it is designed to entrench forever the existing principles of constitutional structure with one important exception. The exception is a new power to delegate legislative functions between Dominion and provinces, which is spelled out with detail, precision, and care, but also with a patent conflict with the present text – a conflict that will add one more net of constitutional categories to the equipment of the lawyer who fishes this pond. It could be an open season for the pedants.

The principal aim of this book is to propose a renewal, a rebirth, of the constitution of Canada, not indeed as a revolutionary departure in all things from the existing structure but as a sign and a sacrament of the completion in Canada, by Canadians, of our own foundations of government.

For this is the crux of the matter: if the plans at present to the fore are accomplished, the result will be fundamentally new, actually, if not in appearances. Full and final control of our own processes of government will be for the first time vested in us in theory as well as in fact. In discarding legal subordination to the British parliament (not, of course, to be confused with allegiance to the Crown, which remains unaffected) we shall be starting a new legal life, and this is coupled with an important practical consideration. For the first time a definite means of changing the constitution will be determined by law rather than by custom and convention.

To commemorate this great change, it is just and proper that the constitution be new also in organization and structure. Not indeed radically different: there is no need or demand for that. But it is time that the debris of Imperial Statutes, Royal Instructions, Orders in Council, and the battered hulk of the British North America Act and its train of amendments be replaced by a clear, concise, readable instrument, 'made in Canada', containing the essentials of the law of Confederation and designed for efficient and just government in modern conditions.

In other words the fundamentals should be sought out and propounded in a document accessible to all, teachable to the youth of the nation, comprehensive yet compact, expressed in a distinct manner in dignified but understandable language, so that the people will have a charter that they can know, understand, and cherish. In a word, the importance of the constitution demands that, if possible, it should attain legal *elegance*.

Such a clearing away of the present jungle of enactments need not destroy any good that has been achieved to date. It would rather be the carefully chosen fruit of the past constitutional experience.

But another reason for clearing the ground and re-building is that some things do need to be changed. The years have made it quite plain that the original establishment was made on a mistaken basis in many instances. The powers and duties of the governments were not wisely distributed in every case and especially with regard to commerce, domestic relations, and taxation. To these initial misconceptions have been added the judgments of the Privy Council, which to some extent altered the original purpose and balance of the B.N.A. Act (largely, but not altogether, to the aggrandizement of provincial powers), but whose most serious contribution lies in their modification of the original scheme of mutually exclusive jurisdiction. This scheme has proved fallacious in concept and should be abandoned.

In the years around 1867 it was thought that a firm line of demarcation could be drawn between Dominion and provincial powers and that subjects for law-making could be placed on one side or other of this line with little or no difficulty. Thus, John A. Macdonald (later Sir John A.) said in February 1865, in the debate on the Quebec Resolutions in the Provincial parliament of Canada:

> We have given the General Legislature all the great subjects of legislation. We have conferred on them, not only specifically and in detail, all the powers which are incident to sovereignty, but we have expressly declared that all subjects of general interest not distinctly and exclusively conferred upon the local governments and local legislatures, shall be conferred upon the General Government and Legislature. We have thus avoided that great source of weakness which has been the cause of the disruption of the United States. We have avoided all conflict of jurisdiction and authority. . . . [10]

The years since have amply revealed the difficulty of avoiding such conflicts quite apart from the fundamental frivolity of the idea of the division of exclusive powers between the legislatures. This scheme is known in legal circles as the 'watertight compartment' doctrine[11] and has been much execrated of late because it prevents delegation of authority between the governments. In 1950, the Supreme Court of Canada decided that the legislature of a province cannot give the parliament of Canada power to make laws concerning a matter that is within the exclusive jurisdiction of the provinces.[12] Perhaps the better statement of the proposition is that Canadian legislatures resemble statutory corporations and differ from common-law corporations (and, by analogy, the Imperial parliament) in this: they cannot exceed the powers given them by statute, and therefore they cannot receive or exercise powers not given them by the B.N.A. Acts. Probably the major premise of the decision is that fundamental changes should not be brought about by ordinary legislation and, although change by delegation would not be immutable, it would be profound and drastic.

In the result, the 'watertight compartment' doctrine should be in ill favour with those who want to effect wide legislative changes. Strangely enough, however, it seems not to have been critically examined in essence. No one seems to have said 'Is it necessary?'. No one seems to have proposed a distribution of functions on another basis that is sensible and workable; some indeed may have done so, but no such proposal would appear to have attracted the attention of the constitution-makers. The Fulton Formula, the plan of constitutional amendment worked out by the representatives of the attorneys-general of Canada, purports to keep the exclusive-powers basis but to work around it by a peculiarly laborious and complicated process of legislation. It is extremely odd that the preservation of exclusiveness should be considered so important; it is not operative in other federal constitutions such as that of Australia or that of the U.S.A.

This book will put forward an alternative scheme with the reasons for preferring it. It will be the most important of the changes proposed. But these changes are built into an edifice the materials of which are taken from the existing law and custom of the constitution. There is no radical departure from those foundations that have remained firm, but on them there is erected a new temple having unity, truth, worth, and, in a measure or so the author hopes, beauty, in place of the scarred and shaken monuments of past legislation.

CHAPTER 1

What is a constitution?

The word 'constitution' is used with several different meanings of which four only need concern us. The four meanings are distinct but allied. In the first sense, the constitution of a state is its supreme law or theory of government. In the second meaning, it is the body of laws that are considered of basic importance and to which all other laws and institutions are, by law or custom, subordinate. Since such laws usually define the structure and functions of the essential organs of government, the third sense of 'constitution' denotes these structural laws. And in the fourth meaning, a constitution is the body of laws (whether basic or not), conventions, and institutions that make up the government of the state, that is, the structure and organization of the state.

In the first sense, that of supreme law, the constitutions of many states can be expressed quite succinctly. For instance, the fundamental law of Great Britain is the supremacy of parliament, which means that parliament can make any law (except one that binds future parliaments) and law so made is supreme. Parliament can bind even itself by changing its structure or procedure. In 1911, the British parliament deprived one of its parts, the House of Lords, of its absolute power to stop legislation and thus governed future parliaments.[1] This could be reversed, of course, and so could practically any other change, so that it is said parliament cannot bind itself.

States with 'rigid, written constitutions' may be based on theories of government fully as simple as those of the 'flexible, organic constitutions'. Italy and the United States have written constitutions, but in each case the supreme law is the one that regulates the amendment of those documents. The French Republic has had several written constitutions, but the theory of government and manner of amendment do not deviate too far from British practice. On the other hand, the Roman Republic had a flexible, organic constitution, but it would be very difficult indeed to express its supreme law in a few words.

The second sense of 'constitution', as the body of basic laws to which institutions and other laws are subordinate, is a wider and more useful one than the first. Such laws are usually also supreme and fundamental ones, and in this second sense, if it is restricted to laws that are both basic and supreme, the constitutions of Australia, France, Germany, Ireland, and the United States (and of nearly all states, other than Great Britain) are superior in kind to and override the ordinary laws of the legislatures. The legislatures also are subordinate to these superior laws and usually cannot alter them in the normal course of legislation. Canada has such a constitution.

As previously noted, basic, superior laws usually deal with the organization of the government of the state in its principal divisions and with the limits within which the divided functions are exercised. The third meaning so expressed is probably the usual one outside of the British Commonwealth. Within the Commonwealth the emphasis is on the fourth meaning, despite the number of written constitutions involved, because of the pre-eminence of the parliamentary theory of government and because the second and third meanings of 'constitution' are not as suitable for dealing with the political facts in Great Britain as is the fourth. In this fourth and widest meaning, 'constitution' is defined by MacRae as consisting

> . . . of institutions and rules; by institutions meaning such things as Legislatures, Courts and Governments (including various departments and agencies of executive government); by rules meaning rules which have to do with the form, functions and powers of such institutions.[2]

It is apparent that no limit can be given to such a concept. It may be coextensive with what is called public law as opposed to private law (which deals with relations between private persons). It may take in more than law. Conventions – that is, rules having no sanction enforceable in a court – are held to be an important part of the British constitution. One such convention is that the Crown acts only on the advice of its ministers. Another is that the government 'falls' on a vote of lack of confidence and must call for an election or hand over to another ministry.

The fourth definition of 'constitution' is not suitable for the purposes of this book, for we are not concerned with conventions but with the *necessary, desirable,* and *essential** fundamental laws of a federal structure of government.

The constitution, then, as considered in this discussion, is the supreme law of the land defining the fundamentals of government and delimiting the functions of the principal institutions. An occasional departure from this usage need not cause any confusion as any instance of that kind will usually be explained by the context.

*For a discussion of the use of these three terms, see page 53.

CHAPTER 2

What is the constitution of Canada?

The fundamental law that establishes the government of Canada and of the provinces is the British North America Act. It is not the only law to be considered, but it is the main one, and it is usually what is meant when we refer to the Canadian constitution in a restricted or a popular sense.

The British North America Act (commonly called the B.N.A. Act) is not a single act but a series of statutes. All these statutes, except an amendment to Section 51 of the B.N.A. Act, 1867, were enacted by the parliament of the United Kingdom and not by any Canadian legislature. The usual process has been for some Canadian body to prepare a statute or an amendment that the British parliament passes on request. Except for the Act of 1867, the British parliament has not questioned or changed any such proposal.

The background of the Act is briefly as follows:

In 1791, Quebec was divided into Upper and Lower Canada (the present Ontario and Quebec) with separate governments, but in 1840 these were reunited in the Province of Canada. A unitary form of government for such diverse legal and cultural entities proved unworkable, and when Upper Canada became more populous, the threat of an effective demand for representation by population in the bicameral legislature strained to the utmost the *entente* that existed between the leading politicians.

The processes of government began to bog down. But certain elements of this constitution, principally the settlement of the school question, have survived and were incorporated by reference in the B.N.A. Act, 1867.

Meanwhile the Maritime provinces were agitated by a proposal for union. Delegates met at Charlottetown in 1864 and these were joined by representatives from Canada (where deadlock had been reached) with proposals for a larger union. Further talks were held at Quebec, and seventy-two Quebec Resolutions were adopted by the delegates from Canada, New Brunswick, Newfoundland, Nova Scotia, and Prince Edward Island. Newfoundland and Prince Edward Island decided not to have any further dealings with the proposals, but the other colonies went forward. In 1866, commissioners from Canada, New Brunswick, and Nova Scotia met in London and revised the Quebec Resolutions and thus brought forth the sixty-nine London Resolutions, which formed the instructions for drafting the British North America Act, 1867.[1] The Quebec Resolutions had been approved by the Canadian Provincial parliament as the basis for the union and the Canadian commissioners in London were not authorized to depart from them. The Maritime provinces did not approve the Quebec Resolutions in the same sense and their commissioners were instructed to seek better terms. As a result, the Maritimers considered the London Resolutions the true basis of the agreement, but the Canadians made light of them in Canada – with the curious consequence that they dropped out of sight and were ignored by constitutional lawyers, the courts, and the Privy Council until the time of the O'Connor Report.[2] O'Connor suggests that this attitude was a deliberate policy of Sir John A. Macdonald in order to forestall criticism that he had gone beyond his authority.[3]

Confederation united New Brunswick, Nova Scotia, and Canada, dividing Canada into the present Quebec and Ontario. An immediate problem was the addition of more provinces and territories, and an incredible legal tangle went with the admission of the first one, Manitoba. In 1868, an act[4] of the British parliament enabled the Crown to take over the North-Western Territory and Rupert's Land from the Hudson's Bay Company. In 1869, the Canadian parliament provided for the temporary government of the territories by an act of its own[5] and forwarded a joint address to the British parliament for the admission of the territories (as provided in Section 146 of the B.N.A. Act). In 1870, Canada enacted the Manitoba Act in anticipation of an Imperial Order in Council which was promulgated June 23, 1870. So Manitoba was brought forth. But this was not yet the end. To quell any doubts, the Canadian government requested legislation, the Canadian parliament adopted a joint address, and the British parliament passed the 1871 Amendment[6] to the B.N.A. Act. This confirmed the Canadian legislation and gave the Dominion power to establish new provinces and to alter boundaries.

British Columbia and Prince Edward Island entered the Confederation in much simpler fashion. In each case, the Canadian parliament and the colonial legislature passed the addresses to the Queen required by section 146 of the B.N.A. Act, and the necessary Imperial Orders in Council were issued on May 16, 1871, and June 26, 1873. Although the latter was after the 1871 Amendment, the Amendment did not figure in the process.

The 1886 Amendment[7] to the B.N.A. Act was also concerned with the territories. It permitted the Canadian parliament to give them representation. The opponents of the 'compact' theory of Confederation consider this amendment a precedent in favour of their view because the provinces were not consulted before it was requested and apparently they did not ask to be. Of this, more later, but the next three amendments are also pertinent to this question.

The first, in 1907,[8] revised the system of grants payable by the Dominion to the provinces. The procedure was quite different from that previously adopted. The provinces were consulted, and conferences extending from 1887 to 1907 were held in an effort to achieve a 'final and unalterable settlement' of the fiscal problem. The second, in 1915,[9] altered the constitution of the Senate and increased the number of senators; but this time the provinces were not consulted, and representations made by Prince Edward

Island to a House of Commons committee were rejected, as were suggestions that the other provinces should be consulted. And a similar procedure resulted in the 1916 Amendment[10] which extended the life of the Canadian House of Commons. Again the provinces were ignored, but the War was sufficient reason for that.

Meanwhile, in 1905, Alberta and Saskatchewan were established as provinces by the Alberta Act and the Saskatchewan Act respectively; these acts of the Canadian parliament were both given royal assent on July 20, 1905.

The 1930 Amendment[11] was passed to confirm property settlements made between the Dominion and the four western provinces. It underlines in a rather striking way the dependence of Canadian legislators on the British parliament for the final word even in such an essentially internal matter as an agreement between Canadian governments. This dependence continued despite the Statute of Westminster, 1931,[12] enacted by the Imperial parliament to confirm and ratify declarations made by the Imperial Conferences of 1926 and 1930. By it the Imperial parliament recognized the autonomy of the dominions in constitutional usage, and all restrictions on the dominions' legislative power, with certain exceptions in each case, were removed. In the case of Canada the exception was the B.N.A. Acts, 1867 to 1930, which were reserved to the Imperial parliament by Canada's own request embodied in a joint address of the Senate and House of Commons.

The depression of the '30s left a legacy in the 1940 Amendment,[13] which gave the Dominion power to deal with unemployment insurance. The provinces were all consulted and all agreed to the amendment, which was made necessary when the courts held *ultra vires* (beyond the powers of the Canadian parliament to enact) a Dominion statute[14] dealing with unemployment insurance.

World War II produced the 1943 Amendment,[15] which postponed revision of the representation in the House of Commons until the end of hostilities. Here again the provinces were not consulted, or so it would appear, and the Quebec legislature voted a protest. Following this, the 1946 Amendment[16] recast Section

51 of the B.N.A. Act, 1867, which defines the method of apportioning representation in the House of Commons among the provinces. Previous apportionments had been based on giving Quebec a fixed number of sixty-five and allotting the rest in proportion; this act did away with that and based the apportionment on a fixed total of two hundred and fifty-five members.[17]

In 1949 Newfoundland came into the Confederation after extensive conferences between representatives of the federal and island governments, and after a plebiscite in Newfoundland approved entry. A great many special provisions were made in the case of this province; these were confirmed by the first 1949 Amendment.[18]

The 1949 (No. 2) Amendment[19] gave the parliament of Canada exclusive power to make laws concerning:

> The amendment from time to time of the Constitution of Canada, except as regards matters coming within the classes of subjects by this Act assigned exclusively to the Legislatures of the Provinces, or as regards rights or privileges by this or any other Constitutional Act granted or secured to the Legislature or the Government of a province, or to any class of persons with respect to schools or as regards the use of the English or the French language or as respects the requirements that there shall be a session of the Parliament of Canada at least once each year, and that no House of Commons shall continue for more than five years from the day of the return of the Writs for choosing the House, provided, however, that a House of Commons may in time of real or apprehended war, invasion or insurrection be continued by the Parliament of Canada if such continuation is not opposed by the votes of more than one third of the members of such House.

Not only were the provinces not consulted about this amendment, but the federal government evidently thought that it was needed to attain a favourable bargaining position in the fiscal negotiations of that time. The administration took the position that the structure of the federal government is not a matter of proper concern for the provincial governments, that it does not come within their competency at all, and that they are not in any way the guardians of local or provincial interests in the federal field.

A constituent of current history, the Welfare State, is reflected in the 1951 Amendment,[20] which gives the parliament of Canada power to make laws in relation to old-age pensions. This power is explicitly made subordinate to the power of the provinces to deal with the same matter – a much more useful and flexible device than delegation!

The British North America Act, 1952,[21] is a statute of the Canadian parliament passed in virtue of the power acquired in 1949 to amend the Canadian constitution. It is a revision of Section 51 of the B.N.A. Act, 1867, dealing with the apportionment of members in the House of Commons among the provinces. It fixes the total number at two hundred and sixty-three, subject to certain variations.

The British North America Act, 1960,[22] is again a British statute following a humble joint address (the one that caused the Senate to balk) by the Canadian houses of parliament after the concurrence of all the provinces had been given. It fixed a compulsory age of retirement of seventy-five for superior court judges.

In 1964, the federal government had to seek a further amendment in order to put the Canada Pension Plan into effect.[23] All provinces consented.

The acts and ordinances cited are the principal constitutional enactments of the Confederation that concern the central government.[24] The provincial constitutions are of varied origins and need not, for our purposes, be considered because they are generally only of concern to the individual province. The central government and its structure are of universal moment.

CHAPTER 3

Should Canada have
a written constitution?

Should the fundamental laws governing the structure of the Canadian federal union be embodied in a set form of words of authority so supreme that all governments in Canada are subordinate to it? Although the answer here is a decisive 'Yes', the alternative view is not to be ignored and a great many currents of opinion unite to support it. That alternative is the 'flexible, organic constitution' similar to that of the United Kingdom.

There we start with an institution or institutions with supreme power. The institution is free to modify its internal organization and all things external to it, so that it can develop to meet changing times and varied needs. What balance of power there is, and what checks on abuse of power there are, are within the institution, in its parts or members, and these can provide as effective a safeguard of individual rights as any bill of rights. Or so some say: history does not exactly bear this out.

The chief virtue of such an institution, however, is that it does away to a great extent with the binding and confining rigidity of a set form of words and eliminates also the power of the courts of law to wrest the written constitution to suit their own political conceptions – a subject of scandal in the United States and in the decisions of the Privy Council.[1]

Such an institution is called organic because it tends to grow more complex in structure. The British parliament has preserved the same shape for centuries but the substance has undergone many radical changes. This has enabled the government of the country to adapt itself to changing times with the least appearance of revolution. Yet not one element of the parliament now performs its original function.

All courts are, of course, subordinate to parliament and so no judicial decision can permanently bind the government.

Such a system has great advantages. A ministry can be bold and resolute with popular support, without fear of effective opposition. It can meet the exigencies of any day with decision and dispatch. No legal obstacle, for example, could have arisen in England during the depression of the '30s as such obstacles arose in the United States to the N.R.A. plans and as obstacles arose in Canada to similar endeavours.[2] On the other hand, England did not try anything like N.R.A.

A large body of opinion supports this flexible kind of structure for Canada in one form on another. In fact, this is very nearly the case with the provinces and it may now be so in the case of the federal government if the B.N.A. (No. 2) Act, 1949, means what it appears to mean.

There are, however, disadvantages of great moment in the organic form of constitution. Its very flexibility means that harm, sometimes irreparable, can be done in the rush of emergency or by the sheer weight of a precipitous majority. It leaves the protection of minorities and of individual rights to the sense of duty or more frequently the inertia and timidity of the government. And the absolute supremacy of such an institution, which is an essential part of it, means that no rights, no obligations, no human activity is exempt from arbitrary control by the parliament. We see parliaments that are totalitarian in deed as well as in theory: even the British parliament, despite the innate conservatism and common sense of the English people, has on occasion acted in such a manner. During the late War, in England as in Canada, people could be imprisoned without any kind of judicial process. Possibly this was a necessary wartime provision, but the same situation existed in Northern Ireland (part of the United Kingdom) and in Eire in peacetime.

Why, then, should not Canada have a constitution of the organic type? Because a written constitution is essential for a federal state. It is also necessary and desirable.

A federal union must have a written constitution: it cannot exist without a fundamental law defining the division of functions between the governments. Without such a division there is not federation but subordination of one authority to the other. The fundamental law of division cannot issue from a third institution, for in that case that institution would be the ultimate government of the union. Such indeed might be the present situation in Canada, but this state of affairs would not be a true federation or confederation. In fact it is not the present situation in Canada: we have a theoretical federation but a potentially unitary state because of the constitutional practice of amendment.[3] It is by no means inconceivable that a federal government backed by a momentary surge of a majority feeling could secure an amendment that would turn the provinces into truly subordinate bodies in law as in fact. The B.N.A. (No. 2) Act, 1949, went far to establish a precedent for such one-sided action. The sequel of such a course, however unpredictable, would be bitter, with the disruption of the nation as a possible result.

A written constitution is necessary for Canada because it is necessary that Canada be a federal state if it is to exist at all.[4] The history of the legislative union of 1840 shows beyond a reasonable doubt that there are diversities of life and outlook rooted in this country that can by no means be compounded into a unified culture, economy, and polity. Since that day, Quebec not only has not merged with English-speaking Canada, it has grown even more determined to preserve its individuality. But Quebec is not the only, or even the main, obstacle to the unitary scheme. Quebec is the most distinctly and vocally different province, but there are others just as set on preserving their own autonomy and individuality. An important consideration in this respect is that at least nine-tenths of the law that affects the citizen's ordinary conduct and relations is provincial law. This recognizes the fact that what suits the people of Ontario or British Columbia does not necessarily suit those of Nova Scotia or Saskatchewan. There is, of course, considerable similarity in the laws of the provinces, but this similarity is shared with states of the United States and with Great Britain. It is shared even with Quebec, despite the more radical difference of legal background.

The years since Confederation have increased provincial differences to some extent and have certainly increased the number of different provinces. Certainly they have not witnessed any such unification of the English-speaking provinces as was contemplated at that time. Diversity exists in the courts and in their procedures, in the law of domestic relations, in contracts and private wrongs, in local government, in provincial administration, in the law of property. With all the disadvantages of such differences from the lawyer's point of view and the big-business point of view, these diverse things have developed to meet local needs and wishes. It is very true here that what is one man's meat is another man's poison. For example, the judicial organization of Ontario would not be successful in Prince Edward Island nor would the educational system of British Columbia be acceptable to the people of Newfoundland. New Brunswick has for many years leased the fishing rights along its rivers and lakes; in Nova Scotia these are public, and public sentiment is firm for keeping it that way.

Apart from the formal and legal differences between the provinces there are political and economic differences. These differences are reflected in the provincial governments. The evangelistic administrations of the Prairies contrast sharply with the traditional and prosaic administrations of the Maritimes, but even within these groupings there are persevering differences. The economy of each province has a certain unity and divergency from the rest that absolutely demands the protection and fostering of a local autonomous authority. No doubt there is a theoretical virtue in absolutely unfettered trade: it is said that thereby every place would produce what it could best produce and would not waste time and energy and capital on marginal production. We do not live in such a theoretical world and are not likely to. And in any case man was not made for the economy but the economy for man. It is there that we reach the core of the matter, that heart of things that makes it nonsense to talk in merely economic terms.

Patriotism is a form of charity, that is, of unselfish love. It is the natural charity whereby we cherish the land that holds our friends, families, and immediate fellow men. To this we add a good and proper feeling: a *pietas* for the graves and monuments of our fathers, for their achievements and even for their sorrows. Such charity, as with all charity, if it is to have the heart in it, must begin at home. Let it be added that it should not end there, but it will not have any human value unless it is so rooted. And that is why any merely economic or merely political basis for Canadian unity will fail as will any attempt to impose absolute uniformity.

Moreover, while a Canadian outlook and a national feeling is desirable, it is attainable and has been often attained within the limits of the Confederation. But it is neither safe nor desirable to augment this 'Canadianization' (a hybrid word for an illegitimate deed) by a forcing of the constitution. Let national sentiment grow, by all means, but not at the expense of that useful and cherished diversity that has evolved over the years.

For all these reasons and more, it is evident that Canada must remain a federal state and consequently that a written fundamental law is necessary.

But a written law is also desirable. As noted, the alternative is a constitution-making institution – a constitutional convention. The British parliament was probably intended[5] to perform this function, but in actual fact it has refrained from exercising any initiative or exerting any will of its own and consequently the principal agent in amending the B.N.A. Act has been the federal government. This situation arose from many causes of which two are obvious: a desire by the British to grant full autonomy to Canada, best realized by dealing only with the national government; and an inexperience of the meaning of federation and the reality of local autonomy. These attitudes were encouraged in the very beginning by the nature of the first amendments. They were obviously desirable, being little more than making good omissions in the original act, and were clearly acceptable to all Canada.

This attitude of the British government and parliament led the federal government by degrees into a false position. The latter was considered in Great Britain as spokesman for the Canadian nation and thus entrusted to sum up and communicate the consensus of the parties entitled to be heard (not necessarily the provinces: there were also protected minorities transcending local boundaries). While the federal government has never disclaimed this trust it has adopted a practice that is at odds with it, which springs from the doctrine that there are no interests or rights embodied in the constitution that the federal government and parliament is not alone capable of representing. A principal example of this approach is the 1949 (No. 2) Amendment.

It is sometimes assumed that the Canadian parliament is competent to deal with the interests of individual provinces and of minorities in the constitution because these interests are represented in the Senate. But this view is fallacious for three reasons: firstly, because the Senate operates by ordinary bare majorities and no group has a determinant deterring voice; secondly, because the senators are picked by the successive federal administrations and not by the groups concerned; thirdly, because the Senate was not designed and has received no mandate to scrutinize constitutional problems as such, its office being to act as a board of review of measures within the ordinary powers of the central government. It can, and does, of course, take an essential part in the joint address to the Crown that customarily precedes a constitutional amendment.

The parliament of Canada does not competently represent the people with respect to all matters outside provincial jurisdiction. There are matters of importance in the B.N.A. Acts that were intended to limit that parliament and should limit that parliament; they are not numerous but they are of moment. And there are other matters not contained in the B.N.A. Acts that should be in a written constitution – natural rights of the individual, the family, and the citizen that the State should be forbidden to deny.

On the other hand, the bulk of the B.N.A. Act is not sufficiently fundamental to be part of the constitution: in that aspect the 1949 (No. 2) Amendment was amply justified. But this introduces the question: What should the constitution contain?

CHAPTER 4

What should the constitution contain?

The present content of the Canadian constitution, in the sense in which we are using the word, is very uncertain. The 1949 (No. 2) Amendment seems to have reduced it to the following heads:

(a) Matters assigned exclusively to the legislatures of the provinces by the B.N.A. Acts (mainly Section 92, as modified by Section 91, and Section 93).

(b) Rights or privileges granted or secured by a constitutional act to the legislature or government of a province or to any class of persons with respect to schools (Section 93).

(c) The use of the English or the French language (Section 133).

(d) The requirements that there shall be a session of the parliament of Canada at least once a year (Section 20) and that no House of Commons shall continue for more than five years from the day of the return of the writs for choosing the House (Section 50) – provided, however, that the House of Commons may in time of real or apprehended war, invasion, or insurrection be continued by the parliament of Canada if such continuation is not opposed by the votes of more than one-third of the members of such House.

Apparently any other matter can now be changed. The parliament can alter the distribution of the Senate (or abolish it). It can cause the senators to be elected, it can change the basis of representation in the House of Commons, it can abolish the office of Governor General or make it elective. Possibly it can abolish allegiance to the Crown of Great Britain as have other members of the British Commonwealth.

But can the parliament discard any federal power? Probably not, because of the 'watertight compartment' doctrine.[1] That is, since all power is divided between the central government and the provinces and since the central government is still prohibited from interfering with exclusive provincial powers, it is likely that it cannot add to those powers. This must seem fantastic to the non-lawyer.

Suppose, for example, that in order to enact Senator Pouliot's suggestion, parliament repealed Clause (26) of Section 91, 'Marriage and Divorce'. Would the provinces then acquire jurisdiction in matters of this class? Possibly the class would then be held to fall within 'Property and Civil Rights in the Province', i.e., Class (13) of Section 92, a provincial jurisdictional subject-class. But Class (12) of Section 92 gives the provinces legislative power in relation to 'The Solemnization of Marriage in the Province', and by an illogical but much used rule of statutory interpretation,[2] this might be held to exclude 'Marriage and Divorce' from provincial legislative power!

The parliament certainly has power to alter the provisions relating to the courts.[3] Section 97 requires provincial judges in Ontario, New Brunswick, and Nova Scotia to be appointed from the bars of their respective provinces. This is of some importance to those provinces and to lawyers who are members of those bars, but the appointing is not a right or privilege secured to the legislature or government of a province (still less a right with respect to schools – a possible reading of the second exception in the 1949 (No. 2) Amendment, despite the rule that attributive clauses apply in general to the near and not the remote words).[4] It might be possible for the central government to assume control of appointments to all courts instead of to the superior, district, and county courts as at present.

The provision for the parliament of Canada to make uniform

laws (Section 94) does not appear to come within any exception of the 1949 (No. 2) Amendment, nor does Section 95, which gives the parliament and provinces power to legislate concerning agriculture and immigration, with the federal power predominant.

In substance, the central government is now limited, not by defining its functions, but by defining an area of jurisdiction upon which it must not encroach. That is, provincial powers are defined and the residue of power is left to the federal government. This means that the bulk of the B.N.A. Acts has been superseded by the amendment, and the remainder now defines only temporarily the structure of the Confederation. Is this a tolerable situation? Should the limits of the several jurisdictions be more definite and of wider scope? In order to get a satisfactory answer it is prudent to consider the nature of parliamentary government.

Its prime tenet is the supremacy of parliament: that is, a parliament can make laws on any subject whatever and to any effect whatever, and these laws are not impeachable, for being lies or for being unjust or for any other reason. The sole limitation is that a parliament cannot bind itself. Such a system is in striking contrast to that of the United States where laws can be successfully challenged as beyond the powers of the legislature or as denying fundamental rights. Such a system demands a balance of legislative and judicial powers to function, although not necessarily the same balance as exists in the United States.

Parliamentary government also achieves a balance, as does all stable government, but at a lower level. That is, it is avowedly based not on any system of recognized rights and duties but on the wishes of a determinant majority. This is an unworkable theory in a federal state where distinct minorities are more numerous and coherent and yet more likely to be attacked because of the lack of universal agreement.

In fact, it is quite debatable which régimes – the parliamentary, or the constitutional as opposed to parliamentary – have the worst or best records in relation to respect for human rights and dignity. The United Kingdom parliament on the whole would score high but not perfect marks, while certain states of the United States would score rather low.

The excesses of parliamentary governments are permitted and encouraged by their theories of government because those theories confess nothing to be an excess. The sins of limited governments arise not because of defects of theory but through imperfections of the enacted limits or through violation of them. The limited governments are thus more just in fundamental structure although they may be quite as inequitable in practice as the parliamentary polities. But the object of this book is to ascertain the preferable structure or constitution, which is patently that of the governments limited by recognized and undeniable rights.

One rather forceful objection to constitutional guarantees is that they can be used against the state. We see criminals and traitors and others taking refuge behind the Fifth Amendment to the Constitution of the United States, and this has the effect on some minds of casting discredit on that Constitution. No doubt the wisdom of the Fifth Amendment is questionable: we have amended the somewhat similar principle of our common law.[5] But this little irritant cannot by any means offset the great value of constitutional guarantees that exist for the benefit of all, not only the obnoxious. One can conceive what might happen in the United States in the grip of a Red scare if the parliamentary principle were in full force.

Canadian government is not fully parliamentary and there is no prospect of its being so. It is parliamentary in operation but it is not parliamentary in scope, because of the division of powers of legislation;[6] this limitation contradicts the parliamentary principle. The mechanics of government in Canada follow the British model but in essence and jurisdiction Canadian governments are more akin to those of the United States. We do not have their complete balance of legislative, executive, and judicial powers, but we do have the division of powers that is essential to any federation.

It is not necessary that the division be 'watertight'. Because of the impossibility of delegation between the governments a very complicated organization is needed to deal with matters that straddle the line of division: labour relations, marketing, the criminal courts, liquor control, Sunday observance, religious freedom, insurance, monopolies, and the law merchant.

This difficulty could be solved by leaving the whole or the bulk of legislative matters within the competence of all the legislatures, with a fundamental set of traffic rules to decide which authority would prevail in case of actual conflict. This would not eliminate the difficulty of characterizing under what class of subjects a particular matter falls. But it would eliminate the danger of legislation being held *ultra vires* although not in conflict with any law of another government, and would mean that necessary laws could be enacted where now the various law-making bodies fear to tread because of the danger of passing invalid acts. The only restrictions on legislative powers would be the entrenched rights.

For example, 'Interest' is presently an exclusive subject-matter of federal legislative power, under Class 19 of Section 91, but the Canada Interest Act by no means deals fully with the topic. Various provincial enactments contain sections dealing with interest, notably on judgment debts, but these provisions, although needed, are possibly *ultra vires*.[7] Under the system proposed in these pages, both would be in force but the central government could override a provincial act if it appeared desirable to do so. That is, the system would not eliminate conflict but would solve it and would do away with deadlock.

Again, because provincial enactments ordinarily do not operate outside the province, there is a legislative gap that it might be useful to have filled by the central authority. Then if a province wanted changes in the federal law it could enact them for the province. This is particularly desirable in the field of contracts but it could apply to many things, such as domestic relations, motor vehicle drivers' permits, insurance soliciting, and all matters where a degree of uniformity is desirable without prejudice to local wants.

Finally, in dealing with legislative powers, a written constitution should not make them unlimited. Basic rights should be formulated and made inviolable – those rights that governments may not justly transgress, those rights that, in fact, no one has the right to surrender: the rights of human beings, of families, of the societies that exist for ends independent of the State, of free citizens.

Besides the foregoing essentials of a federal constitution for a free society, there are other matters that it is necessary or desirable to include in such a constitution. These are chiefly:

(a) The definition of the structure of the central authority in so far as it is of moment to the separate member states of the union or to interest groups.

(b) The division of the central power into legislative, executive, and judicial functions.

(c) Rules governing the relations between the authorities, especially in regard to taxation.

(d) Limitations on the constitutions of the member states in so far as they affect the central government or the citizens at large.

(e) Provisions defining the citizenship.

(f) A process of amendment.

Since it is easier to discuss such topics in relation to a concrete proposal, further treatment of them is postponed until the constitution advocated in this book has been spelled out. But before doing that there is one further question we might usefully consider: What shape should the constitution take?

CHAPTER 5

What shape should the constitution take?

The melange of British North America Acts and others that constitute our basic laws is composed of ordinary statutes of the British parliament, and the tendency has been to interpret them as such.[1] This has had serious results in the development of the organs of our governments because the ordinary rules of construction of statutes contain many quirks and peculiarities not suitable or sufficiently broadly based for the task of reading the meaning of a constitution. Not that the interpretation of the B.N.A. Acts has been at all uniform. Cases have varied from the most rigid literalism to the 'living tree' approach. Constitutional law is full of these metaphorical tags.

The 'living tree' view was voiced in 1930 by the Privy Council thus:

> The British North America Act planted in Canada a living tree capable of growth and expansion within its natural limits. The object of the Act was to grant a Constitution to Canada. 'Like all written constitutions it has been subject to development through usage and convention': Canadian Constitutional Studies, Sir Robert Borden (1922), p. 55.[2]

The court held that this justified a 'large and liberal interpretation' rather than a 'narrow and technical construction'.

In general the rules of interpretation seem to have been used by the courts to effect what they thought should be done. In the event, neither the centralists nor the provincialists have been satisfied: this proves nothing. On the whole, the Privy Council tried to keep a balance, to keep in mind certain modern developments that necessitated giving to the central government powers not explicit in the Acts (such as control over radio and aeronautics), while finding perhaps more in the provincial powers than the Fathers of Confederation, or a great many of them at any rate, would have admitted.

One main defect of the common approach to the constitution has been the refusal and indeed the inability of the courts to look beyond the text. This is inherent in the status of the constitution as a set of statutes. This status is in British law not peculiar to statutes: if you make an agreement to buy a house and subsequently get a deed, the agreement is held to be perfected and exhausted by the deed and your rights thereafter will depend on the deed and not the agreements; you cannot even, in the ordinary case, look to the agreement to explain what the deed is intended to mean, although this rule is not absolute.

Somewhat the same situation exists with respect to the B.N.A. Acts and the preceding agreements known as the Quebec Resolutions and London Resolutions.[3] For the most part the courts have ignored the two sets of Resolutions and have never explicitly based any decision on them.[4] This may be justified in the case of an ordinary statute, but our constitution is different. It was a compromise between delegates of the original provinces, sanctioned by the Imperial parliament. The 'compact' theory of Confederation has been much derided, mostly for the wrong reasons. Thus it is said that the B.N.A. Act is not a treaty – a platitude. But it is the expression of something very like a treaty. Others point out that not all the present provinces were represented at the preliminary conferences and that, in fact, Quebec and Ontario were not separately represented. But the like situation arises in other treaties and compacts, which, nevertheless, can be taken advantage of by states that adhere to them. The history of the achievement shows that all present interests were virtually represented and provision made on their behalf.

Again it is argued that the post-Confederation provinces are new entities, creatures of the B.N.A. Acts, and, not representing the same interests as the pre-Confederation provinces, are not entitled to be heard in their places – that the original provinces no longer exist, their substances having been divided between the Dominion and the new provinces.[5] But what can represent provincial interests, whether old or new, unless it be the new provinces? Surely not the Senate, at least as presently constituted, and the House of Commons was not designed with that in mind.

The attitude that provincial boundaries are 'administrative' is based on this legalist approach to the constitution:[6] that the Confederation is the creation of the Imperial parliament and must be looked on solely as such. Rather, the Imperial parliament was the catalyst of the elements existing in this country; it was the honest notary that committed the agreement of the colonies to authentic and binding form. It is only just to the origins and existing elements of the nation to recognize that the B.N.A. Act was merely a method of bringing about Confederation, putting the seal of authority on it if you will, but sanctioning the acts and intentions of men here.[7] It cannot be a true or valid rule of interpretation to treat a document as what it is not, nor can such an approach yield true or valid results: it omits too much of the picture.

It will assist a more suitable interpretation and will offset judicial and legal conservatism in this arena if the shape of the 'made in Canada' constitution departs from the statutory form to show two things clearly: firstly, that it is a constitution and should be interpreted with all the means available to show the true intent of the makers; secondly, that it is a federal constitution and is intended to maintain the existence and interests of the component states as well as those of the whole.

The shape proposed is similar to that of a treaty. It departs from ordinary statutory language in the conciseness of its phrases and in the use of ordinary language. It also uses technical terms, such as 'Article', not usually found in our domestic laws. The name 'Articles of Confederation'[8] might just as well have been 'Constitution of Canada', 'Federal Charter', or any such name. The name chosen does have this significance: it indicates that the document so named is the result of agreement, that it represents a consensus of the views of distinct entities, and that these entities, though united, are not swallowed up in the result. Which is as it should be.

It remains to reiterate that Canadian nationality and unity will not be fostered by ignoring true differences and permanent distinctions in the national society. If these diversities are given their due, the unifying forces will in the end have less particularism to contend with. Opposition breeds opposition; patriotism is the fruit of mutual respect and esteem.

Admitting this, it is possible even for a professed separatist to reserve judgment. Until an organization is adopted that permits the survival and growth of all the provinces, it is not right to say that true Canadian unity is impossible – unless it is indeed found impossible to achieve such an organization.

Bearing this urgently in mind, let us turn to the proposed solution.

CHAPTER 6

Articles of Confederation

PREAMBLE

All Authority comes from God through the Consent of the People, who alone may found the Conditions under which they will be governed, to which their Princes, Parliaments and Judges are naturally subordinate;

And since the Ends of Government are the Happiness and Welfare, the Freedom and Security, of the Citizen and not the Aggrandizement of the State or of any Instrument of the State;

And in as much as These Ends are best secured where Freedom, Brotherhood and Equal Laws are safeguarded and nourished and where the Violence, Greed and Corruption of public Functionaries and private Persons are alike restrained;

And because the most effective Safeguards and Restraints are an enlightened Citizenry, a Government divided and balanced as to Function and a certain Law;

The People, Parliament and Provinces of Canada, so that their Institutions may serve the Common Good and so that Men may know the Law, constitute and confirm a Confederation of their Provinces and Territories by These Articles.

ARTICLE 1

The Name, Form and Languages of the Confederation

1. The Name of the Confederation is Canada.

2. The Form of the Confederation is a Union of the Peoples of autonomous Provinces in one Nation with a federal Government.

3. The national Languages are English and French. Any Person may use either Language in the Debates of the Houses of the Parliament of Canada and of the Legislature of any Province and in any Pleading or Process in or issuing from any Court in Canada. Both Languages shall be used in the Records and Journals of the Houses of the Parliament of Canada and the Acts of the Parliament of Canada shall be printed and published in both Languages.

ARTICLE 2

The Citizenship

1. Every Person born in Canada or to a Citizen of Canada has the Right to become a Citizen of Canada unless he freely renounces the Citizenship.

2. No one who freely renounces the Citizenship or who is a Citizen of another Nation may become a Citizen except by Naturalization.

3. No one shall be deprived of the Citizenship except of his free Choice in accordance with predetermined Law.

4. Every Citizen of Canada shall be a Citizen of the Province or Territory where he last resided for one Year and every Citizen has the Right to reside in any Province or Territory.

5. No Citizen shall be denied elective public Office or the Right to vote therefor except for Immaturity, established Insanity or wilful or wanton Crime.

6. Every Citizen has the Right to publish peaceable Comment on public Affairs and on public Officers and Servants and to join in peaceable Assemblies to discuss Matters of public Concern.

7. Peace Officers and Troops used to maintain the Peace in
Canada shall consist only of Citizens.

8. Every Citizen has the Right to keep Arms for the lawful
Defence of his Dwelling.

ARTICLE 3

The Parliament

1. The Parliament of the Confederation shall have two Houses,
the Senate and the House of Commons, and shall be called the
Parliament of Canada.

2. Every Province shall have an equal Number of Senators
from among its Citizens, to be appointed or elected by the provincial Government, Legislature or Electorate, as the Parliament
or the Legislature of the Province may determine, and at least
Two Thirds of the Senate shall consist of such Senators. The
Number of the Senators shall not exceed One Hundred and Five.

3. The House of Commons shall consist of not less than Two
Hundred and Fifty Members and not more than Four Hundred
and Thirty Two Members, each of whom shall be elected by a
distinct territorial Division. No Division shall have more than
twice the Population of any other or overlap provincial Limits
and each Province shall elect a Number of Members proportional
to its Population: no Province, however, shall have less than
Two Members. A Census to determine the Divisions shall be
taken at Intervals not greater than Ten Years.

4. No House of Commons shall continue for more than Five
Years from the Day of the return of the Writs for choosing the
House except that in time of apprehended or actual War the
Parliament may continue the House of Commons if the Continu-
ation is not opposed by the Votes of more than one Third of the
Members of the House.

5. The Parliament shall meet at least once in every Year and
so that Twelve Months shall not elapse between the last Sitting
of a Session and the first Sitting of the next Session.

6. A Senator or Member of the House of Commons may be
ousted from Office only by process of Impeachment.

7. No Measure that imposes any Tax, authorizes any Loan or Guarantee or appropriates any public Funds shall originate except in the House of Commons and then only for a Purpose that has been recommended to that House by Message of the Governor General in the Session in which the Measure is proposed.

8. No Measure shall become law without the Concurrence of both Houses with the exception of a Bill that the Senate has failed to approve as approved by the House of Commons, which, if again approved by the House of Commons at the Session of the Parliament first ensuing after the General Election next after the failure of the Senate to approve it, shall not require the Concurrence of the Senate to become law.

9. Every Measure approved by both Houses of the Parliament and every Measure approved by the House of Commons that does not require the Concurrence of the Senate to become law shall be presented in Parliament for the Assent of the Sovereign and no Measure with respect to which the Assent is withheld shall become law unless, at the same Session or at the next ensuing Session, each House approves the same Measure by a Vote of Two Thirds of the Members present, whereupon it shall then become law.

ARTICLE 4

The Executive Government

1. The Executive Government of the Confederation is vested in the Sovereign but the Governor General shall exercise it in the Name of the Sovereign and all executive Officers and Servants of the Government of the Confederation, other than the Censor General and his Officers and Servants, shall be subject to his Command.

2. The Governor General shall hold Office, unless he dies, resigns or becomes permanently incapacitated, until his Successor takes Office or until he is removed by the Parliament, which may only be by process of Impeachment, and he shall be immune from all civil and criminal Process while in Office.

3. The Governor General, in relation to any Matter within

the Competence of the Government of the Confederation, may
exercise the prerogative Powers of the Sovereign and may make
Orders having the force of law but such Powers and Orders shall
be subordinate to the Acts of the Parliament and shall not impose
any Tax.

    4. The Governor General may

        1. Call the Parliament into session at any time, recommend
Laws and other Measures to it, prorogue or dissolve it,
and decree General Elections;

        2. Enter into Communications and make Treaties with
the Governments of other Countries and with international Bodies;

        3. Dismiss any executive Officer or Servant of the Govern-
ment of the Confederation who does not have the Right
by Law to hold Office during good Behaviour, other than
the Censor General and his Officers and Servants; and

        4. Appoint Commissioners with plenary Powers to investi-
gate Matters of public Concern;

but the Powers enumerated in this Section shall not be construed
to limit in any way the executive Powers and prerogative Powers
that the Governor General may exercise.

    5. The Censor General shall be appointed by the Governor
General on the joint Resolution of the Senate and the House of
Commons and shall hold Office for Twenty Years. He shall conduct the Census and all Elections to the Parliament and shall
ensure that every Expenditure of public Funds by the Government of the Confederation is lawful. He shall be removable from
Office only by process of Impeachment and the Expenses incurred
in the due Performance of his Duties shall be a first Charge on
the public Funds of the Confederation.

ARTICLE 5

The Judiciary

    1. Every Judge of every Court, whether constituted by Canada
or a Province, which has Power to fine and imprison for a Contempt committed out of the Court, shall hold Office on judicial

Tenure, that is, he shall hold Office during good Behaviour for a Term of not less than Ten Years or until the Attainment of a predetermined Age or for Life, whichever the Authority that constitutes the Court may decide, and while in Office he shall not suffer any Diminution of his Term of Office or of his Salary or Allowances and shall be removable only by process of Impeachment.

2. The Supreme Court of Canada shall consist of the Chief Justice of Canada and Eight associate Justices, who shall be appointed by the Governor General and shall hold Office on judicial Tenure. The Salaries and Allowances of the Chief Justice of Canada and of the Justices of the Supreme Court of Canada shall not be at lesser Rates than the Salaries, Indemnities and Allowances of the principal Ministers of the Executive Government of the Confederation and shall be paid out of, and be a first Charge on, the public Funds of the Confederation.

3. The Supreme Court of Canada shall have final Power to determine any Question with respect to These Articles and any Controversy between the Governments of Canada and a Province or Provinces or between the Governments of Provinces and shall have such further Jurisdiction with respect to the Laws of Canada or of any Province as the Parliament or the Legislature of the Province may enact.

4. The Parliament of Canada or the Executive Government of the Confederation may establish Courts or judicial Bodies with respect to any Matters within the Competence of the Government of the Confederation, other than Courts for the ordinary Administration of criminal Justice in the Provinces, or it may confer such Jurisdiction on Provincial Courts or judicial Bodies.

5. There shall be for each Province a Court consisting of the Chief Justice of the Province and at least Two associate Justices, who shall be appointed by the Head of the Executive Government of the Province, subject to Disallowance of the Appointment by the Governor General within One Month after he has received Notice of it. The Judges of the Court shall hold Office on judicial Tenure and their Salaries and Allowances shall not be at lesser Rates than the Salaries, Indemnities and Allowances of the

principal Ministers of the Executive Government of the Province and shall be paid out of, and be a first Charge on, the public Funds of the Province.

6. The Court shall have final Power in the Province to inquire into any Imprisonment, any Proceeding of an executive or judicial Body or Functionary, whether public or private, and any Claim or Use of public Office or Function, and to correct or end any such Imprisonment, Proceeding, Claim or Use that it finds to be unlawful. The Jurisdiction of the Court shall not be subordinate to that of any Court other than the Supreme Court of Canada.

ARTICLE 6

The Provincial Governments

1. The Laws and Institutions of each Province shall continue, subject to alteration by the Legislature of the Province, but so that the Legislature shall include a representative Assembly elected by the Citizens of the Province at Intervals not exceeding Five Years; where, however, the House of Commons has been continued beyond Five Years, the Legislature of the Province may continue the representative Assembly for an equal or lesser Period.

2. Each Member of the representative Assembly shall be elected by a distinct territorial Division and no Division shall have more than twice the Population of any other.

3. A Member of the Legislature may be ousted from Office only by process of Impeachment.

4. No Measure that imposes any Tax, authorizes any Loan or Guarantee or appropriates any public Funds shall originate except in the representative Assembly and then only for a Purpose which the Head of the Executive Government of the Province has recommended to the Assembly in the Session in which the Measure is proposed.

5. Every Measure that has been approved by the representative Assembly in three consecutive Sessions of the Legislature, where the first and third Approvals are at least Eighteen Months

apart, shall become law although it has not received the Assent
of the Sovereign or of any other Part of the Legislature.

ARTICLE 7

Legislative Powers

1. The Parliament of Canada may make Laws for the Peace,
Order and good Government of Canada in relation to any and
all Matters; except as provided in the second Section of this
Article, every Law of a Province that conflicts with a Law of the
Parliament of Canada shall be inoperative to the Extent of the
Conflict and, notwithstanding the second Section of this Article,
every Law of a Province that conflicts with a Law of the Parliament of Canada made in relation to any Matter coming within
the following Classes of Subjects shall be inoperative to the Extent
of the Conflict:

1. The Parliament of Canada, the Constitution and Powers
   of the Senate and of the House of Commons, including
   the Representation of the Territories therein, and the
   Qualifications, Appointment or Election, Payment and
   Privileges of the Senators and of the Members of the
   House of Commons;

2. The Office of Governor General and the Qualifications,
   Appointment or Election, Term of Office, Powers, Payment and Privileges of the Governor General;

3. The Constitution, Jurisdiction, and Procedure of the
   Supreme Court of Canada and of the Courts of the
   Confederation, and the Qualifications, Terms of Office,
   Powers, Payment and Privileges of the Judges thereof;

4. The public Service of the Confederation and the Persons
   engaged therein, including the creation of Corporations
   therefor;

5. Lands and other Things for the public Service of the
   Confederation;

6. The Erection of new Provinces in Lands not within a
   Province or which are ceded by a Province and the
   Government of Territories not within a Province;

7. Canadian Citizenship and the Admission to Canada and Naturalization of those not Citizens;

8. The aboriginal Inhabitants of Canada and their Property and Protection;

9. Relations with other Countries and with international Bodies;

10. The Protection of Canada from foreign Enemies, civil Strife and from national Perils arising from Famine, Pestilence or great Movements of natural Forces;

11. Criminal Law and Procedure, including the Punishment and Reformation of Criminals, but not including the Constitution of the ordinary Courts of criminal Jurisdiction in the Provinces or the Administration of Justice in the Provinces;

12. Health and the Prevention of Disease;

13. Unemployment Insurance and Assistance;

14. The postal Service, Telephones, Telegraphs and Communication by Radiation;

15. Transportation Systems that serve more than one Province or that extend beyond the Limits of a Province and public Works and Undertakings that are, or that are declared by the Parliament of Canada before or after their Execution to be, for the general Advantage of Canada or of more than one Province;

16. Weights, Measures and the Calendar;

17. Money, including Coinage, Currency, paper Money and legal Tender;

18. The Law Merchant, comprising Interest, Bills of Exchange and negotiable Instruments, Copyright, Trade Marks, Rights to Discoveries and Inventions, Trading in Shares and Securities, and Bankruptcy and Insolvency;

19. Banking, including the Incorporation of Banks, and the Acquisition and Management of insurance or investment Funds;

20. Import, export and interprovincial Trade and Commerce;

21. Navigation and Shipping on Water or through the Air, including Quarantine, marine Hospitals, Beacons, Buoys, Lighthouses and Sable Island;
22. Fisheries not within the Limits of a Province and migratory Birds;
23. The Census and Statistics;
24. The Recognition and Enforcement within each Province of the Laws and Judgments of other Provinces, Territories or States.

2. In each Province, the Legislature may make Laws for the Peace, Order and good Government of the Province in relation to any and all Matters; with the Exception of Laws made in relation to Matters coming within the Classes of Subjects enumerated in the first Section of this Article, every Law of the Parliament of Canada that conflicts with a Law of the Legislature of a Province made in relation to any Matter coming within the following Classes of Subjects shall be inoperative in the Province to the Extent of the Conflict:

1. The Constitution of the Province and of the Provincial Legislature, and the Qualifications, Election or Appointment, Payment and Privileges of the Members of the Legislature;
2. The Head of the Executive Government of the Province and his Qualifications, Appointment or Election, Term of Office, Powers, Payment and Privileges;
3. The Administration of Justice in the Province, including the Constitution, Organization and Maintenance of Provincial Courts, both of civil and of criminal Jurisdiction, and including the Procedure in civil Matters in those Courts;
4. The public Service of the Province and the Persons engaged therein, including the creation of Corporations therefor;
5. Lands and other Things for the public Service of the Province;
6. The Punishment and Reformation of Offenders against

the Laws of the Province by Fine, Imprisonment or other
Penalty not of a capital Nature;

7. Public Works and Undertakings;
8. Local Government;
9. Education;
10. Hospitals, other than marine Hospitals, Asylums, and
other eleemosynary or charitable Institutions, and Charities;
11. Fisheries within the Limits of the Province and Lands,
Forests, Agriculture, Mines and the natural Resources
of the Province;
12. Private Law, including the Law in relation to Persons,
Associations, Corporations, Marriage and the domestic
Relations, Obligations, Wrongs, Contracts, Property
and civil Rights.

ARTICLE 8

Fiscal Powers and Institutions

1. The Government of Canada may borrow Money and may
impose Taxation of any Kind and by any Mode or System.

2. The Government of a Province may borrow Money and
may impose Taxation of any Kind and by any Mode or System
but not so as to tax the Bringing of Goods into the Province,
the Passage of Goods through the Province or the Taking of
Goods out of the Province.

3. No Lands or Property belonging to Canada or any Province
shall be liable to Taxation.

4. In the case of any Provincial Government that by prudent
and efficient Use of its Powers to tax and to borrow is yet unable
to provide the public Services of the Province according to the
average Standard enjoyed by Canadians, the Government of
Canada shall pay to the Government of the Province in each
Year an Amount sufficient to enable the Province, using its
Powers to tax and borrow prudently and efficiently, to provide its
public Services at that Standard. Payments so made shall be
excluded, however, in determining the Standard.

5. The Federal Council shall consist of Delegates of the Governments in Canada. Each Provincial Government shall appoint one Delegate and the Government of Canada shall appoint Delegates not exceeding in Number the Provincial Delegates. The Chairman shall be elected from the Delegates of the Government of Canada and the Council shall meet at the Call of the Chairman or of any Five Delegates. The Council may make a binding Allocation between the Government of Canada, on the one Hand, and the Governments of the Provinces, on the other Hand, for any Period not exceeding Ten Years, of the Powers to tax and borrow and may determine the Limits of Rates or Amounts that shall apply to the Allocation; but to do so a Majority of Delegates of the Government of Canada and a Majority of the Delegates of the Provincial Governments, representing a Majority of the Population of Canada according to the latest general Census, must concur.

ARTICLE 9

The Relations between the Governments

1. In any Controversy between the Governments of Canada and a Province or Provinces or between the Governments of Provinces, the Government of Canada may be sued in any federal superior Court established to hear and determine Claims for or against that Government, and the Government of a Province may be sued in the Court established for the Province pursuant to Section 5 of Article 5 of These Articles; but the Parliament of Canada or the Legislature of the Province may confer concurrent Jurisdiction on any other Courts in Claims against the Government of Canada or of the Province respectively.

2. The Court having Jurisdiction over any such Controversy may enforce any Agreement between Governments, order the Performance of any needful Act, prohibit any Breach, award Damages and punish for Contempt any Person who is not entitled under These Articles to Immunity from civil and criminal Process or who is not the Head of the Executive Government of a Province.

3. The Parliament of Canada may alter the Limits of any Province but only with the Consent of the Legislature of the Province; any Provinces may alter a Limit that they have in common by Agreement.

ARTICLE 10

Impeachment

1. The House of Commons shall have the sole Right to prefer a Bill of Impeachment in relation to the Government of Canada and the Provincial representative Assembly required by These Articles shall have the sole Right to prefer a Bill of Impeachment in relation to the Government of the Province.

2. The Senate of Canada shall have the Duty and the sole Right to adjudicate on any Bill of Impeachment.

3. The Senate, after hearing all the Evidence for the Parties and Argument thereon, may dismiss the Bill or, if satisfied that the Person impeached has been guilty of wilful or wanton Crime, infamous Conduct or culpable Neglect of Duty, may vacate the Office or Appointment of that Person and may decree that he shall be liable to the ordinary Processes of the Law for any Wrongs or Crimes for which he has been impeached and of which he has been found guilty.

ARTICLE 11

The Limits of Government

1. Nothing that conflicts with These Articles shall have the force of Law in Canada.

2. No Law shall be enforceable until it has been published and made accessible to those subject to it.

3. No Court may command or enjoin the Parliament, a Provincial Legislature, a House of the Parliament or of a Provincial Legislature, the Governor General, the Head of the Executive Government of a Province or a foreign Sovereign or his recognized Representatives, but otherwise every Person and Body in

Canada, whether public or private, shall be subject to the Law and to the Courts.

4. None shall be denied the equal Protection of the Laws but no Law made to offset Inequalities in Strength or Capacity, due to Age, Sex or other social or economic Condition, is thereby invalid.

5. No public Office or Function and no Title of Honour shall be the subject of Property or Heritable, other than the Crown.

6. Every human Being is a distinct legal Person and full private Capacity shall not be denied to any Person except for Immaturity, established Insanity, Profligacy, Bankruptcy or wilful or wanton Crime.

7. No Law shall impose the Beliefs or Practices of any particular Religion or require any religious Tests for the exercise of any civil Right or public Function, but this shall not prevent public Homage to Almighty God, the setting apart of the Lord's Day or governmental Favour and Support for religious and moral Principles and Activities, if offered without Discrimination between the various religious Bodies.

8. Slavery is unlawful; and no one shall have a proprietory Right to the Person or Services of another human Being, nor shall the specific Performance of any private Contract of Service be decreed or enforced.

9. Everyone has the Right to be secure in his Person, Reputation, Houses, Papers, Communications and Effects against unfounded Interruptions; and no one, without the Authority of a judicial Order or Warrant, shall arrest or detain any adult Person, or forcibly enter a House in the peaceable Occupation of another, unless with a reasonable Belief that it is necessary to do so to prevent the Commission or Concealment of an Offence or the Escape of an Offender or to preserve human Life or Property; nor shall any Warrant issue but upon reasonable Cause, supported by Oath or Affirmation, and sufficiently describing the Place to be searched and the Persons or Things to be seized.

10. Whoever arrests or detains anyone shall, as soon as it is reasonably possible, tell him the Reason for his Arrest or Deten-

tion, permit him to retain and instruct Counsel and bring him before a judicial Magistrate; nor shall reasonable Bail be denied without just Cause.

11. All Trials shall be speedy and public, unless the Law otherwise permits for the Protection of Children or for public Safety or Decency; and everyone is entitled to have his Rights and Obligations determined by an impartial Tribunal, constituted in the ordinary Course, to be heard in Person or by Counsel, to have compulsory Process to obtain Witnesses in his Favour and to have an Interpreter when needed; and no one shall be deprived of Life, Liberty or Property without a reasonable Opportunity to learn the Nature of the Claim or Charge against him, to prepare his Case, to confront and question the Witnesses against him and to make a full Answer and Defence.

12. In every criminal Prosecution, the Accused shall be presumed innocent until proven guilty according to Law; if charged with a treasonable, seditious, homicidal or libellous Offence or one punishable by Death or Whipping, he shall have the Right to be tried by a Jury; if lawfully acquitted or convicted of an indictable Offence, he shall not again be put in jeopardy therefor; and he shall not be compelled to be a Witness against himself; nor shall any Answer given by a Person compelled to be a Witness in any Proceeding be used against that Person in any other Proceeding (unless it be for Perjury in the Answer) if he objected that the Answer might criminate him or if he was denied Counsel.

13. Everyone has the Right to Integrity of Mind and Body and none shall be deprived against his Will of bodily Parts or Functions, for any Cause, or be subjected to mental or physical Torture.

14. No Law shall impose a Penalty for any Act or Omission that was lawful when done or omitted or any new or increased Penalty for any Offence committed before the Time of Enactment.

15. For every Deprivation of a Right there shall be a Remedy enforceable in some Court.

16. Everyone whose Property is taken for public Use, other than by a lawful Tax or Penalty, has the Right to full Compensation as for a Trespass, but if the Taking is lawful he shall have no Right to punitive Damages.

17. Everyone has the Right to work or to refrain from working and no one shall be prevented from working at any Occupation, except for Incompetence or Misconduct therein.

18. Everyone has the Right to acquire Land and other productive Property sufficient for the proper Support of himself and his Dependents and to take and convey it by Deed, Will or otherwise.

19. All Persons have the Right to associate for any peaceable Purpose but Associations resulting in the private Control of great Wealth or Power or tending to restrict economic or political Freedom may be prohibited or limited, and no one shall be compelled to belong to any private Association.

20. Everyone has the Right to marry and to have Children or not to marry; Marriage shall be monogamous and for Life; the Status of a Marriage shall be determined by the Rules of the Religion in relation to which it was made or, in the Absence of such Rules or in the case of a civil Marriage, by the Laws of the last marital Domicile of the Spouses.

21. The Family is the naturally fundamental Society and has the Right to exist intact; the Duty and Right of Parents to keep, rear, discipline and educate their Children shall not be diminished except for Insanity, Depravity or wilful or wanton Neglect.

22. Everyone has the Right to Education, according to his Capacity, for at least Twelve Years at public Expense; and no one, whether he attends a public or a private School, shall be deprived of the equal Benefit of public Funds for educational Purposes; nor shall anyone be denied the Right to maintain or attend private Schools.

23. The Rights and Privileges of any Class of Persons which now exist or which may hereafter be established with respect to Denominational, Dissentient or Separate Schools shall not be prejudicially affected.

24. All religious Confessions and their subordinate Societies shall be recognized as corporate Bodies, not dependent on any Law or Act of Government for their actual or legal Existence and not subject to Law with respect to their Constitutions, Choice of Officers or religious Purposes; they shall have the Right to practise, profess and preach their Tenets peaceably, to communicate with their Members abroad and to own and enjoy Property reasonably sufficient for their religious, educational and charitable Purposes free of Taxation; and Persons engaged chiefly in the Service of Religion shall be exempt from armed Service.

25. The Parliament of Canada may suspend all or any Provisions of this Article in time of actual War for an ascertained Period not exceeding One Year and the Governor General may do the same by Proclamation where a Majority of the Judges of the Supreme Court of Canada is satisfied that Warfare is taking place or imminent on Canadian Soil.

ARTICLE 12

Amendment and Transitional Provisions

1. These Articles may be changed only by an Act of the Parliament of Canada that is ratified by the Legislatures of at least Two Thirds of the Provinces containing Three Quarters of the Population of Canada according to the latest general Census; but any Amendment to this Section, to Article 1 or to Article 11 shall require ratification by the Legislatures of all the Provinces.

2. Every Obligation and Right of the Government of the Confederation now existing in relation to one or more but not all of the Provinces, by virtue of any Provision of the British North America Acts, of any Act of the United Kingdom or of any Imperial Order in Council, shall continue unless repugnant to These Articles and may be changed only by an Act of the Parliament of Canada that is ratified by the Legislature of every Province to which the Provision relates.

3. The Parliament of Canada and the Legislatures of the Provinces shall continue until each is dissolved in the ordinary

Course and the Parliament and each Legislature may provide by Law for any other transitional Matters that may arise in relation to its constitutional Functions or Jurisdiction; but the existing Courts corresponding in Function to those required by These Articles shall continue until altered by Law and the Judges of such Courts shall be deemed to have been appointed hereunder.

4. When These Articles have been enacted by the Parliament of Canada and ratified by the Legislatures of all the Provinces, they shall come into force on a Day to be fixed by the Parliament of Canada.

CHAPTER 7

The Articles in General

There are some general points worth making about these twelve Articles before beginning a detailed discussion. In the first place the Articles are much shorter than the B.N.A. Act, 1867. The Act has one hundred and forty-three unrepealed paragraphs of an original one hundred and forty-seven, together with schedules. The Articles have seventy-eight. Despite this trimming, achieved by deleting a great deal of temporary, local, or secondary matter, the proposal has much that is new and fundamental that we now lack. This is especially true of Articles 2 and 11. Moreover, even where the substance of a provision is carried forward completely there are frequent verbal changes. Legislative draftsmen today prefer the active voice to the passive because the use of a passive or an impersonal construction (such as this clause is) makes it too easy to omit the answer to the important question '*Who* has the duty to do the thing that is commanded?'.

A great deal of wordy detail has been cut out without impairing the effect of what remains. Detail is singularly dangerous in a constitution unless it is capable of being expressed in general terms. One should not have to struggle with such questions as whether Eskimoes are Indians or whether Radio Transmission comes under the class Telegraphs.[1] Detail is usually not sufficiently important or fundamental for the relatively immutable law that a constitution should be.[2] For the most part it can be safely left to the legislator or the judge to supply the practical means of implementing the fundamental law. If a constitution is to last it must be flexible enough to permit growth in its meaning. Thus, the Articles are couched in very general terms for the most part: so general, indeed, that the more prudent solicitors will probably be tempted, even if they agree with them in spirit, to dot many i's and cross many t's. But a constitution should not be a straitjacket. For sure, clothing is not an apt metaphor as it is too superficial. A constitution is rather the principle of an organic structure, the sapling or even the seed, from which the 'living tree' develops.[3] To bear that in mind is to approach the particular clauses in a spirit of reasonable criticism.

On the other hand, the expressions used, although general, are intended to have some content and are not intended to be merely flowery piety or to be filled out by the courts in their discretion without their being given any clues as to the meaning. Such phrases as 'Freedom of Speech, Freedom of Religion, Freedom from Fear, and Freedom from Want' have been avoided because, although they have a significant place in the politics of freedom, they are too Humpty-Dumptyish to form the settled bases of legal rights. Moreover the ideas they denote have been around for a long time and are capable of more meaningful expression. Accordingly, the draft is aimed at philosophical breadth similar in principle to mathematical generality rather than at poetical or oratorical diffuseness.

We proceed to the discussion of the Articles in the following way. In dealing with each Article and section we first of all turn to this point: How fundamental is this proposition? Is it *essential*? That is, is it so much part of this constitution that the enactment would be a different thing, possibly not even a thing of the kind we were going after, without it? Is the proposition *necessary*? Must we have it in order to preserve the character and content of our political system although it may not be an essential part of a fundamental law? Is it *desirable*? Is the purpose of the clause important enough to warrant putting it in a law intended to be paramount, impressive, and difficult to amend?

These are the key questions and to answer them in the affirmative is to justify the particular provision; other remarks deal only with secondary problems. Yet, so primary are most of the matters dealt with, so close are they to first principles, that there is little scope for argument or persuasion. In most cases, a man will either recognize the worth of an idea because it fits into his scheme of things or he will reject it outright as absurd. This is regrettable, for these ideas are capable of rational justification: for every word written here in explanation, a thousand might be added in defence and in promotion. But this would make the book what it cannot be and still fulfil its first object – to put forward the proposed Articles for the consideration of the Canadian people. Nevertheless, it will probably be required at some time to give an account of the spirit of the proposal, and it might as well be now. For the Articles purport to be the expression, in a Canadian setting, of the political wisdom of the Western world.

That world is an outgrowth of Christendom and its extensions, and its political ideals spring, in part, from the morality and theology of Christianity. There are remoter sources in Greek philosophy and, beyond that again, in Judaism. Moreover, modern political thinkers have given them secular bases that, added to the traditional ones, have won them almost universal acceptance in our day. Rousseau's concept of the Social Contract, itself a product of earlier concepts, was particularly persuasive to his generation and is not wholly lost on ours:

> Each of us puts his person and all his power in common under the supreme direction of the general will, and, in our corporate capacity, we receive each member as an individual part of the whole.[4]

The older and the newer views yield some differences. Thus, the traditional philosophy and religion unite to hold that obligations precede rights and that rights derive from them in this way: that we have the right to do what we have the duty to do. So, man has a right to life because God has given him the function and duty of living, growing, and filling the face of the earth. Man has the right to liberty because his Creator endowed him with free will and the function, and hence the duty, of using it to perfect himself. Man has the right to happiness, if he can achieve it, because every creature has the function and duty of pursuing its own perfection. These rights are fundamental because they derive from the fundamental law of human nature, natural law.

The virtue of a written fundamental law is that it can combine such potentially divergent views. For it represents a consensus and hence a social contract; and it can also be the expression of our understanding of justice and thus bring into a single charter ideas of Moses and Samuel, Plato and Aristotle, Augustine and Aquinas, Hobbes and Locke and Rousseau, and of all, indeed, who have added to our concept of the just commonwealth. The living political ideals of this tradition are the complex growth of over three thousand years.

CHAPTER 8

The Preamble

The Preamble, while not of the essence of fundamental federative law, is necessary and desirable. For it sets out the political theory upon which the document is based and thus is a constant reminder to the people of the ideal to which the constitution is a means. As the judicial history of the B.N.A. Acts has shown, the legislatures and the courts can steer the machinery of state created by the law in a great many diverse directions, depending upon their ideas of political theory. The Preamble is thus a signpost, showing the direction that the people has chosen.

The political theory actually embodied here may be summed up as religious, liberal, and democratic. That is the political character of the Canadian people and it is what their first law should express. Accordingly, the first paragraph acknowledges God as the source of all authority: this homage is due to our Creator and it adds another dimension to our inherent rights. It does not involve any prejudice to those who think differently but enlarges the freedom of all.

But then, as the text next indicates, no man attains authority without some method of human selection. God does not nominate and appoint kings or governments. The method of selection must ultimately arise from the consent of the people. This is possible, although rather difficult, to establish, even in the case of a tyranny: so the Stalinist régime, after its usurpation of power from the moderates in the time of Lenin, established stable conditions and a semblance of law and, to the extent that the Russian people acquiesced in this rule and no longer as a people opposed it in act and spirit (which was very largely the case, it seems), it can be said that the rulers had authority. One is not happy with such extreme examples, however, and it gives a more probable appearance to the proposition and makes it more acceptable to us to refer to those revolutions of which, on the whole, we approve, such as the English Civil War, the Restoration, the ousting of James II, the American Revolution, and the French Revolution. The ceremonies of the English coronation, coming down from medieval days, illustrate not only that the Crown is heritable, as of right, but that it represents a compact between ruler and people.

While governments receive their authority through such methods of selection or through constitutions, it is stated that persons in authority are subordinate, not to the people, but only to the conditions of government ordained by the people. Thus the people can lawfully change magistrates, not arbitrarily, but only in conformity to the law. Rousseau describes magistrates as in a middle position, being subject to the constitution but having authority over the people,[1] and this, with a rather larger theory of government than his, is what is meant here.

The second paragraph of the Preamble rejects all those mystical visions of the state that see a corporate beatitude, rather than the good of the individual, as the end of politics. Since we have rejected totalitarianism in its Nazi and Fascist forms abroad we should have the consistency and courage to do so at home. The proposition is a warning against the pyramid-builders of this generation. They exist. In fact, we all probably have a little of that spirit if we share the usual human instinct to manage other people's affairs for them.

The third paragraph of the Preamble sets out the essence of liberal political philosophy, that part that is valid, true, and permanent, with its accidental excesses sloughed off. Many crimes have been committed in the names of Liberty, Equality, and Fraternity, and yet, who can doubt that in a very real sense they are the heart of a just society?

Freedom is the first condition of a true polity. No other principle – not beneficence, not security – can supply the lack of it. Freedom is essential to the citizen: a man without freedom has no just title to the name citizen and without citizens there can be no state. But if there is a state, there must be law.

The essence of a just law is equality. Caste, privilege, and all official and legalized snobbery are repugnant to a free society. We feel this in our bones. We do not resent calling the judge 'Your Honour', but we do resent the manner of the judge that assumes that he is different flesh from us. Our gorge rises at the people who can fix tickets, or who get low-number licence plates. We feel a hearty civic revulsion at any idea that there is one law for this class and another for that. Equality does not mean that everyone has the same quality of mind or the same size of virtues any more than that everyone has the same size of feet. It means that every law has this element of equality, that it does not distinguish between persons on accidental grounds having nothing to do with the merits of the case. Equality in the law is thus compatible with laws dealing with different groups of people, such as men and women, parents and children, in different ways, when these laws are based on the social functions and relations of the groups concerned. But it is not compatible with denying the vote to Uncle Tom because he is black. Equality, in short, means an equal law.[2]

Now law and liberty clash, frustrate each other, and are sterile unless they are reconciled by a third element, brotherhood. Where brotherhood is absent, liberty does not accept law, although law is essential to true liberty, and law crushes liberty, although human law without liberty is a contradiction. It is probably not the best name for what we mean, but it is near enough, and it is sanctioned by long usage in the context.

Brotherhood is a certain act of the intellect and a consequent act of the will. Freedom in solitude is barren. To accomplish any but the most modest desire, to fulfil all but the most meagre appetites, we need the co-operation of our fellows. We can attempt this in an absolutely self-centred world by arrogating to ourselves all liberty and rejecting all law, or we can accept civil

society and law and pursue our liberty as a citizen. In this latter
alternative we know that all citizens are entitled to the like liberty
and that our liberty does not extend to infringe theirs. It follows
that the law both enlarges our freedom, that is, our possible
action, by making civil society possible and fruitful, and at the
same time it circumscribes it to what is innocent in relation to
our fellows. The act of intellect is a recognition that true liberty
is freedom to choose what is good, and that society fulfils its
prime function by amplifying the field of choice for our benefit.

It is one thing to know such a principle: it is another, more
difficult thing to accept it and apply it to ourselves. It requires
an act of the will, indeed many acts of the will, until the acceptance becomes a habit. Such a habit can only be achieved through
a certain virtue that we know by various names such as love,
natural charity, benevolence, or good will. For though the habit
has a rational, prudent basis in the individual's own benefit, to
be real, so as to prevail over the immediate advantage of acting
against the law and society, it must be more than selfish. It is of
the same nature as patriotism, which is the unselfish love of one's
country. The unselfish love of our fellow man requires that we
try to understand him and that we respect his rights. This spirit,
when it is the mark of a society, may fairly be called brotherhood.

It involves positive civic virtues, a realization of the proper
scope of our own conduct, and a heartfelt acceptance of law,
especially the moral law, but also any just civil law. It does not
involve, of course, any surrender to the ignorance or malice of
those who will not accept or obey the law. On the contrary, the
spirit of brotherhood requires that malefactors and those who
would subvert liberty be restrained and corrected.

It follows that this third paragraph of the Preamble demands
more than mere tolerance: it demands active mutual good will.

Apart from that, it represents a position on which all main
parties in the country are agreed; platforms differ merely as to
the means to carry it into effect. It is true that in the last century,
restraints on private greed were not considered a function of government, unless it took the form of theft or embezzlement. This
has passed; greed is now recognized as a potent danger to the

public peace and good order. Great private powers (from which unions are not excluded) threaten governments themselves, and every modern state to some extent controls the unlimited accumulation of wealth, unfair competition, and monopolistic practices.

In the fourth paragraph of the Preamble the structural plan of the constitution is set out. It makes a clear choice of a written basic law and a balance of powers rather than the Old World solution of a sovereign legislature, which is not suitable for a federal system. In this, the proposal seems to refer to the constitutional separation of powers[3] in the United States or even to the extreme form of the Massachusetts constitution.[4] But it should not be forgotten that the term 'separation of powers' was first used, although somewhat mistakenly, with reference to the British constitution.[5] In any case it is implicit in the present Canadian structure to a large extent, for our executive governments have always exercised powers apart from the parliament and legislatures, and our judiciary has acted constantly to limit the other functionaries of government to what is lawful. The Preamble of the British North America Act, 1867, makes an explicit distinction between the legislative authority and the executive government of the Dominion.

The division of powers by function is a very old device and a very reasonable one. It would seem that the Romans had some notion of it when they elected a variety of independent magistrates such as the consuls and the censor. Aristotle propounds a more scientific idea where he discusses at length the powers that the assembly, the magistrates, and the courts should have.[6] Separation of powers is as reasonable and efficient a guarantee of freedom as can well be devised and it is absolutely necessary to a confederacy in order to resolve those clashes that overlapping jurisdictions evoke.

But the proposed division is no more absolute than the one we have. The executive government will retain its present law-making powers (it may have more), the legislature will keep its control of judicial procedures, and the judiciary will have rule-making powers. It is the principal functions of each that will be separate and the separation will be embedded in the constitution.[7]

We come to the last paragraph of the Preamble. This, besides serving as a statement of enactment, sets out the parties that enter into the action, 'the People, Parliament and Provinces of Canada'. It is thus recorded that all have had a hand in the product and an interest in the result.

From the Preamble the courts should understand that the constitution represents not only the practical decision of the people and governments of Canada but also a statement, however imperfect, of reason and justice. It is not mere will but an intelligent will, mind that has discovered and endeavoured to express truth. It is not only an edict: it is the summation of the best things of our diverse traditions in a paramount judgment.

CHAPTER 9

The Name, Form and Languages of the Confederation

SECTION 1

The Name of the Confederation

This section does for the Articles what Sections 3 and 4 of the B.N.A. Act, 1867, do for that Act. Section 3 of that Act states that the Provinces

> ... shall form and be One Dominion under the name of Canada; ...

And Section 4 now reads,

> ... unless it is otherwise expressed or implied, the Name Canada shall be taken to mean Canada as constituted under this Act.

The latter clause is merely an interpretative one, made necessary by the pre-existence of the Province of Canada, which was split into Quebec and Ontario at Confederation; but it makes superabundantly clear that Canada's name was 'Canada'.

Nevertheless, for most of its existence, the Confederation has been known popularly and to a great extent officially as the 'Dominion of Canada', despite the express words of Section 3, and despite the fact that the word 'Dominion' is not used as part of the name in the B.N.A. Acts. Indeed, it does not seem to appear in the B.N.A. Act, 1867, except in the preamble and in Section 3.[1] And yet, when the Liberal administration in the mid 1950s made several overt moves to drop the word 'Dominion' from the title, there was considerable outcry. This indicates, at any rate, that there are people who think the name of their country to be a matter of some importance, unless, of course, it is an indication that some people will oppose any change whatever. The section as proposed should put them in a dilemma because it does not propose any legal change, however new it may appear.

It is not essential or even necessary but it is certainly desirable that the fundamental law contain the name of the nation, if only to give stability to that name. One need only think of the many changes in the names of other nations in our time and it will fully appear that this section is well worth while. Fortunately, the alternatives to 'Canada' are not apparent, nor has anyone seriously attacked it.[2] The possibilities are endless, of course, but they are not attractive. We shrink from a descriptive title such as 'The Confederate Provinces of British North America', and we would shrink the more from the more likely products of this age of initials and portmanteau words, such as 'CPBNA' or 'Britnoram'.

The noun 'Confederation' and the adjective 'federal' are used throughout wherever 'Canada' would be ambiguous. Most constitutional authorities now agree that 'Dominion' is no longer apt to express the status of the nation, which has evolved beyond 'dominion status'.[3] Other expressions might be used, but 'Confederation' and 'federal' are probably the most accurate and are in well-established common use.

SECTION 2

The Form of the Confederation

The whole of the British North America Acts must be considered as material corresponding to this section of Article 1, but if any portions are more particularly related to it they are the preamble and Sections 3, 5, 6, and 7 of the B.N.A. Act, 1867.

The chief criticism to be made of these provisions is that the role of the provinces is not clearly stated. This has been the point of departure of many attacks on provincial autonomy and of as many efforts to weaken the federal power. Did the B.N.A. Act create new provinces? If so, do these new provinces continue the old in any way? Have they any rights under the agreements made before the Act of 1867? The effect of these questions and the answers to them suggested by the preamble and the structure of the B.N.A. Act, 1867, is that Canada is not a true federal union, that the provinces are creations of the Act, that all governmental powers in Canada come from or through the Act (and its subsequent amendments), and that the residue of powers not explicitly stated lies with the central government.[4] This appears to be the view of O'Connor if one bears in mind his ruling principle that the intent was to divide powers between the Dominion and provincial governments on the basis of a division between national and local legislation.[5] On the other hand, Clement held that there is a residue of unexpressed powers for both the central government and the provinces, and this may be what O'Connor meant also.[6]

Much of the trouble stemmed from the need to resurrect the old provinces of Lower and Upper Canada (under new names) without reverting to the legal situation of 1840 when they were united as the Province of Canada. The device adopted of creating new provinces fitting the limits of the old had the result of reducing the continuing provinces of Nova Scotia and New Brunswick to the like status.[7] The result is fortunate from the point of view of simplicity of structure but unfortunate from the viewpoint of historical continuity and the sanctity of agreements.

Another part of the 1867 preamble that is subject to criticism as inappropriate and nebulous is the phrase 'Constitution similar in Principle to that of the United Kingdom'. As previously remarked, the true principle of the United Kingdom's constitution is the supremacy of parliament, and that principle cannot be applied to the Canadian scheme or to any truly federal union as a dominant theme. In Canada it has a subordinate effect: the parliament and legislatures are parliamentary in function but not in scope and cannot exceed the limits of their respective law-making powers.[8] The phrase under discussion has probably had some effect in the occasional tendency to overstress the parliamentary nature of the parliament of Canada.

The phrase was intended to have force, however, and to mean that political action in Canada should follow the same rules as in Great Britain. Undoubtedly what the colonial delegates and the Colonial Office both had in mind was the system called 'responsible government', in which the sovereign, or chief of state, does not actually administer the executive government, which function is rather that of the prime minister or other head of the administration. The executive is responsible to the legislature in the sense that the executive cannot rule for long without the support of the legislature because of the latter's control over taxation and expenditure. In practice the executive does not try to rule without that support. In its turn, the legislature is responsible to the electorate through general elections.[9]

While not essential, it is desirable as it is necessary, to avoid misunderstanding, that the constitution should state the *form* of the union. That is, it should be made clear that it is a union; that the provinces are autonomous; that, on the other hand, the provinces are not separate nations and that there is but one nation; and that the union is federal. The ambiguity, obscurity, and contradictions of the B.N.A. Acts on these points have caused much litigation and, as some think, a warping of the original structure. If these rather important propositions are left to be implied, some court may decide, quite sincerely and lawfully, that they could have been expressed, and since they were not, they were not intended. While this reasoning is even weaker and more illogical than the exclusion rule mentioned above[10] it is a common method in the case law. Our constitutional history affirms that the matters contained in this section are important enough to be stated in the Articles.

The word 'nation' has become contentious since this book took its final shape. To avoid becoming involved in the current dispute, the significance of the word in the section should be made clear. It has the same meaning as when we speak of the American nation, the Indian nation, the Belgian nation, or the nation of any other state containing a number of ethnic nationalities. It relates to nations only as the sources of nationality in international law, a neutral sense. It does not prejudge whether there is a Canadian nation composed of English-speaking and French-speaking nations any more than it prejudges whether there is a British nation composed of English, Scottish, and Welsh nations, or whether such nations within nations should have distinct political institutions.

SECTION 3

The National Languages

The partnership of two cultural traditions expressed in the French and English languages is an essential part of Confederation. Every proposal for giving Canada power to amend the constitution has treated this partnership of languages as essential, entrenched, and not to be changed without the consent of all provinces. The section reiterates the law and proposes that it be extended to all the legislatures and to all the courts: to all the legislatures because the law is not truly equitable if it applies only to Quebec; to all the courts because our judicial system is at once federal and local in character.

On the other hand the provisions for printing that are contained in Section 133 of the B.N.A. Act, 1867, are omitted as unnecessary and discriminatory. They are not necessary because Quebec has a well-established tradition of fairness to the English-speaking population. They are discriminatory because they apply to no other province.[11] To apply them universally would only cause friction without any useful result. It is better to leave them out.

After an initial attempt by the British régime to substitute English civil law and customs, the French culture established by the first colonists of Canada was guaranteed by the Quebec Act, 1774, and this guarantee was continued by subsequent constitutional acts, including that of 1867. That culture survived and is a present fact, different in quality and right from the cultures of other ethnic groups in Canada, who came here subject to its existence in fact and law. It is a fact that cannot be suppressed justly or by any civilized process, however angry either side may be about its existence. It can be got rid of only by the withdrawal or expulsion of Quebec (and probably New Brunswick) from Canada, and hardly then. But it is quite clear that Canada would not survive this parting, even physically.

But Canada has a spiritual need for the French as well. They add a necessary element to the amalgam that is beginning to be known as the Canadian. Moreover, those who combine the two cultures are our most urbane, our most civilized, our most reasonable citizens. It would be a sad error to put asunder the sources of such qualities.

A loyal adherence to the spirit of this Article would exorcize the ghosts of separatism and secession in Quebec, British Columbia, and the Atlantic provinces.

CHAPTER 10

The Citizenship

It is not essential that a federal constitution should deal with the citizenship. Such a law may omit this particular and yet fulfil its purpose. That is, in fact, the case with the B.N.A. Act. The Act, by Class 25 of Section 91, gives the parliament of Canada exclusive legislative authority over matters in the class of subjects 'Naturalization and Aliens'. By Section 95 the central government and the provinces have concurrent legislative powers with respect to immigration (and agriculture) and these powers are what are called in this book *dominant* powers of the central government. That is, a provincial law on such a matter is ineffective to the extent that it is repugnant to federal law.

The sections cited do not define the body of citizens and their basic rights: on the contrary, if they touch the citizenship at all, they make it completely subject to the parliament and the legislatures. It is a moot point whether they give any power over native Canadian citizens or subjects. At first glance, the words *naturalization, aliens*, and *immigration* would not be applicable to native Canadians. On the other hand, until recently there was one sole nationality, British, for the whole Empire, and it is not doubted that the parliament and legislatures could deal with British subjects under the immigration powers of Section 95.

The B.N.A. Act does not use the word *citizen*, probably because in 1867 the term, and even the idea, was alien to British legal thought.[1] We now have the Canadian Citizenship Act,[2] which deals mainly with naturalization but does define the native body of citizens.[3] If federal legislation dealing with native Canadian nationals is valid, either under Section 91, Class 25, or Section 95, or under the general power to provide for the peace, order, and good government of Canada (exclusive of provincial jurisdiction), it is a fairly positive conclusion that, whatever their legal rights, Canadians have no *constitutional* rights to the citizenship or to the usual rights consequent upon the citizenship such as the right to return to Canada after going abroad.

So it would seem very desirable and even necessary that the body of the citizens be constitutionally defined. It should not be left to ordinary law, made in the ordinary parliamentary way, to determine who are the members of the political society. This is not because parliaments or governments would usually abuse their powers, but because they might. It was not unknown in the recent past for states to transport subjects forcibly as punishment or even as colonial reinforcement. It is surely not an impossibility in our heartless age. There is therefore a good case for the inclusion of this Article.

Section 1 gives a common method for determining the native body of citizens.[4] It does not, of course, say that such persons are citizens, but only that they are entitled to become citizens. Thus, the mere accident of birth in Canada would not automatically make a citizen of a person who had spent all the rest of his life elsewhere. He would have to take some action to become a citizen, but citizenship could not be denied him unless he had renounced it or had become a citizen of another country. Ordinarily a resident native of Canada would become a citizen through automatic processes of law. Section 1 is somewhat wider than the provisions of the Citizenship Act, but there is no strong repugnancy between them. It would be imprudent and short-sighted to try to incorporate the detail and complexities of the Act in the Articles.

Section 2 makes it clear that the process of naturalization applies not only to the admission of aliens to the citizenship but

to the readmission of those who have given it up. Article 7, Section
1, Class 6 makes this a matter of dominant federal legislation
and hence of ordinary law, and thus distinguishes it radically
from native entitlement to the citizenship. This also is a common
provision,[5] generally accepted, and should cause no heart-burn-
ing. It is of course not essential, but it is a necessary complement
of Sections 1 and 3.

Under Section 3, once anyone becomes a citizen, whether by
native right or by naturalization, he cannot be denationalized
without his consent, which may, however, be implied. This could
happen if he freely became a member of another state, or renounced the citizenship, or if he committed treason or the like
crime that showed that he had transferred his loyalty. Section
3 is desirable as being in accord with international law and
justice.[6] In fact, the only status for a person deprived of citizenship is outlawry, which is repugnant to modern jurisprudence.
Article 15 of the Universal Declaration of Human Rights shows
that this principle has international approval:

ARTICLE 15

1. Everyone has the right to a nationality.
2. No one shall be arbitrarily deprived of his nationality nor
denied the right to change his nationality.

There is, of course, a distinction between nationality and citizenship, but the provisions of the Articles make them synonymous
for Canada.

Section 4 enacts a uniform principle of provincial citizenship.
This does not now exist and there are instances on the statute
book of discriminatory laws in this respect.[7] The division of
powers here has resulted in uncertainty and some injustice, not
so much in the policies the legislatures have followed in fixing
voters' qualifications, but in collateral matters, such as taxation
and freedom to work and trade. The section, in consequence, may
meet some opposition from those representing provincial interests,
but the need for it is the need for unity on the citizenship, a root

matter. The object is to establish beyond cavil what appears to be the existing practice, which is, however, threatened by too narrow a provincialism. The section will help to avoid the legal snarls that have arisen in the United States because they have no uniform rule of state citizenship. It will permit the free interplay of cultural forces and tend to prevent excessive particularism. It is part of a context that withholds from the provinces certain negative means of self-protection, such as customs tariffs and linguistic monopolies, while ensuring that they have the utmost positive autonomy and freedom in their control over civil rights, education, local government, and the like. Section 4 is not, of course, essential or even necessary but, in view of the history of this country and of the United States, it appears to be most desirable.

In Section 5, universal adult suffrage is chosen, with the usual exception of mentally or morally deficient persons, as the voting rule. Others might be excepted: for example, illiterates. It is trite that the citizenship and the franchise are distinct privileges and the latter does not necessarily go with the former. Membership in a political society does not necessarily connote the right to vote. In some states it might be rational and prudent to deny the franchise to whole classes of adult, sane citizens because they are too ignorant or too savage to understand how to use the function properly. No doubt such an argument can be used for selfish motives and often is. It is a question that need not trouble us further. In our society, which is politically homogeneous and has a long tradition of universal adult suffrage (long enough at any rate to make any alternative absurd), there is no ground for a further limitation of the right to vote. A limited franchise is too fertile a soil for the growth of oligarchy, which is, of all political systems, the most opposed to democratic ideals. We need not refer to the poll tax laws and the literacy tests of the southern United States to see how such laws can be abused and too partially applied in favour of an ascendency group. Like things have happened nearer home. However there are other states that use this device quite fairly and impartially.

One might call Section 5 necessary for the kind of democracy we have and want to continue to have without characterizing it as essential.

The much-debated matter of free speech in Section 6 is, without being essential to a federal constitution, necessary to our conception of democracy. If anything, the section will appear to many to be too docile through the reiteration of the adjective 'peaceable'. But it is an attempt to express succinctly and accurately the just limits of freedom of expression while ensuring that the freedom is real. Anything less would be an illusory liberty but anything more would license sedition, and this a democracy can tolerate no more than can any other form of government. A common-sense interpretation, jealous of legislative and executive authority but more jealous of the common weal and civic rights, would establish this section as the first principle of orderly political development. That is, the government would not be able to prevent such comment and such assemblies unless they offered a real and present danger of disrupting the peace.

Two things should be noted about this provision. Firstly, it treats freedom of speech and assembly as a political right and not as a human one. Secondly, it incorporates what may or may not be a fundamental right in Canada.

The truth of the first point is obvious but seems to have been submerged lately by waves of emotion. Both the Universal Declaration of Human Rights, Article 19, and the Canadian Bill of Rights, Sections 2 (d) and (e), appear to conceive of these freedoms as human ones, not merely political, and so not limited to the members of the political society in which they exist. This notion is at odds with international law so far as political comment and contacts by resident non-citizens are concerned. If a foreign envoy, for example, makes political speeches on our soil, as one sometimes does, that can be a subject for protest to his government and even for his recall, and if a foreign national should indulge in the like he is subject to expulsion. This is entirely just and proper; constitutional freedom of political action should be restricted to citizens. Recent decades have emphasized the folly of any other course, except when it is an act of grace by the host state.

The second point arises from a 1938 decision of the Supreme Court of Canada,[8] later upheld by the Privy Council,[9] that an Alberta bill setting up some measure of control over the press was invalid. The court did not deny that the provinces had some right to curtail freedom of speech when it amounted to a private wrong or an infringement of individual rights, but it was held that they could not deal with excesses of speech as public wrongs or crimes, and that this was what the bill tried to do. It was thus an unlawful invasion of the field of criminal law, which is a subject exclusively within federal powers under Class 27 of Section 91 of the B.N.A. Act. This does not, of course, establish free speech as a constitutional right but leaves it subject to the usual law enacted by the parliament of Canada.

Chief Justice Duff, however, went further. He held:

> Under the constitution established by *The British North America Act*, legislative power for Canada is vested in one Parliament consisting of the Sovereign, an upper house styled the Senate, and the House of Commons. Without entering in detail upon an examination of the enactments of the Act relating to the House of Commons, it can be said that these provisions manifestly contemplate a House of Commons which is to be, as the name itself implies, a representative body; constituted, that is to say, by members elected by such of the population of the united provinces as may be qualified to vote. The preamble of the statute, moreover, shows plainly enough that the constitution of the Dominion is to be similar in principle to that of the United Kingdom. The statute contemplates a parliament working under the influence of public opinion and public discussion.[10]

He goes on to say that the 'right of public discussion is, of course, subject to legal restrictions. . . . Even within its legal limits, it is liable to abuse and grave abuse . . .', but:

> . . . it is axiomatic that the practice of the right of free public discussion of public affairs, notwithstanding its incidental mischiefs, is the breath of life for parliamentary institutions.
>
> We do not doubt that (in addition to the power of disallowance vested in the Governor General) the Parliament of Canada possesses authority to legislate for the protection of this right. That author-

ity rests upon the principle that the powers requisite for the protection of the constitution itself arise by necessary implication from *The British North America Act* as a whole. . . .[11]

In the same case, Mr. Justice Cannon said:

> . . . As stated in the preamble of *The British North America Act*, our constitution is and will remain, unless radically changed 'similar in principle to that of the United Kingdom'. At the time of Confederation, the United Kingdom was a democracy. Democracy cannot be maintained without its foundation: free public opinion and free discussion throughout the nation of all matters affecting the State within the limits set by the criminal code and the common law. Every inhabitant of Alberta is also a citizen of the Dominion. The province may deal with his property and civil rights of a local and private nature within the province; but the province cannot interfere with his status as a Canadian citizen and his fundamental right to express freely his untrammelled opinion about government policies and discuss matters of public concern. The mandatory and prohibitory provisions of the Press Bill are, in my opinion, *ultra vires* of the provincial legislature. They interfere with the free working of the political organization of the Dominion. . . . The federal parliament is the sole authority to curtail, if deemed expedient and in the public interest, the freedom of the press in discussing public affairs and the equal rights in that respect of all citizens throughout the Dominion.[12]

This case does not hold that the central government cannot abrogate freedom of speech; indeed it goes far to say that it can. But the themes chosen for the judgments cited, 'the working of the parliamentary institutions of Canada as contemplated by the provisions of The British North America Act'[13] and 'the free working of the political organization of the Dominion',[14] suggest very strongly that the constitution is the source of political rights that are essential to parliamentary democracy, so essential that no Canadian government can lawfully do away with them. Such a political right would not be inalienable in the United States sense, but it might be inviolable in a new, tenuous, and unpredictable Canadian sense. That is, if it should exist: the case gives only tentative and uncertain hope that it does. Indeed, three of the six judges explicitly reserved any such question until it should arise in more concrete form.

Section 6 of Article 2 would therefore be not only eminently more desirable than the present doubtful situation but, in view of the reasoning of the judges and especially of the scope that they were willing to allow to the federal power to deal with free speech as a matter of criminal law, the section is necessary and even essential for a free people.

There are those who might consider Section 7 as an echo of the eighteenth century and about as suitable for a twentieth-century constitution as a minuet in a jazz cellar. It smacks of the complaints against the Hessians in the England and New England of the first Georges. The purpose of this paragraph is to make sure, as far as any law can, that our domestic political matters remain such, even to the extent of keeping a civil war in Canada within the Canadian family. It is repugnant to the dearest beliefs of free man that any party in the state, even the government, should rely on alien forces. It is a truism that any government that needs the help of our friends the Russians, or the Americans, or the English, or the Utopians, is not our government: it does not belong to us.

Section 8 is, in a certain way, a corollary, an immediate consequent of the preceding section. It has somewhat the same air of the times of Rousseau, Paine, and Jefferson. It would, indeed, be much too mild for them, but it is designed to deal with very different social conditions, in an unarmed, urban, and urbane society. Where rebellion against the government is virtually impossible we have the seeds of tyranny, a tyranny not too remote from fact in the instability of modern politics. It could happen here, not only by a conspiracy but even if an average government should take its evangel too seriously. We all can recall that fascism had its admirers in Canada during the '30s, some in high places.

Rebellion is impossible when the people are unarmed. It is therefore desirable and necessary for the protection of our democratic laws and institutions that the citizens have the right to arms. The problem was solved in the United States by giving the states the constitutional right to maintain state militias.[15] This is contrary to our tradition in Canada and it would probably not be acceptable to any Canadian interest, federal, provincial, or otherwise. But the right can be preserved to the citizens themselves. For what purpose? To resist the government? By no means: that must always be contrary to the law. The purpose stated in the section, however, is a legitimate one and has weighty reasons of its own to commend it. For the police are not always with us to protect us from murderers, rapists, robbers, and those who would do us grievous harm. There are some police officials and public men who would willingly have all private fire-arms confiscated, not for any sinister motive but out of zeal for the public peace. How many people, how many members of parliament indeed, know what the most recent provisions of the Criminal Code contain or even when they were passed? A single amendment, sponsored by an overzealous or short-sighted minister of justice, could give legality to a general prohibition of fire-arms. On this ground – the security of the home – the proposed section is a useful and desirable provision; for the reasons first given it is necessary for the stability of our freedoms.

None of the eight sections of this Article, as we have noted above, appear in form or matter in the British North America Acts. Some have counterparts in other organic laws and in bills of rights, such as the Universal Declaration of Human Rights. This may lend some weight to the argument that they should be in the Canadian constitution, but it is better to consider them on their own merits. In that light, each is a substantial, desirable, and even necessary addition to the laws that guarantee the just scope and dignity of our citizenship.

CHAPTER 11

The Parliament and the Senate

The third Article propounds the elements of the principal law-making body of the Confederation. Since the constituent states have a vital interest in the composition and powers of this institution and since such an institution there must be, the Article is an essential one. The elements of the central legislature in which the provinces have an interest must be set down. So also must those things be set down on which the general political rights of the people depend, in particular the political system that we desire to maintain.

Our political system is representative democracy, which itself is divisible into two chief species. We have favoured the type usually known as responsible government, that is, the cabinet system where the real executive is part of the elected legislature and rules with the *confidence* of that body. If the government loses the confidence of the legislature, it must either make way for a different government or seek a general election. Usually, however, it can appeal to the electorate by a general election at a time of its own choosing on the issues that it considers most favourable.

This system contrasts with that of constitutional government, the type of democracy that prevails in the United States and in most of the western hemisphere. In that system legislature and executive may, and often do, represent opposed political parties, and the executive can neither anticipate nor delay the appeal to the electorate. The continuation of the executive government is provided for by the constitution rather than the confidence of the parliament.

Responsible government is written into our provincial constitutions by the provisions of Class 1 of Section 92 of the B.N.A. Act, which forbids the provinces to legislate with respect to the 'Office of Lieutenant-Governor'. The prohibition is a merely inferential one but this simple phrase effectually prevents any radical change in the system. Despite the declared intention of the Canadian delegates to the Quebec Conference of 1864 to build responsible government into the fabric of the central government[1] (a deliberate choice between responsible government and the United States system) and despite the elaborate detail of the 1867 act in dealing with the central government, there has not existed since the 1949 (No. 2) Amendment any similar restriction upon the federal government; a departure from responsible government to some other basis of representative democracy is now legally and theoretically possible.

Accordingly, while it is necessary and essential to preserve and fortify the bases of representative democracy in Canadian government, there does not seem to be any need to reinstate responsible government, as opposed to constitutional government, in the constitution. Because of this and in order to keep the constitution as flexible as possible, consistent with its federal nature, the Article has been limited to the essentials of representative democracy as practised in the Confederation. Responsible government, whatever its virtues, is not essential either to representative democracy as such or to any provincial or minority interest in the constitution; so the Articles are silent on the subject.

This contrasts strongly with existing legislation. The organization and powers of the parliament of Canada contained in Part IV of the B.N.A. Act, 1867, originally consisted of forty-one sections. Of these, three have been repealed and one added. The thirty-nine survivors vary considerably in importance: at least six are no longer operative in law, being what are called 'transitional provisions' designed to bring the Confederation into being. Section 19, for instance, enacts that the first parliament shall be called together within six months after the union.

Sections 56 and 57 deal with the reserving of acts of parliament by the Governor General for the 'Queen in Council': that is, the United Kingdom government is given a right to refuse assent to such acts. This is a dead letter and is recognized as such as a result of the Imperial Conference of 1930.

The remaining sections deal with a great many matters that might well be left to the parliament itself to determine, such as the number of members of the House of Commons and their qualifications, the election of the Speakers, the terms of the senators, resignations, manner of counting votes, and similar topics, most of which are not of sufficient importance to take up space in a fundamental law the amendment of which should require a much greater than usual concurrence of assent.

But things of such fundamental importance do exist. Two of them are recognized in the 1949 (No. 2) Amendment: the right to an annual parliament and the limitation of the House of Commons to a five-year term. These are of general interest and are essential to representative democracy. But while one can feel considerable sympathy with the desire of the federal government to control its own structure, because the B.N.A. Act is too minute, too detailed, and deals with too many non-essentials, on the other hand the 1949 (No. 2) Amendment goes too far. In particular the power of the purse should be a constitutional one, the members of the parliament should be immune from summary ouster, and if the Senate is to continue as now, not subject to electoral control (as it may under the Article), there should be some method of carrying the will of the electorate against the veto of that house.

SECTION 1

The Composition of the Parliament

The parliaments and legislatures of the British Commonwealth consisted, until recent years, of the sovereign and one or two houses of parliament. Now there are several member states where the place of the Queen has been taken by a president or other functionary. In the sixth Quebec Resolution it was proposed that

6. There shall be a general Legislature or Parliament for the Federated Provinces, composed of a Legislative Council and a House of Commons

without mention of the Queen. This was probably an oversight, although Sir John A. MacDonald gives a plausible explanation of the wording in the pre-Confederation debates of 1865 in Canada,[2] because the omission was repaired in the London Resolutions (also Number 6) and in Section 17 of the B.N.A. Act, 1867.

Although it may trouble those whose transoceanic loyalties commonly override their Canadian ones, there is no essential need to mention the sovereign as a component part of the parliament. It is a matter of established law that the Crown is a part of parliament so that the section is, as Sir John A. Macdonald pointed out with respect to Quebec Resolution Number 6, not designed to exclude the Crown.[3] But the essential function of the sovereign with respect to parliament and as part of it is to give the royal assent to bills as the formal means of making them law; this is dealt with in Section 9, which is so phrased that it is effectual under either type of representative democracy.

The function, the essential function, of Section 1 is to establish a bicameral legislature, which is the part of the matter that is of federal concern. In other ways, the section and the Article permit wide limits of composition. The arguments of Sir John A., however they may have been inspired, retain their force, and the section accordingly restores the substance of Quebec Resolution Number 6.

Well, why two houses? In a unitary state it is conceivable that a very satisfactory legislature could, for example, be composed of two types of lawmakers who would meet as one body, subject to whatever rules proved necessary to carry the popular will into effect. Thus, to the elected representatives could be added people of experience, special knowledge, or useful talents, who could bring their gifts to bear directly on their elected colleagues rather than trying to impress each other and the empty air somewhere else. Such a unicameral legislature would have many of the advantages that appealed to Aristotle in his *Politics*.

But in a federal state there is a vital need of just such a balance as is provided by two legislative chambers chosen on different principles: the one to represent the electorate at large, and the other for the sole or chief purpose of representing the interests of the component states. The perfect type of this balance is that of the Congress of the United States: the perfection, balance, and theoretical beauty of the scheme is to a large extent carried into practice. This type was copied rather freely in the Australian Constitution and very imperfectly in our own. The difficulty with the Canadian compromise is that, if it suited 1864, when it was arrived at, and 1867, when it was enacted (and this is subject to doubt), it does not suit today. In the result, the Senate is held in low esteem, but it is more urgent than ever that the provinces as such should have effective and equal representation in the parliament.

SECTION 2

The Senate

The Canadian Senate is like vice or the weather: everyone has something to say about it, usually derogatory, but no one is sure what should be done about it.[4] Our senators are, on the whole, men and women of well above average ability and achievement. It is doubtful that any such concentration of talent and intelligence could be gathered together either by popular election or by the lottery of noble birth. Despite the quality of its membership, the Senate lacks the prestige of either the House of Lords or of the Senate of the United States. The reasons for this lack of esteem are not far to seek. Popular election gives the accolade, as does the aura of being born into a great name and presumptive great wealth, in ways that are acceptable to the citizenry. Mankind recognizes merit that it has itself helped to create or that is vouched for by its having held on to property for several generations. Mankind begs leave to differ with the selections that are made by a professional politician however eminent, especially in view of the widely harboured suspicion that senatorships are granted to placate newspaper publishers and to pension fellow politicians. It is obvious that the public has difficulty in relating the resultant composition of the Senate to its proper functions, and it withholds its respect.

Moreover, the Canadian Senate has played the part of the House of Lords rather than that of the United States Senate. The latter body is a dynamic one that frequently initiates major laws and is a full partner in the government of the country. The House of Lords, on the other hand, sees itself as the helpful critic, the brake, the warning voice, the organ of second thoughts. It is not too unkind to describe it as the sleeping partner that rouses itself on occasion to prevent the more venturesome member, the House of Commons, from putting the firm in bankruptcy.

This role was planned for the Canadian Senate at its conception. In the words of the Honourable Alexander Campbell, he

> . . . would have that House conservative, calm, considerate and watchful, to prevent the enactment of measures which, in its deliberate judgment, were not calculated to advance the common weal.[5]

The role was imposed on the Senate by the initial conditions of Confederation, the very strong imperial sentiments then prevalent in the governing group, the power of the executive government to obtain constitutional changes, and the parliamentary habits adopted at that time. In addition, such a role is implicit in the phrase of the preamble to the 1867 Act, 'a Constitution similar in Principle to that of the United Kingdom', and in Sections 53 and 54 of that Act which require that money bills originate only in the House of Commons and then only on a message by the Governor General.

But the Senate has not had enough weight to sustain its part as so conceived and the public does not accept its intervention as necessary or even useful. So, reform of the Senate is a persistent bass note in Canadian politics, never a strident one but always part of the background noise.[6]

A second chamber in the Canadian parliament is not only desirable but necessary for many reasons. The chief reason is the need to give a distinct, representative instrument to those elements of the Confederation that exist in addition to the citizens as individuals. The main elements of this kind are the member states, but in a federal state there are bound to be other distinct minorities whose interests should be protected and preserved. This cannot be done through a unicameral legislature based on ordinary popular representation where each lawmaker represents a roughly equal number of citizens.[7]

Nor is there an acceptable alternative in leaving the interests of the member states to be protected in the legislature by their own state governments. If these were to try to intervene, advise on, and review federal law the process would become totally inoperable.

The choice is clearly a body of representatives constructed to give an effective voice to the member states and to other special interests concerned. The relative importance of such states and interests cannot be gauged by their numbers: to the extent that numbers are important the Commons chamber represents them quite adequately. Indeed it has been the undue emphasis on numerical importance that has warped the structure of the Senate. The only solution, because it is the only practical solution as far as the member states are concerned, is equal representation.

In Canada, we do not now have equal representation of the provinces in the Senate, but a compromise whereby the country is divided into four regions – the West, Ontario, Quebec, and the Maritimes, with Newfoundland as an appendix. Each region has twenty-four senators, which number may be increased to twenty-five or twenty-six. Newfoundland has six. The peculiarity of this division can be seen more clearly in tabular form:

Nova Scotia	10			Manitoba	6
New Brunswick	10	Quebec	24	Saskatchewan	6
Prince Edward Island	4	Ontario	24	Alberta	6
Newfoundland	6			British Columbia	6

Why was this curious distribution adopted? Or why was not the United States system or the British used for the chamber instead of this odd mixture?

From the *Confederation Debates*[8] it appears that the Newfoundland and Maritime delegates to the Quebec Conference (with the exception of those from P.E.I.) objected to the election of senators, fearing that the elective principle would provide a lever to bring in representation by population in that chamber. The Province of Canada had been experimenting with an elected upper house containing a residue of appointed members since 1856, but this idea was no more acceptable to the Atlantic provinces, which, except for P.E.I., had experienced only the system of Crown appointment to such a body. It was also thought that an elected Senate would more readily work itself into conflict with the House of Commons, especially in money matters, on the principle that elected senators had an equal right to speak for the people. These were the chief obstacles to the United States plan.

On the other hand there was also a strong feeling against the establishment of an hereditary body in Canada. British aristocrats were tolerable with their presumably long lineage and inherited wealth, especially since the advent of responsible government had confined their Canadian activities in a large degree to governorships and the Imperial forces. But the thought of neighbour Joe Doakes, who made his pile in landgrabbing, shipbuilding, the West Indies trade, or usury, becoming first Baron Doakes of Chebucto was a little too much for the stomachs of either the colonials or the British government. It was not republican ideals that saved us from this fate but a mixture of good taste and envy, or perhaps, more prosaically, a universal realization that you cannot create a nobility overnight. Nevertheless, the demand that the members of the provincial legislative councils should share in the political spoils of the Confederation was also a factor not to be ignored.[9]

But the foregoing reasons do not account for the divisions adopted. The Fathers were unable to rid their minds of 'representation by population'. They were obsessed by the discrepancy between the populations of Prince Edward Island and Ontario and the potentially greater discrepancy because of the vast difference in areas. Yet neither then nor now were these differences out of proportion to those between the smallest and largest states of the Union, whether in number or land size.[10] They could not see the justice of equal representation of the provinces in what was to be essentially an advisory chamber. But the agitation for representation by population was one of the main reasons for the foundering of the Province of Canada, and the statesmen of the time considered that Quebec, because its differences were obvious, had to be brought into the new union on some basis of equality with the other members. In that respect, a ratio of two to one was fairer than three to one or an eventual ten to one.

This reasoning is losing its validity, because the individualities of the provinces have developed and become more important than the regional differences. There is now no solid reason why each province should not have equal membership in the Senate, the distribution demanded by the functions of that body.[11]

Primarily the Senate, like the House of Lords, should be a reviser and a voice of caution. It is not designed to propagate measures but to protect interests.

Since the Senate should be the body where the corporate interest of the province is to find a voice in the national forum, this Section 2 of Article 3 enacts that each province is to appoint or elect an equal number of senators, to constitute at least two-thirds of that body. If each province were entitled to six, the most popular number at the moment (half of the provinces now have six senators each), the Senate would be limited to ninety members. Such a limitation is desirable: when an assembly becomes too large the ordinary member is a cipher and only one or two leaders have any persuasive effect. The chamber should be large enough to maintain diversity and even conflict – we desire no imposed oligarchy – but small enough to make every individual count. Six members to each province would meet the various requirements with the least strain and the least violence to the present structure.[12]

The provincial senators might be elected or appointed in a variety of ways. The simplest and most direct method would be to divide each province into senatorial districts each of which would elect a senator at every general election. Such an elected Senate would tend to resemble the United States Senate rather than the House of Lords. This has advantages that are worth considering; in particular it would tend to curb the modern preponderance of the executive over the legislature.

What of the remaining third or less of the Senate? How should it be chosen? Various political, economic, and cultural interests (such as the French language) transcend provincial limits and are important enough to warrant representation. Labour, capital, and ethnic and aboriginal groups come to mind. Religion is another interest that logically comes in here, but it appears impractical and too contentious to urge the direct representation of religious groups in the Senate. It would be impossible to do the job both fairly and adequately. Also, too often the political parson is neither a good priest nor a prudent statesman. This interest will probably be best represented by the members of parliament as such and not by specifically religious delegates.

The universities would provide a useful constituency for some number of senators. University M.P.s in England have included some exceptional people.[13] These great schools could provide Canada with legislators able to stand for a variety of higher interests such as science, letters, and philosophy.

Finally, there might be a number of *ex officio* senators, such as former governors general and prime ministers, and Canadian privy councillors of a certain seniority. If the eligible were only those who had served the nation on a high plane requiring very superior qualities, there would be no danger of the public regarding the method of selection as a political pension plan.

Some such provisions as are contained in Section 2 of Article 3 must be made to rebuild the Senate on a substantial foundation of popular support and to make it a genuine organ of provincial representation. The section is designed to leave the detailed composition of the Senate to be worked out by parliament and the executive government with some scope for provincial law, subordinate to federal legislation. The section replaces some seventeen sections of the B.N.A. Acts, which deal with the number of senators, the division of the number among the provinces, the qualifications, age, nationality, property, residence, tenure, resignation, and vacation of office of senators, and related matters. The proposed section does not attempt to match this detail, which is all in the dominant field of the powers of parliament under

Section 1 of Article 7. Once the parliament has adopted its own particulars of structure and function the organization is ensured a relative permanence by the forces of tradition, habit, and the balance of its parts.

CHAPTER 12

The Parliament and the House of Commons

Fifteen sections of the British North America Act, 1867, deal with the structure and functions of the House of Commons, and this in considerable detail, most of which is not fundamental or even desirable. In fact, four of these provisions were alterable by the Canadian parliament from the very beginnings of the Confederation. The remaining sections set out such minutiae as the function of the Speaker, the number of members, the quorum, voting, and the like. There are about four of these sections fit to be included in a constitution.

Rather than simply restate these remnants it seems better to inquire whether the principle of the Commons chamber cannot be discovered and set down. This should suffice to guard the vital interest of the people in this house.

In modern times the function of the Commons that distinguishes it from other governmental bodies is that it represents the people in controlling the public purse. This principle is at once severable into two elements – representation and fiscal control.

The representative nature of the chamber is ensured, it is thought, by making it elective. It is arguable that a body, more representative because it would be a better cross-section of the population, could be attained by the drawing of names out of a box, such being the way a jury panel is drawn. Before the mid nineteenth century local government was carried on by the general sessions with the aid of the grand jury. The only solid argument against a House of Commons selected by lot is that it could not be expected that the members would act as tribunes, active in questioning and in searching out what is amiss, eager to serve their constituents, and responsive to public opinion. This is what we have come to expect and this is what we mean by representation – rather than a purely statistical resemblance to the body to the population. Indeed, few members of parliament are average individuals. Belloc has very justly remarked somewhere that the British House of Lords is a much more representative group in the sense of ordinary or average, being mostly selected by the accident of birth; the Commons members on the whole are uncommon in their ambition, determination, persuasive powers, education, and other virtues and vices too numerous to catalogue.

Representation means to us also territorial representation: that is, each member is elected to represent an area of the country containing roughly[1] the same order of population or electors as every other.

In Article 3, Sections 3, 4, 5, and 6 deal with the representative aspect of the parliament and especially of the House of Commons. Section 7 shares fiscal control between the executive and the House of Commons.

SECTION 3

The Composition of the House of Commons

The original membership in the House was one hundred and eighty-one and this has increased to a basic membership of two hundred and sixty-three with some more members for the territories. The distribution and limit of this number is determined by Sections 37 and 51 of the B.N.A. Acts which complement each other although they appear to conflict. Section 51 is a rather elaborate set of rules that could be expressed mathematically in several different ways, for working out the provincial allocations of membership in the Commons. With a few changes, these would still be workable under the Article as drafted.

The size of a representative assembly is a serious matter to the extent that the size affects its character. Too large a group reduces the ordinary member to the status of nonentity. The United States House of Representatives, with four hundred and thirty-five members as of 1960, must be crowding this limit although the members are remarkable for their vigour and parliamentary independence. There are reasons to believe that the equivalent British and French chambers, with six hundred and thirty and five hundred and forty-six members respectively, are beyond the limit. They have only this to recommend them, that the larger they become, the more closely they come to resemble a cross-section of the population. But such an assembly is far from being deliberative; only the leaders persuade – in fact, only the leaders get a chance to say anything that is important.

The danger of too small an assembly, apart from inability to man the necessary committees, is that the individual members are too much under the influence of the executive, too subject to party coercion, and too subject also to the pressure of human respect in the parliamentary society to fulfil the standards of independent judgment we desire in the ideal parliamentarian. In such case there is no danger of a revolt or even strong opposition between elections. There is probably a lower limit in this respect, however, and when an assembly is very small, the individual members are important enough to be able to challenge the leadership. Shrewd observers from Plato to Parkinson[2] have noted the influence that the size of a group has on its cohesion and on its capacity to act as a unit or to evolve an effective opposition to the dominant inner group.

Most Canadian legislatures have between twenty-four and a hundred[3] members, and we have the word of the Privy Council that the provincial legislatures are parliaments.[4] They tend, however, to be parliaments of the cosy[5] type that do much of their work in the committee of the whole house, and spend a lot of the public time on local and private bills.

A hundred members must be in the neighbourhood of the

limit for the chamber of this type, with its almost familial atmosphere, its spirit that we call (in Nova Scotia) 'clannish'. The
Canadian and United States Senates have both come to this
limit. Once it is exceeded, the member merges into the mass and
the character of the assembly changes, becomes colder, less
self-sustaining and more dependent on exterior support and
response.

Between the limits one hundred and four hundred we may
expect the group to exhibit the tendency both to assert its independence and to display sensitivity to the wishes of its constituents. The mid point, however, is two hundred and fifty, and
the Canadian House of Commons, which is not far in excess of
this at two hundred and sixty-five, is not notable for either virtue.
This may be a passing phase and in that hope we have proposed
the limits of the House as between two hundred and fifty and
four hundred and thirty-two; the latter figure must be somewhere
near the limit where the individual member ceases to count at
all.[6] The lower figure should be a safe distance above any number
that would threaten us with a parliamentary oligarchy.

Constitutional limits within which the number of legislators
may vary are not, of course, fundamental; but they are desirable
because of the possible changes in the character of the legislature
that great increase or decrease in the number would bring. The
proposal for single-member divisions may not please those who
favour the single-vote multiple-member division system of proportional representation. In this, a single large division returns
a number of members on the rule of a single choice for each
voter. This scheme does distribute the seats in very much the
proportions of the resultant popular vote, but at the price of
inviting those unstable administrations dependent on even more
unstable assemblies for which France was so lately and so deser-
vedly in bad repute. This system also dilutes the relationship
between a representative and his constituents to a much greater
degree than any other (except the state representative at large)
and it is not any more equitable in the end. The main argument
against it, however, is that only a strong executive can survive it
or live with such an assembly, and in the result it encourages

imbalance in the parts of the body politic. If the Canadian constitution were to contain explicit provision for an elected executive directly responsible to the people, this extreme form of proportional representation might then be palatable and even welcome to ensure proper criticism of the government; but where
an elective ministry or chief minister is only a possibility, the
dangers of the multiple-member system are too great to give it
any leeway. The single transferable ballot for single-member electoral divisions has this, at least, to commend it: the elected
member has a majority in favour of him. This system of proportional representation is both lawful and feasible under Section 3.
Hence the proposed division is the single-member one. It is a
small thing, but the system will also simplify the computation
of the number of divisions and the application of the rule concerning their size.

This is that no division shall have more than twice the population of any other. Equality in this aspect was not always the law,
and it took a rather rough and bitter struggle in England in the
last century to bring about the present practice of comparative
equality. Vestiges of the old attitude survive, not too surprisingly, in the United States, where there is currently going on a
constitutional struggle against the gerrymandering of urban districts to favour rural ones. This is being carried on, as is the
fashion, in the courts; the outcome may be of more than passing
interest to this country.[7] But representative equality, within the
limits of the draft Section 3, is now so basic to our accepted
concepts that it should be in our basic law.

The next provision, that no division shall overlap provincial
boundaries, is not in theory of fundamental importance because
in practice it would be the rule in any case. It might also
be argued that the Commons represents the purse and the taxpayers at large rather than the provinces. Still, any departure
here from the established law would stir up the suspicion that
provincial integrity was being ignored. It is also in line with the
following rule, which is also the established one, that each province returns a number of members proportional to its population.
There are some exceptions to this in the laws that we have that

might have to go. One is the fifteen-per-cent rule in Section 51 of the B.N.A. Acts as enacted by the British North America Act, 1952,[8] which provides that no province is to lose more than fifteen per cent of its members in any one readjustment of the membership of the House of Commons. It is debatable whether this exception is just or even expedient, but on the assumption that it is, it is also probable that the word 'proportional' is elastic enough to permit it to stand. The same word was used in the former section to describe a not dissimilar concept.

The provision for a minimum number of two members for a province is designed to take the place of the present Section 51A of the B.N.A. Act which enacts that a province is entitled to at least as many members in the House of Commons as it has senators. In the past this was important only to Prince Edward Island, which was in this manner assured of at least eight parliamentary spokesmen. Now it has become quite important to New Brunswick and Nova Scotia: the first named is actually now entitled to only nine seats on a population proportion and Nova Scotia to just above ten. The lower limit for both provinces pursuant to Section 51A is ten in each case. Moreover, Rule 5 of Section 51 (the Rule that includes the fifteen-per-cent rule) also has a clause that will prevent any western province from having fewer than ten members. In the result, under the present law (which may, however, be changed by ordinary acts of the Canadian parliament), Prince Edward Island is entitled to at least four members in the House of Commons, Newfoundland to at least six, and Nova Scotia, New Brunswick, and the four western provinces to at least ten. These results are anomalous.

Rather than try to incorporate these elaborate and radically unjust rules in the constitution – rules that would fester and promote disunion – the two-member minimum was introduced. This is not at odds with the federal nature of the constitution because the representation of Prince Edward Island, the only province to which our measure is now applicable, will remain at least eight in the parliament, but the bulk of its representation will be in the Senate where the interests of the province as such are intended to be looked after. And two is not a disproportionate number for membership in the Commons, for a single member would not be capable of watching all the necessary matters at all times.

The provision for a census every ten years is an anti-gerrymandering rule of sufficient importance to warrant inclusion. Section 8 of the B.N.A. Act, 1867, requires a census in the first year of each decade. The draft provision is more elastic in allowing a census to be anticipated but not postponed. If this is not acceptable the clause might read: 'A Census to determine the Divisions shall continue to be taken in every Tenth Year from the last such Census.'

SECTION 4

Duration of House of Commons

The federal government saw fit to exempt the provisions for a five-year limit on the life of the House of Commons contained in Section 50 of the B.N.A. Act, 1867, from change by the Canadian parliament in the drastic amendment of 1949. This is undoubtedly a rock-bottom principle of the constitution in the sense that the Commons and, through the Commons, the parliament and the administration, shall be made responsible to the electorate at short intervals. Five years is the period that has come to be accepted in our national political life as the most expedient and useful for this purpose; some term should be embedded in the constitution and there is no demand or overriding reason to choose any other. The wartime exception is that enunciated in the 1949 (No. 2) Amendment with some verbal changes. Thus 'actual' is substituted for 'real' in deference to those philosophers and purists for whom 'real' includes not only 'actual' but 'possible', and 'invasion or insurrection' is omitted as comprehended within the meaning of 'war'. The changes are in the interests of a more exact and concise style, and it is inconceivable that any court would deny to any government the powers intended to be given by the provision in either form of words.

SECTION 5

Yearly Session of the Parliament

The principle of annual parliaments contained now in Section 20 of the B.N.A. Acts was also preserved inviolable by the 1949 (No. 2) Amendment. It is almost superfluous to discuss the constitutional necessity for this rule. Although not theoretically necessary for the federal form of government it is practically very much so. The only possible objection to it is that parliament has so much business that the government needs no coercion in this respect. This may not always be the case, however.

The 1949 (No. 2) Amendment did not make any exception for wartime, and such an exception would seem to be inadmissible. Wartime governments acquire despotic powers and need the check of the tribunicial chamber so much the more. One should keep in mind the content of Section 25 of Article 11 which permits that article to be suspended for a year. This demands an annual reconsideration.

This is a good stage at which to comment on an argument frequently proposed against written constitutions: that they are useless against administrations with the force to overrule them. But the same argument applies to institutional constitutions to an even greater extent. For in the latter case, control of the institution means complete power over the constitution itself. It is then that sentiment and ill-defined custom are the only barriers to tyranny or revolutionary change. But a written charter of liberties has this advantage: it makes plain to all when the government is acting illegally and when it is usurping power, with the result that all right-minded citizens will be in some degree opposed. They may not on all occasions be a majority, but justice, fortified by law, is a powerful political weapon: in the end, men are ruled not by physical power but by moral and mental forces, of which law is perhaps the strongest. It is as simple as that.[9]

Of course, in countries where the populace does not respect the law, especially the public law, because it has never been firmly established in their tradition, no law, fundamental or otherwise, is safe from subversion by the administration.

SECTION 6

No Ouster but by Impeachment

The established immunities and privileges of the members of the parliament are not now constitutionally founded but are left to the parliament with the limit imposed by Section 18 of the B.N.A. Act, 1867, that they may not exceed those at the time enjoyed by members of parliament in Great Britain. The same applies to the immunities and privileges of the houses of parliament.

This deserves two comments: firstly, the limit thus imposed is repugnant to the present status of Canada in the Commonwealth and in the world and should not be retained; secondly, there is now no provision explicitly forbidding an arbitrary ouster and there should be. With respect to the first comment, it is clear that the 1949 (No. 2) Amendment has made this section part of the law that the parliament can change; it is not within the reserved topics. It can therefore be left to the parliament to deal with in its discretion.

But the dismissal of a member from the parliament is not so much a matter of privilege as it is the concern of the constituency that it be represented by the member of its choice. Consequently, the dismissal of a member is not a proper power for a majority in the chamber in question. In fact, it should only be done by a solemn process of a judicial nature such as is the process of impeachment.

Immunity from being arbitrarily unseated should be the only constitutional privilege of the members of the parliament, but it is a necessary one. The only reasonable alternative to impeachment is to commit the question to the judiciary; this raises problems arising out of the division of powers and the independence of the houses of parliament from judicial control that it is better not to raise.[10]

SECTION 7

Taxation and Money Bills

The ultimate source of power of the House of Commons is its control over taxation and spending. In medieval times the Commons had to be consulted because a tax that was not volunteered by a body speaking for the taxpayers could not have been collected: the government was too weak. Modern governments find little difficulty in collecting taxes or in having legislatures authorize them: they are much too strong. It is not so long since an illegal tax was imposed in Canada and was later ratified by the parliament.[11]

A modern tax structure can be heavy to the point of crushing the economy, and yet all protest is feeble and ineffectual except over protracted periods. The laws to enforce payment are summary and ruthless[12] and the means used to collect far outstrip those available to the private creditor against his debtor. This is proper, at least to some extent, even in the present universal alienation of mankind, but certainly no safeguard of popular right should be omitted. Wherefore the control of the House of Commons over taxation and public expenditure should be retained and enshrined in the Canadian charter.

In the United States Constitution there is a clause[13] that provides that money bills shall originate in the House of Representatives. This was designed on the principle, apparently, that he who pays the piper calls the tune: that is, the direct representatives of the taxpayers should be the only ones to initiate taxation measures. This would imply that the Senate might obstruct such a proposal but has no right to advance one of its own. But the clause goes on to give the Senate the power to propose or concur with amendments as in other bills. This has been taken to mean that the Senate can substitute its own bill for one that has originated in the other house and it has often done so. In particular, the Senate has not scrupled to increase appropriations or taxes. The incentive for this is the 'pork barrel', the mass of public works and expenditures that congressmen hunger to have apportioned to the benefit of their own constituencies. Thus the representatives of the states have gone over the heads of the representatives of the individuals, the citizens, the taxpayers, often enough to cause serious confusion and uncertainty in the nation's fiscal policies. This means that there is no real executive control over the budget.

An extremely stringent curb on this was put into the Australian Constitution, which is a compromise between constitutional and responsible government. The device used[14] was to forbid the Senate to amend money bills; if it wishes an amendment it must propose it in a message to the House of Representatives. But Australia has had no real trouble with this aspect of fiscal responsibility because it shares with us a constitutional provision that the United States lacks: the provision that taxation can be imposed only for a purpose that is proposed by the government.[15]

The Australian expedient does not seem necessary, although it probably expresses a constitutional convention. If our government and Commons have to agree on raising and spending any money item there seems no good reason why the experience and critical powers of the Senate should not be available to amend a bill if it needs amendment; and there is every reason why the special interests represented in the Senate should have a real voice on the question – and so much the more so if the Senate is to be chosen by, as well as for, the interests it is designed to represent.

Thus, Section 7 contains only the substance of the existing law and does not attempt to put into concrete form any of the conventions or customs that relate to this topic. This is one more step in keeping the constitution flexible within the limits of what is essential or necessary.

SECTION 8

General Election to Override Senate

The purpose of this section is to put into the law the convention that the Senate shall not continue to oppose a measure passed by a Commons that has survived a general election.[16] Great Britain has such a law in the Parliament Act, 1911, but we do not. There is some question whether the proposal, if enacted, would not do violence to the federal nature of our government. The United States does not have any such measure. On the other hand, Australia has an extremely elaborate means of resolving such conflicts as may arise between the Representatives and the

Senate. This is a joint dissolution of House and Senate, when both must submit to a general election. This solution does not convey any immediate impression of superiority: it would have done just as well to make both Senate and House elective at the same time and for the same term.[17]

Indeed, the last proposal is probably the best way to make both houses in Canada equally independent and responsible. It would be a step towards responsible government without undue preponderance of the executive, and it is feasible under the draft Articles. After all, the Senate, in addition to its function as critic, is meant to represent a different balance of interests than the Commons; this balance is conceived to have as vital a part in legislation other than the initiation of money bills as the purely popular representation. If the Senate were elective the proposed Section 8 would be wholly unnecessary and incongruous. Since it may not prove to be elective in the event, the draft section would then be necessary to ensure the ultimate sovereignty of the people.

SECTION 9

Overriding the Governor General

In Canada, as in England, there is no legal method for parliament to pass a law despite the refusal of the royal assent to the bill by the Queen or the Governor General. In theory, should either say no, that is the end of the proposed law. Of course, that does not happen, and the reason that it does not happen is because we function under the cabinet system of government which is an integral part of responsible government as we know it. In this the actual executive is the ministry, in which the prime minister has the chief part, and the Queen or Governor General acts only on the advice of the ministry.

There is no danger, while this lasts, of a bill passing the parliament and coming for the royal assent with the ministry opposed. If a bill, or any measure, is passed by either house against the wishes of the government it constitutes a vote of non-confidence, and that means that the government, by a convention, must either make way for a new ministry or procure a general election. Section 55 of the B.N.A. Act purports to give the Governor General power, in his discretion, to disallow or reserve a bill; but since 1930[18] it has not been doubted that this is a dead letter, that the Imperial government has no function in respect to Canadian legislation, and that the Governor General may disallow only on the advice of the Canadian cabinet (which, as noted, would only be given in most extraordinary circumstances). It would appear that any provision for overriding the executive veto is unnecessary.

Nevertheless, cabinet government may not last the life of the constitution: it has shown signs in our day of growing old, especially in those parts of the world where revolutionary ideas have gained popular acceptance. It is at its weakest in a state with many political parties, and to operate well it requires a fairly even balance between two established parties who do not differ fundamentally on the bases of the state. It is a queer but very human quirk of politics that the American constitution, so designed and balanced that it can function with any number of parties, exhibits the most firmly entrenched two-party system in the world, while the British system, which needs two strong, evenly matched parties to be effectual, has been the one most often copied by those countries where party spirit is at once most multiplex and intense. Where the two-party system breaks down, an executive independent of the legislature (and consequently, a legislature independent of the executive) is the natural restorative of stability. Such a restorative is now possible in Canada; it continues to be possible under the Articles and for that reason draft Section 9 is inserted to permit the legislature to overcome an executive veto on legislation. The two-thirds rule is taken from the corresponding rule in the United States Constitution[19] but our draft makes it possible to continue the matter to the next session of the parliament. This is because we may continue the practice of the general election as occasion arises instead of at set intervals, in which case, the conflict between parliament and the executive could well fall to be resolved by the voters.

The nine sections of Article 3 all deal with principles that are not only vital to the structure and dynamic of the parliament but are, of their very nature, prior to that structure. Without them a very different kind of parliament would emerge, but that, speaking strictly, is not the point. The point is that they are not ordinary rules concerning the substance and procedure of the parliament; they are the sources from which it derives its unique essence and movement. Especially, they fit the parliament into its proper place in the federal plan: they are the norms which show the relationship of the parliament both to the provinces and to the people. In short, in a federal nation, these rules are *constitutional*.

And it is important to remember that not all of them are now, or have been since 1949, part of the constitution of Canada as we have been using the term. If these limitations are truly necessary we have lost ground; it is urgent that we restore them to our political foundations.

In reviewing this Article 3, it has also been shown in general and in detail that the organic type of constitution, the institution, is not sufficient for the Confederation, at least where the central government is concerned: it ignores too many elements of importance to the component parts. The Article, however, preserves the organic character of the parliament to the fullest degree in all that is properly its sole concern and thus blends the best of both the organic and the statutory principles in a harmonious concept. The result should be a free, living, growing instrument of government based on firm and lasting ideals.

CHAPTER 13

The Executive Government

While the British North America Acts are very full and detailed concerning the parliament of Canada, they are quite concise and general about the executive government. Besides the eight sections in Part III of the 1867 Act, which deal with it specifically, there are a score more that set out particular powers. Most of them are inserted out of gross excess of caution.

The reasons for this difference in treatment lie in the characters of the two powers. The parliament of Canada was a new thing in a new context and had to be erected from the ground up. The position of a colonial governor, on the other hand, was one with many precedents, and though the Canadian government was to have wider powers than any colony to that time, the executive position was not different in kind from that existing in other places.

Even so, some of the provisions under this head relate to matters not at all fundamental. On the whole, however, this part of the Act is more in the nature of a constitution than other parts, and so many items have found a place in Article 4.

SECTION 1

Vested in the Sovereign

The Crown of Great Britain is the focus where the lines of connection of the Commonwealth meet. The connection with the Crown is a thing held very dear by many Canadians. It would not be true to say 'all Canadians'. But this affection gains something from the very remoteness of the monarch. It is different in kind from the English sentiment; it is not directed to the Queen as part of our national life but is partly nostalgic, partly pride of race and ancestry, partly deliberate policy, and partly ingrained habit. It is uncertain how many are opposed to the Imperial connection. Everyone who is not deaf knows that there are some so opposed, as the Newfoundland plebiscite discussions showed. But it is probable that the present feeling among Canadians is that the membership in the Commonwealth should not be disturbed. As this is a fundamental matter, affecting as it does both the central government and the provinces, it should be included in the constitution.

The Crown is also the head of the executive power of each Commonwealth government.[1] This headship is largely titular but not absolutely so: the Sovereign still has powers, although these are largely in the nature of reserve forces and are not used in the day-to-day administration. The Royal discretion only comes into play when a change of administration is in question, and even in that case the right of the Queen to refuse a dissolution of the House of Commons to a prime minister whose government has lost the confidence of the House is disputed.[2]

It is said[3] that the Crown has 'the right to be consulted, the right to encourage, the right to warn . . .'. That is, the Crown does no public act of government except in accordance with the advice of a committee of ministers called the cabinet, but in general this committee must act through the Queen or, in Canada, the Governor General. The Queen must be told what is being done and has the right to express an opinion of it.

In England this has had some weight. George V is reported[4] to have affected the course of events on one or two occasions of crisis by such an opinion. After all, he was an Englishman, vitally interested in English affairs and yet set apart and above ordinary politics. He had facilities for a full grasp of public business and his education was designed to make him a leader. On the whole, the distinction between the titular executive and the actual has proven satisfactory in England.

While the Queen enjoys in England considerable personal respect and influence as head of the government, it is doubtful that the advice of Canadian governors general has carried anything like the same weight. They have been, until lately, distinguished strangers, usually here for a few years only, alien in education, culture, and outlook to our people. Some have adapted themselves well, some not so well; some have achieved social influence in the widest sense; but it is obvious that they can speak with little personal authority. And the same is true of the very distinguished Canadians who have held the post, despite their outstanding services to the country.

The Governor General is, in fact, in the position of an umpire. His task is to call the result of the play by superintending the changes of administration as they occur. Otherwise he is ornamental only. The same is true of the provincial office of lieutenant-governor.

Many Canadians, although otherwise 'loyal' to the Crown, cannot see any sense in the office of Governor General *as at present constituted*. They cannot see any need of this coat-holding position whose tenant has no real discretion and only nominal functions. We are too near to the spectacular and dynamic example of the United States presidency to appreciate fully the English practice. Consequently, many consider the office of Governor General wholly superfluous.

We may yet need to make something of the office to preserve representative democracy. For honest, democratic government and for individual liberty, the executive and legislative branches should be truly distinct so that each, for the common good, may enjoy a measure of independence. In cabinet government, the distinction is theoretical only. Walter Bagehot thought, in 1867,[5] that parliament controlled the executive. Today the executive frequently controls parliament. Modern perils have made this easy: the immense demands of defence and social security have meant equally great demands for taxation and administrative powers. Too often the needs of the era for strong government have resulted in an unhealthy degree of cabinet control over the legislature. Any question of importance to the executive is discussed and voted on according to straight party lines, and the lawmakers' independent actions are often reduced to three rights reminiscent of the Crown's: to question, to publish, and to delay. On such questions, effective criticism is voiced only in the secret party caucus, which may be dominated by narrow or unworthy motives.

In contrast, the United States Congress affords the heartening spectacle of many independent legislators who cross party lines to vote for what they think right (or expedient). The Congress is not often cited in Canada as an example of what should be done. We are prone to take too literally the satirical or comic-strip view of the congressman because the citizens of that country are merciless with their public men, often with good cause. But even with a solid majority of its party in both houses, the administration does not control the Congress. It has to 'sell' its proposals to the legislature and its committees, which go into them in great detail, hear evidence and experts, and scrutinize them very thoroughly, not just to persuade the government to modify its plans here and there (as is our custom) but to see whether they should be accepted at all. Party lines exist, but so does enough true independence to override them.

The easiest and most direct way to separate the legislative and executive functions is to make the Governor General the actual head of the administration. In a democracy, this implies that he would be elected. We would then have a constitutionally independent executive government with its immense possibilities for action but still subject to parliamentary control of the purse and to the electorate in general elections. On the other hand, stable government would be possible even with three or more equally numerous parties in the Commons. Nor would we find the executive and the legislature challenging each other to general elections for trivial causes or on frivolous non-confidence motions.

Such a structure offers the advantages of both the British and American systems without the extreme of cabinet dominance to which the British system tends or the extremes of irresponsibility and antagonism between the branches that may occur in the United States. It avoids also the fluidity characteristic of the French party system.

It is not necessary to include this plan in the constitution. It is not essential to Confederation. It does not affect allegiance to the Crown or the rights of the provinces or of any particular group or class, nor would it require any change in the legal powers of the Governor General as they now exist.[6] Parliament could set it up if we wanted it. What is necessary is to provide freedom to adopt it, by the constitution, because we may want it very much indeed if our party system remains fragmented.

Section 1 of this Article thus preserves the Imperial connection with the Crown of Great Britain, puts the executive power where it is now, in the hands of the Governor General, and makes him the chief executive officer, at least in title. This is at the same time more general and more explicit than Sections 9 and 15 of the B.N.A. Act, 1867.

(The reference to the Censor General is an anticipation of Section 5 of this Article.)

SECTION 2

The Governor General

In 1867 the Governor General was conceived to be the representative of the Crown in a more personal sense than is now the case; this may account for the lack in the B.N.A. Act, 1867, of any mention of his term of office. The office is assumed in the Quebec Resolutions and London Resolutions although they are silent on many aspects of it that appear in the B.N.A. Act. O'Connor argued, even in 1939:

> The B.N.A. Act *mentions* him many times and in a few instances confers upon him powers, but he is treated by it, throughout, as an appointee of the sovereign who is to act on the sovereign's behalf.[7]

But he points out (at page 160),

The status of the Governor General of Canada and of the executive government of Canada has been considerably altered since 1916.

O'Connor was there discussing a Privy Council case[8] in which the Judicial Committee, although not rejecting the doctrine that the Governor General is a *viceroy,* were at pains to say that it was doubtful. By *viceroy* they meant a substitute for the Crown with the full powers of the Crown.

Today the Governor General is in fact a viceroy, albeit a pallid one. He exercises the powers, such as they are, of the Crown, and he exercises all of them, except the power to appoint his successor. The office, from being that of an intermediary appointed by the British government for its own purposes, has become a purely Canadian one and is thus entitled to serious consideration in its own right. Even if the Governor General remains no more than an umpire it is both desirable and necessary that his position be secure and free from pressure. Even his present function is surely as important as that contemplated for a senator or member of the House of Commons, and he should be entitled to the like security. The parliamentary balance should secure that the powers given by Class 2 of Article 7, Section 1, to the parliament are not used to debase the office; it should be possible to leave the term of office and the salary and allowances to the parliament. In view of the constant onset of inflation it is certainly desirable to leave money matters to ordinary legislation if it is safe to do so. This has proved to be the case in the United States.

The Article omits the references in the B.N.A. Act to the Canadian Privy Council. As long as this body continues its present mode of operation it is much better and safer that it should be governed by convention rather than by law.[9] It is of the essence of the cabinet system that the Privy Council does its real work behind a sort of façade of law. Even the mention in the B.N.A. Act does not purport to govern it in its operation but refers to the existing practices of the Governor acting with or without the Council. It is better left at that or even less than that, for while the cabinet is basic to the modern British scheme of government it is not basic to representative democracy, nor is it essential, necessary, or desirable to enshrine it in a fundamental law. Indeed, parliamentary government will probably long retain the fiction of cabinet rule after the fact has become something else, and this may even be the case in countries where British political principles are by no means so deeply entrenched as they are in Canada.

Prerogatives and Powers

The royal prerogative is a great stamping-ground of constitutional-law writers. It is a great and serious mystery and no two authorities quite agree on its scope. It is defined by Dicey as

> the residue of discretionary or arbitrary authority which at any given time is legally left in the hands of the Crown.[10]

Another definition:

> the Common Law rights, privileges, powers, capacities and immunities of the King.[11]

The latter is more meaningful to the lawyer because the mention of the common law tells him at once that this is stuff that is not governed by statute. Another way of stating the thing is that the Crown's prerogative consists of all the royal authority that it has left after all the acts and deeds of parliament have had their effect. Even this does not tell the full story because most of what is left of the prerogative is exercised under the cabinet convention.

We start with the theory of the supremacy of the king, who in earlier times called in lords and commons to grant him taxes and so gradually surrendered most of his authority to this new supreme body that he had thus created, the parliament. The theory operates to this day, although it is debated whether the Crown has actually kept any authority. So, Section 3 of Article 4 is designed to express the present state of the prerogative in theory subject to its two essential exceptions: firstly, that acts of parliament are superior to the prerogative, and secondly, that the Crown, the executive, cannot impose any taxation of its own accord. The latter fact was a result of the state of practical politics in medieval times and became the recognized highway to parliamentary supremacy in the Petition of Right (1628) and its consequences.

SECTION 4

Specific Powers of the Governor

The enumerated clauses in Section 4 set out the most basic executive powers – most basic, that is, in the relations of the executive government with the parliament, other states, the public service, and questions of public importance. The last clause, giving power to commission investigations, may seem to differ in importance from the other three, but it has many things to commend it. There is a sort of intuitive realization that this power is very important for a government in its dealings with the parliament and the public; it is an instrument of great persuasion and public appeal. But its mention at this place can be justified in a more mundane fashion by recalling to mind the very real services that royal commissions have performed for Canada. As of now they are regulated by statute, but the executive should have an indefeasible right to this fruitful and potent tool.

SECTION 5

The Censor General

This office is an innovation, although the germ of it exists in several public offices of the present structure. In particular, the chief electoral officer and the auditor-general now perform functions that should be fortified by an independent position. To do this for each in a constitutional law would appear to require an excess of detail. It seems better to combine the offices in one independent magistracy of limited functions.

There should not be too many independent magistrates in a state, but there should be some. If too many, they weaken each other and the executive, so that the separation of powers becomes diluted and diminished. But the concentration of this fundamental supervisory jurisdiction in one official gives his position great strength and power to resist unlawful procedures. Since his executive action is confined to the elections and auditing, its effect will be preservative rather than assertive.

Now it is not a long step from such an office to that of the Speaker of the Commons who, in England at any rate, is a great public officer and personage. It would be natural to suggest that the Speaker's office be combined also with the Censor General's, because the complex of functions involved is all of one piece. This is the more important in some minds because the Speakership in Canada has been considered a stepping-stone to a cabinet post rather than a high dignity in its own right. The practice of alternate English- and French-speaking incumbents weakens the office by making it impermanent and not attractive as a career, but this could be modified if it were made a statutory office of long duration to which the Deputy Speaker would succeed in due course. In such a case the legitimate interests of the two-language partnership could be met by having the Speaker French-speaking and the Deputy Speaker English-speaking, with the languages reversed on the next election of a Speaker and Deputy Speaker.

If the parliament is to maintain and, indeed, regain its ultimate power to check and overrule the executive, it is essential that the Speaker be in as independent a position as a judge. This can only be done by a convention, as in England, or by law. In Canada, the existing convention of changing Speakers does not favour the stability necessary to independence so that law is the obvious corrective. A mere change in the convention, not enacted even as a statute, would be subject to the whim of the next majority of a different political party.

Some might reasonably contend that such a law should be a fundamental one such as we contemplate in this book. But so many things – the historical background of the Speakership, the changing nature of parliamentary government, the uncertainty of the outcome of combining the office, which has traditionally been held by an elected member of the Commons, with an office with a fixed term – all these weigh against including the Speakership in the Articles. It would be all the more unwise to give the

Speakership to the Censor General by the Articles. Some thought should be given to the proposal in the sphere of ordinary legislation as part of the evolution of the House of Commons.

Article 4 drops some of the detail of the B.N.A. Acts respecting the executive government, such as the power to appoint deputies and administrators and to appoint the Speaker of the Senate. Article 7, Section 1, Class 2 gives the parliament, however, full authority to make laws concerning the office of Governor General and the details of that office. There should be no fear that the parliament will be unable to deal with any aspect of the central government that is not expressly withheld. What is designed is not, like that of the United States, a government of limited and enumerated powers, but a government with general power, subject to certain express bounds.

CHAPTER 14

The Judiciary

Judicial Tenure

Under a proper constitution, a judge should not need a habit of courage in giving any judgment, nor should he be at the mercy of the executive or the legislature. In other words, he should have secure judicial tenure.

The obvious first condition of judicial independence is that the judge cannot be arbitrarily fired as James I fired Sir Edward Coke, Chief Justice of the Common Pleas,[1] nor removed by act of parliament, as it was proposed to remove James Coyne (who, though not a judge, was entitled to hold office during good behaviour[2]). In a federal state the central legislature is necessarily subject to the federative statute and to the courts that administer it (ultimately all ordinary courts)[3] to the extent that its acts may be declared illegal or void. But an impasse is not admissible in this country. It is essential that such a conflict be juridically determined without a summary termination of the judge's office; otherwise the confederation has become a unitary state.

For security of tenure, a set term of office, if it is long enough, is as good as an appointment for life or until the fixed age of retirement. But if it is so short that the judge will anticipate one or more reappointments then the renewal of the term becomes a means of applying influence to the judge. To avoid this a minimum of ten years is suggested: judges are usually appointed to the bench rather late in life, and while it is conceivable that a ten-year term might be renewed twice, it is not very likely in the circumstances. A seven-year term offers much more likelihood of two renewals and it is thus to be avoided as the minimum.

A corollary of the first condition of judicial independence is that the judge's term of office should not be subject to radical curtailment by law. One hesitates to cite Mr. Diefenbaker's 1960 Amendment[4] as an example of this as there was some demand for the change, not only on political grounds, but in legal circles, and the régime of constitutional judicial independence does not now exist in Canada.[5] There was therefore no theoretical objection to the amendment and it was certainly not designed to influence the judiciary, except, perhaps, to alter its political complexion by filling the vacant places on the benches with men more sympathetic to the administration. Even this is scarcely a dominant purpose of the change, as some of the judges displaced had been appointed by the Bennett government.

It is possible that Prime Minister Diefenbaker chose the method of constitutional amendment rather than ordinary legislation, which appears to have been a lawful alternative under the 1949 (No. 2) Amendment, because he did not wish to subvert the idea of judicial independence, for even if that becomes constitutionally guaranteed, it will still be possible to deal with it by amending the constitution. But it should not be possible to take away the security of a judicial office by ordinary legislation.[6]

The second condition of judicial independence is that the judge should not be subject to financial pressures from the government. The best way to fix this is to enact that his pay shall not be cut.[7] No doubt there are many other pressures of a moral or social nature that a determined executive can exert on a judge; they can be resisted well enough if the law is preserved. But an attack on the judge's pay undermines his position and defences in so many devastating ways that it is insupportable.

The third condition of judicial independence is that a judge should be ousted for bad behaviour, not by arbitrary decision, but only after a trial conducted according to the formulae of the law, and as far as possible according to its spirit, by an impartial tribunal.

There is no concrete reason why such a trial could not be conducted by other judges: no doubt it would be competent and fair in such hands. Nevertheless, to do so would permit one of the functional elements of the government to be the final arbiter of its own virtue, and the possibilities of professional or fraternal bias might invalidate the process in the public estimation.

It might also be possible, in many cases, to entrust such a trial to an executive committee, but, again, such is the public mistrust of the motives of politicians that this process would not engender any confidence in its fairness. This is probably unjust: most people when called on to act judicially, for example as jurors, make a conscientious effort to do so. But this is one case where it is politically necessary to employ the principle that justice must not only be done but be plainly seen to be done.[8]

It is for such reasons that many states have entrusted this problem to be solved by the legislature, sitting, however, as a judicial body. In the British system this is called a joint resolution, a name that does not connote that the parliament must act judicially; in the United States it is called impeachment and the judicial nature of the process is very clearly spelled out in the United States Constitution.[9]

Should all judges hold office on judicial tenure, as so defined, or as it might be modified in the case of the less exalted, for example, by substituting a judicial inquiry for impeachment? This is desirable but it is not a constitutional essential. To make a judiciary independent in the fundamental law it is only needful to give judicial tenure to enough of the judges in the higher levels so that anything done out of turn in the lower courts can be surely and easily corrected.

Supervising the lower courts (not by appeal but by prerogative writs) is a recognized department of common-law powers distinct from both original and appellate jurisdiction. This function is exercised by courts of a certain status, historically the superior common-law courts in England (especially the Queen's Bench) and their equivalents overseas. And these are defined also as 'superior courts of record'. The peculiar property of all courts of record, whether civil or criminal, is that they have power to fine and imprison for contempt, and the superior courts of record have the further property that, unlike inferior courts of record, they can fine and imprison for contempt committed out of court.[10]

What we want are the judges of the superior courts of record. The section would then begin:

> Every judge of every superior court of record, whether constituted by Canada or a Province, shall hold office on judicial tenure, that is....

Unfortunately this involves the word 'superior', which has acquired in Canada a very slippery connotation. The kind of jurisdiction exercised by a superior court in 1867 is almost the only criterion by which to decide whether or not a particular body is or is not a superior court.[11]

Considering the vast change in conditions in the intervening century one is tempted to call this test absurd; it is, in fact, a source of great confusion and uncertainty and has outlived any use it once had. The general jurisdiction of a superior court in 1867 is no longer relevant to the jurisdiction and hence the specification of such a court today. But the supervisory jurisdiction is still relevant and still useful to distinguish such courts.

The supervisory jurisdiction is used as the basic one of the essential provincial court required by Section 5. As such it is the most suitable for the purpose, the most important jurisdiction such a court can exercise. But it is not, in terms, the most adaptable to describe the group of judges who are traditionally given security of tenure. It would require a rather involved formula to designate the various trial and appeal courts to be included by means of the canon of supervisory jurisdiction. Accordingly a more concrete definition of the judges to be protected is used, based on the power to punish for contempt committed out of court.[12] This is reasonably precise and avoids the kind of question that the word 'superior' has provoked in Canada. It is also a good practical standard for the minimum scope of guaranteed judicial tenure, because only the most important courts are given the authority to punish for contempt committed out of court.

The Supreme Court of Canada

The parliament of Canada was given power, by Section 101 of the B.N.A. Act, 1867, to provide for 'a General Court of Appeal for Canada', and this power was used to create the Supreme Court of Canada. The Court is thus the creature of the parliament and could, in theory, be radically altered by the same authority. This is not likely, but it is not impossible, should a Canadian ministry find itself in the mood of President Franklin D. Roosevelt in the '30s with respect to the Supreme Court of the United States.

The purpose of Section 2 is to recognize the Court as a constitutional fact and to embed enough of the elements of it in the Articles to secure its permanency and continued authority. It now consists of nine judges – a sufficient minimum for constitutional purposes. Indeed, the present number is necessary so that a reasonable number of Quebec judges may sit in civil cases appealed from that province. But it is not impossible that the common law and the Quebec civil law will eventually obtain a fusion of principles: they are merely beginning to act on each other these days, but each system has much to offer the other. Even in such a case, however, there should be at least nine judges to give a broad spectrum of judicial views.[13]

The Jurisdiction of the Supreme Court

The Supreme Court of Canada was designed as a 'General Court of Appeal for Canada'.[14] An appeal court for private civil suits is not an essential body in a federal state. In fact there is much to be said against it as in many cases it protracts litigation beyond what is reasonable in time and expense. The idea of a general court of appeal was part of a plan to make uniform the laws of the common-law provinces. This plan has not succeeded and is not likely to: uniform laws are of some value to lawyers but even this value is overrated. There is no essential need for such a general court of appeal.

What is essential is a judicial tribunal that is on a par with the other national organs of government and that will have power to preserve the federal balance by enforcing the principles of the Confederation. So, the chief jurisdiction of the Supreme Court must be to guard, interpret, and put into effect the constitution. Of course this is what it is doing now, and since the right of appeal to the Privy Council overseas was abolished, the Supreme Court has become in fact what it should be in law, the bulwark of constitutional integrity.[15]

Some people do not find this to their taste. They distrust courts as too conservative, too pedantic, too inclined to let words interfere with deeds, and they would entrust the meaning of the constitutional law to a political body. While these objections cannot be ignored or slighted, we must be firm that in our kind of state with its diversity of interests, its protected minorities, its co-ordinate system of governments, the preservation of such interests cannot safely or justly be left to a merely political tribunal; that the better course is to entrust the task to those who are sworn to give true judgment according to law.

The necessary functions of the Supreme Court in relation to the constitution imply a need for it to exercise a final authority, at least by way of appeal, so that any question of law arising between governments in Canada will be settled by legal process. Such conflicts have arisen and will again arise; the judicial machinery that must exist to resolve them should clearly have its apex in the Supreme Court.

Once that the principal jurisdiction of the Court to watch and ward the Articles is granted by them, there seems no objection to giving the Court, by ordinary statute, whatever other jurisdiction the parliament and the various legislatures think to be desirable. By Class 3 of Article 7, Section 1, the dominant power of the parliament extends to the jurisdiction of the Supreme Court, and a collocation of that clause with the present section implies the following propositions:

(a) The Supreme Court will have the fundamental jurisdiction conveyed by Art. 5, S. 3, which cannot be abridged by an act of parliament or of a legislature.

(b) The granting of ordinary jurisdiction belongs to the legislative authority that has power over the laws that apply to the subject-matter.

(c) The dominant law-making power of the parliament with respect to the jurisdiction of the Court will resolve any conflict between federal and provincial law on the subject in favour of the federal law.

Because of this, it should not prove possible for a province to overload the Supreme Court with cases under provincial law. It is rather likely that the eventual result would be to the contrary. Quebec, one would think, would withdraw its civil business from the Court on the Articles coming into force, an idea which has considerable support already in that province. While this might deprive the common-law lawyers of the light and breadth of vision that comes from comparative legal study, it should prove beneficial to Quebec. It is anomalous that the decisions of the appellate courts in that province, manned by men trained and experienced in the civil law, can be overturned by a tribunal the majority of whose members can have only an imperfect notion of that law. It is almost as anomalous, that the Court should have to deal with the odds and ends that linger in nooks and crannies of provincial law, such as the following esoteric question, 'Since a child takes the "settlement" of his father, does he require a new "settlement" after becoming a ward of the state, when the father acquires a new one by removing to another municipality?'.[16] The answer given by the Supreme Court of Canada (No) was of no practical value outside of Nova Scotia and the few provinces, if any, that have kept this vestige of Elizabethan public policy. The provincial courts of appeal are quite capable of giving a satisfactory ruling on this sort of thing, and pressure of business will no doubt soon force its exclusion even without constitutional reform.

SECTION 4

Other Federal Courts

The same section (101) of the 1867 Act that authorizes the parliament of Canada to erect a general court of appeal enables it to provide 'for the Establishment of any additional Courts for the better Administration of the Laws of Canada'. In this context the phrase 'Laws of Canada' means laws validly enacted by the parliament, although Professor Laskin thinks it extends also to common law within the scope of federal competence.[17]

The words 'for the better Administration' express a purpose that governs the creation of federal courts. Hence they are words of limitation. They suggest that if the parliament establishes a court for any other purpose the act may be beyond its powers. It is hard to imagine a concrete case but the ingenuity of legislators and lawyers may yet develop one. The words also suggest that if the federal court does not provide actually *better* administration of the law in question than the ordinary provincial courts it is without power. The Exchequer Court, for example, usually holds trials only once a year in the Atlantic provinces, while all the provincial superior courts sit at least twice a year. Also, in the procedure of this court it is necessary to have an Ottawa solicitor as agent in addition to the local one. It could be maintained, at least in ordinary tort cases in the exchequer court, that it does not provide better administration. The phrase does not add anything worthwhile and there is no need to keep it.

Under Section 101 the parliament has established, besides the Exchequer Court of Canada, various special courts, such as courts martial for the armed services and the R.C.M.P., the Court Martial Appeal Court, the Board of Railway Commissioners, and various other tribunals with judicial functions.

It is debatable whether the parliament can establish courts for the ordinary administration of criminal justice in the provinces. Criminal Law and Procedure are 'Laws of Canada' by virtue of Section 91, Class 27, of the 1867 Act, but the 'Constitution of Courts of Criminal Jurisdiction' is expressly excepted from that class and is included in Class 14 of Section 92, the field of exclusive provincial legislative jurisdiction. Professor Laskin, fortified by the Privy Council's interpretation[18] of the clause 'notwithstanding anything in this Act' in Section 101, holds that the parliament can establish courts of original criminal jurisdiction for the provinces[19] (presumably to supplant the ordinary courts). This is agreeable to the plain and grammatical meaning of the sections involved.

Nevertheless the question is not without considerable doubt. Not only was the point not in issue in the Privy Council decision but there is a long tradition that the B.N.A. Act constitutes the Crown Provincial and its attorney-general the guardian of the prerogative in the administration of criminal justice,[20] and Section 101 can be given ample operation if it is limited to the special courts that have been mentioned and others similar in kind. Possibly also it might be held that the constitution itself contemplates that the ordinary provincial tribunals will in normal conditions provide the 'better Administration' that is the only valid purpose for establishing courts under Section 101.

Such being the state of the question let us at once dispose of it with a decision in favour of the tradition. This is one part of the constitution where the sharing of powers of the central and provincial governments has worked very well indeed, and the solution chosen is in accord with the unitary and unique character of the Canadian judicature as also with the very important liberal principle of local participation in the administration of the criminal law.[21]

The unitary nature of the Canadian judicature which we have just mentioned is distinctive (although the Australian system is not unlike it)[22] in a federal constitution. The basic structure of our ordinary courts is a single thing – not dual, as in the United States. In each province, the superior court of record is part of an organization that leads through a provincial court of appeal to the Supreme Court of Canada, a federal court. The other federal courts exist for special purposes, and the bulk of the laws of Canada are administered in provincial courts. Thus we have avoided the parallel federal and state courts of our neighbours; in view of the integration conflicts and the threats of judicial clashes they have provoked in the United States, we can feel profound relief.

In a way, this is a lucky result and does not follow necessarily from the words of the B.N.A. Act. There is no strong reason even yet to prevent the parliament from establishing federal courts with a variety of jurisdictions, and making them superior courts of record as it has done with the Court Martial Appeal Court. The present system of Canadian courts is a strong example of the contrast between a plan as it exists in words and the concrete detail that it may assume when clothed with flesh. It is not really enough to study a constitution on paper: as a living, breathing thing it will be both more and less.

So, the ordinary courts, other than the Supreme Court of Canada, are provincial courts, and these deal with large amounts of federal law. Similarly, the Exchequer Court, which is a federal court, administers some provincial law, and it has been held that the parliament and the legislature can each confer jurisdiction and impose duties on courts created by the other.[23] The purport of Section 4 is thus the same as the existing law and practice, except where they differ, in which case it chooses the practice in preference to the law.

SECTION 5

The Essential Provincial Court

In accord with the unitary structure of the Canadian court system and in order to emphasize it, the principles of the essential provincial court are put in this Article rather than in the next, which deals with provincial government.

The B.N.A. Act provides for the continuation of existing courts by Section 129, and for the appointment of the judges of the superior, district, and county courts by the Governor General in Section 96. Part VII, dealing with the judicature, consists of six sections, and is brief and bare in contrast with other parts. That is probably why, despite the muddle resulting from the elaboration of the idea of a 'superior court' into fantastic detail,[24] the judicial plan of the Act has worked well. But the Act is weak in defining the necessary and permanent qualities of a superior court with the consequence that any qualities that such courts had in 1867 are in some danger of being perpetuated unduly.

The central government has probably been content to leave the bulk of federal law to be administered by these courts throughout the years, because it can control the appointment and payment of the judges. The parliament has applied the same rates of judicial salary throughout the country with some curious results. Thus the courts of Prince Edward Island cost 127 cents per capita for the judges and those of Ontario cost 30 cents per capita. These are the highest and lowest provincial figures; in between there is great variety.

An undesirable feature of the federal appointment of judges comes to the fore when a political party has been in power for a long time. Then the courts, like the Senate, begin to exhibit a rather one-sided political background. This also stimulates a perhaps undue appetite for judgeships among the opposed partisans who think themselves eligible, and doubtful, harsh, or extravagant courses may be adopted to supply the necessary places when opportunity offers.[25]

This problem, with many others, and in particular the persistent problem of how to erect provincial courts that do not conflict with this prerogative of the Governor General,[26] can be solved by revesting these appointments in the provincial governments, subject to a veto of the central government in the case of one reasonably well-defined superior court of record. This appears to have been the pre-Confederation practice as well as it can be disinterred;[27] the reasons that prompted the change have now long passed away.

The development of the courts since 1867, while partly satisfactory, has produced those irritating and absurd riddles that obstruct the evolution of a fully satisfactory judiciary in the provinces, and long-distance political appointments depend too much on the good sense of the chief federal cabinet minister from the province in question and not enough on the more balanced and broader-based viewpoint of the provincial government and bar. The political experience of the judges, reflecting only that of the two larger national parties, has tended to exaggerate the cautious cast of an occupation that is inherently most cautious. Canadian courts are not noted for creative contributions to jurisprudence.

The positive interest of the province in the proper administration of justice, and especially of those provincially enacted laws that form the bulk of private law affecting the ordinary citizen, argues mightily for provincial-government appointment of the judges of provincial courts. On the other hand, the interest of the central government in those courts is good reason for it to retain some control over judicial appointments. But to give it a general veto over all nominees to magistracies would be cumbersome and a novel irritant to relations between the governments. It should be sufficient if the central government may disallow an appointment to that provincial court that is bound to continue to administer federal law because it has the power to supervise all other courts in the province. The exact machinery for such joint appointments may be debated; the pre-Confederation precedent, while it offers the example of provincial appointment, is unhealthy in that the Imperial government could substitute its own choice. The veto should be sufficient, and there is reason to think that federal and provincial co-operation in this act has existed and can be had.[28]

The judges of superior, district, and county courts are paid by the federal government at uniform rates across the country. In some provinces, the provincially appointed magistrates may receive larger salaries than their judicial superiors, the district and county court judges.[29] The federal government would find it most impolitic to try to differentiate between the judges of different provinces, but such differentiation is entirely appropriate and possible if the payment becomes a provincial obligation. Of course, in such a case, a federal contribution would be just and proper, and it may be advisable to incorporate it in the Articles. It is not essential or strictly necessary, however, and monetary formulae are notoriously short-lived.

The discussion of security of tenure and payment in respect to Section 2 explains the purpose and effect of the similar provisions in Section 5.

SECTION 6

The Essential Jurisdiction of the Court

The permanent and essential jurisdiction of the superior court of record is its supervisory one; this is exercised through the prerogative writs, i.e., *certiorari, habeas corpus (ad subjiciendum), quo warranto, mandamus,* and *prohibition.*

These are common-law writs, and like most elements of the common law they are still in process of evolution and contain imperfections and archaisms that make it imprudent to incorporate them as such in the Articles. To do so would be to freeze part of the law in the text at its present uncertain stage.

It is preferable to state the substance of the law in terms that are precise but sufficiently general to allow the development of this important branch of jurisdiction to continue. It was in eclipse for a while, but of late years it has had a resurgence due to the need to keep special tribunals within the legal scope of their powers. Theoretically, under the present constitution, a tribunal can be placed by the legislature beyond the reach of these writs,[30] but the courts have been most astute to bring back the power by the back door when it has seemingly been ushered out the front. Now that the indignation of the progressives has died down somewhat, it is generally conceded that some such control is as much a basis of civil liberty as is *habeas corpus* itself.

The core of these writs is to determine whether the claim or decision in question is lawful. It is not a question of right or wrong but compliance with the law, lawfulness: that is, whether an official has the authority he purports to use, whether he has a lawful cause for using his authority, whether he uses it in a lawful mode, whether he has produced a lawful result.

The history of these writs (except *habeas corpus*) is not well documented nor are their limitations easy to find out. Let us therefore reiterate that it is wiser to enunciate the principles they seem to stand for, so far as they concern our constitutionally requisite provincial court, than to incorporate them as such into the Articles.

There remains the question 'What other courts should be subject to the supervisory authority of the superior provincial court?'

And the answer, again having in view the unitary nature of the Canadian judicial system, is 'All, except the Supreme Court of Canada.' In this way the character of the system is preserved and in the same stroke those distressing conflicts of courts of co-ordinate powers that occur in some federal countries are avoided.[31]

The purpose of this Article is to preserve the unique and satisfactory character of the Canadian judicature while deleting those features that have developed as weaknesses or defects in the administration of justice. This the Article does by instituting the chief federal court and the chief court of each province, under the basic régime of an independent judiciary, and on terms sufficient to satisfy the just interests of all parties. For the other courts, adequate provision is made in this Article and in Article 7.

CHAPTER 15

Provincial Government

The dominant mind in the construction of the Confederation, Sir John A. Macdonald, did not conceal his preference for a unitary state, a 'legislative union', rather than a federal one. Recognizing that this preference was not a practical one in Canada, he nevertheless worked hard to incorporate in the plan as much as he could of unitary government.[1] In the B.N.A. Act, 1867, Canada is not a true federation nor yet truly a unitary state. It may be most aptly described as a superior colony that has been given substantial control over its constituent sub-colonies. These, however, are guaranteed their independent existence and some inviolable authority. The central government took the place of the Imperial government with respect to the pre-Confederation colonies that became provinces, but was itself designed to be subject to Imperial control to some extent, as they had been. When the offices and functions of the Governor General and the lieutenant-governor are examined, the hierarchical structure becomes apparent.

Thus the Governor General was conceived to be both the legal head of the Canadian government in the absence of the Queen, and an Imperial officer appointed by the United Kingdom government,[2] charged in his commission to disallow or reserve for that government's consideration several classes of possible Dominion acts.[3] But the Dominion early shed these shackles on its autonomy.[4]

126

The office of lieutenant-governor also was conceived as a dual function: the governor was at the same time a federal super-intendent[5] and legal head of the provincial government. While the office has changed over the years it still retains this double character, and the changes have been mostly in the importance and the activity attached to it.

In the early days, some governors, notably in the new provinces, actually conducted the administration. There were exciting clashes in Quebec and British Columbia between strong-minded governors and their ministries, leading to the dismissal of five cabinets.[6] In the first half-century of Confederation, governors refused assents to twenty-six bills and reserved sixty-four for action at Ottawa.[7]

In the almost half-century since 1917, however, the character of the office has changed. There have been only two refusals of assent and only six reservations.[8] In the last twenty-five years there has been only one of each, and each instance was of a maverick character inspired by the governor's personal views.[9]

In the first half-century the Dominion disallowed ninety-four provincial acts; in the second, seventeen, the last in 1944.[10]

Since the first World War the office, formerly a political plum, has become difficult to fill. The salaries ($9000 for most provinces, with $1000 more for Quebec and Ontario and $1000 less for P.E.I.) were not changed between 1872 and 1963, when they were suddenly doubled; the expenses incidental to the social functions attached to the governorship may exceed those sums two, three, or even four times.[11] The governor's political functions have become increasingly formal and automatic and more and more congruous with the constitutional autonomy to which the provinces have evolved.[12] The term 'figurehead' is not inapt. But the legal powers remain and may happen to be used in unlikely ways.

The federal aspect of the governor's office has already been largely eclipsed; Dr. Saywell affirms:

> As an instrument of federal policy, however, the Lieutenant-Governor has been replaced by the conference, the national political party, the radio, the press, and the telephone.[13]

It has been suggested that the residue of the office could be entrusted to the chief justice of the province (who frequently acts as the governor's substitute in any case), or to a committee of state composed of leading public but not political persons. So, the office is not even necessary to responsible government, to say nothing of being essential to our federal state. We have passed the day when federal control of provincial affairs is either possible or desirable.

The office of lieutenant-governor is well enough entrenched in the provincial constitutions to be safe from merely wanton assault. It does not require constitutional protection, and it would be unwise, in view of the ferment of feeling against it, to try to sanctify it by the federal charter. It has lost its federal significance in the eyes of the people and if it is to continue to be a federal appointment, the governor should act in the name of the sovereign rather than in the name of the Governor General,[14] and as a purely provincial functionary. There is no anomaly here. Many public officers act in the Queen's name.

But the office may not continue, and, as far as the Confederation is concerned, it does not seem to matter whether or not it does. It would thus be an unfortunate obstacle to the evolution of provincial government if it were incorporated in the fundamental law of Canada.

On the other hand, since every Canadian is a potential citizen of every province, there are federal aspects of provincial government worth putting in the Articles. The only essential one that is obvious is representative democracy. Accordingly, this has been built into Article 6 as the core of the provincial constitutions in place of the office of lieutenant-governor, which is the element of the provincial constitutions that is made inviolable by Section 92, Clause 1, of the B.N.A. Act, 1867. The scope of the inviolability is doubtful, but it certainly applies to Sections 58 to 67 inclusive and to Section 90 of the B.N.A. Act, 1867. Section 90 confirms executive control over money matters as well as powers to disallow and reserve bills. Consequently, while provincial legislatures have wide powers to amend their constitutions, they may not discard responsible government nor may they interfere with the supervisory powers that the federal government retains over them by law.

The purpose of this shifting of the centre is to make the provincial constitutions more democratic and at the same time to found them on more basic, because more essential, conceptions. The proposed Article is concerned with the same field of topics as the existing law and imports into the provincial constitutions some, but not all, of the corresponding provisions of Article 3. These have been sufficiently discussed in general in the treatment of that Article and these remarks deal only with their specifically provincial aspects.

The requirement of an elected assembly, in Section 1, and the limitation on its term are essential to popular control of the legislature and to representative democracy. The Constitution of the United States of America in dealing with the constitution of the states requires only that

> The United States shall guarantee to every State in this Union a republican form of Government. . . .[15]

The courts of that country have not been willing to attempt to define this and it has not been a fruitful provision. It is preferable to spell out the necessary particulars rather than rely on such a slippery phrase as 'republican form of government' or, in our case, 'responsible government'.

The requirement in the second section for equal single-member divisions is not essential, but the example of our neighbours again warns us that it would be prudent to avoid the rural versus urban struggle already mentioned. For some reason local gerrymandering can be even more gross and unprincipled than national.

Again, the danger of local excesses is much greater in respect to unpopular legislators, and the provision for security of office, while not essential, would seem to be necessary.

Section 4 is the dynamic counterpart to the structural elements of Section 1. It is the essential power of the purse which the legislature and executive control in concert; if they do not act in concert they must reconcile their differences in order to raise or spend money. This is the heart of prudent, democratic administration.

It is arguable that the fifth section is essential. It is designed to provide that the popular chamber, if it persists over a rather lengthy period, can carry any proposal into law against the objections of the governor and any 'upper house' that may exist. This makes the will of the electorate ultimately sovereign. It may also be necessary in order to make sure that the province can reconstitute, if it desires, the office of lieutenant-governor. For the existing provincial constitutions will continue until altered, and it is conceivable that the lieutenant-governor, as a federal officer (which he will continue to be until that is changed), might refuse assent to a bill, or reserve it, if it touched his office. The power to refuse assent and to reserve bills (and possibly the power of the federal government to disallow), being part of the provincial constitutions, would continue under the Articles until altered by provincial law.

But it does not seem necessary to require an intervening election in this case. In the federal situation the problem is to override the Senate which, as now constituted, is not responsible to the electorate. In the provincial case, such a conflict is not possible in most provinces, nor is a lasting clash between the executive and legislature, under responsible government. But there is a possible collision with the federal government, and there the province should be able to carry its point and should not need a repeated mandate from the electorate to do so.

The Articles should deal only with such aspects of provincial government as concern the whole nation. In all other respects the provinces should be left to work out their own constitutions on the existing foundations.

CHAPTER 16

Legislative Powers

The plan of Article 7 is similar to Part VI of the B.N.A. Act, 1867, not only on the surface and in much detail but also very substantially. It adheres, for example, to the existing distribution of classes of legislative matters between the governments, with one or two important exceptions; it also yields the residue of power to the central government as the 1867 Act was intended to do.

Yet here is one of the chief objects of this book – to excise the idea of exclusive legislative jurisdiction from the federal structure. This is a profound change but a most necessary one if we are to shake off the shackles on governmental initiative imposed by that idea and by the interpretive approach that is founded on it.

The alternative proposed is not new to the Canadian constitution. In respect to agriculture and immigration both the Dominion and the provinces have power to make laws, but the Dominion power is the *dominant* one, by Section 95 of the 1867 Act. This device was adopted in reverse in 1951 when the Dominion obtained authority, by Section 94A, to legislate in relation to old-age pensions; in this case provincial laws are the dominant ones.

In fact, are the powers of the several governments as exclusive as they purport to be? There is a good deal of overlapping in the classes of subjects listed in Sections 91 and 92 of the 1867 Act. This is recognized by what is called the 'aspect' doctrine:

... that subjects which in one aspect and for one purpose fall within
Section 92, may in another aspect and for another purpose fall
within Section 91.[1]

But it is possible to argue with some force that some of these
apparently exclusive powers to make laws are, in fact, rather
dominant and *subordinate* in practice. This is particularly striking in three fields: penal law, commercial law, and public works.

In the case of penal law, the central government is given jurisdiction over the criminal law with certain exceptions. In further
derogation of this authority, however, there is a provincial power
to impose fine and imprisonment and an incidental power to
establish procedures for doing so. Such law is commonly called
'quasi-criminal' but, except for the need to preserve the constitutional division, it is indistinguishable from the rest of the criminal
law. The provincial law must be based on some class of subjects
in the provincial field of jurisdiction and the power is not itself
an independent source of legislation as are the other enumerated
classes of subjects in Sections 91 and 92 (including the criminal
law). If there is a clash, the federal statute prevails. But occa-
sionally the implications of the idea of exclusive powers work out
so that a provincial penal enactment will be held *ultra vires,*
although it does not clash with a federal one, because it is not
based on any head of Section 92, or because, though it may be
so based, it deals with a matter on which the federal parliament
has legislated within its power and thus 'occupied the field'.

Most provinces, for example, make it an offence to drive an
automobile imprudently. Mere imprudence is of a quality differing from recklessness in the theory of criminal responsibility,
and so these provincial acts do not clash with the Criminal Code
provisions banning reckless driving: so it was decided in *O'Grady*
v. *Sparling.*[2] Since that case, the parliament has resurrected the
offence of dangerous driving and it is arguable that this imports
the criminal law into the domain of inadvertent negligence, of
which imprudence is a type or species. If this is so, the parliament has occupied the field of inadvertent negligence for penal
purposes, and the provincial prohibitions of imprudent driving
are *ultra vires* although there is no clash between the two and

although they may deal with quite separate kinds of conduct in the field.[3]

In commercial law, there is a federal power to deal with Trade and Commerce in addition to more specific heads in Section 91. The trade and commerce power has been attenuated to a very marked degree, and most commercial transactions not falling within the subjects in the specific heads of Section 91 are governed by the provincial laws of property and civil rights. The fact is, both the parliament and the legislatures are immersed in the material of commercial law, and which enactment prevails in any given case depends upon the traffic rules developed in the case law.

Both federal and provincial governments are occupied with public works, but in this case the dominant power of the central government is quite explicit, although the expression of it is rather involved. Briefly, the parliament of Canada can assume jurisdiction over any public work by declaring that it is for the general advantage of Canada or of two or more of the provinces.

There are probably other examples of actual joint jurisdiction existing behind the façade of separate exclusive powers. Family law, for instance, gets into both fields in a substantial way, but the subject-matters are more clearly distinguishable than in the other cases mentioned.

If this is so, why should it be important and even urgent to get rid of the principle of exclusiveness? Firstly, of course, if the law and the facts do not agree, the law suffers contempt. But even if they agree more fully than we are prepared to admit, it is necessary to eliminate the principle because it imposes a very restrictive and nonsensical rule of interpretation on the constitution.

When, for example, a provincial act is questioned by the courts, the procedure is to look at Section 92, and if authority for the act cannot be found there, it is invalid. But even if Section 92 seems to authorize the act, it may be found to be invalid because of something in Section 91. On the other hand, federal legislation will be generally upheld unless it clashes with some class in Section 92.[4]

In particular:

> . . . the abstinence of the Dominion Parliament from legislating to
> the full limit of its powers could not have the effect of transferring
> to any provincial legislature the legislative power which has been
> assigned to the Dominion by S. 91. . . .[5]

This limits the central government also so that, in theory at least,
it cannot invade and take over an exclusive, although unoccupied,
class of provincial legislative subjects. But the scope of the
federal power is much in dispute, dispute that it would serve no
purpose to get into here.

The first effect of exclusiveness is to impede the legislation of
one body although there is no enactment of the other body to
clash with it. A consequential effect of this principle is the excessive subtlety with which the various heads of power are considered. Where an act of parliament is being considered merely
in the connotations of a general formula and not in contrast to
the enactment of a competing authority, the process tends to general, vague, and hypothetical tests such as the perennial one for
'the pith and substance' of the act.[6] No judicial tests give more
free play to the personal and political prejudices of the courts
or, for that matter, to the metaphysical perplexities inherent in
such an approach.

Another annoying effect of exclusiveness is to bar delegation
of powers between the governments. Delegation is now considered so desirable and necessary that the proposal for the final
amendment of the constitution to be made in the Imperial parliament contains extensive provisions for it: the involved and in-
elegant clauses of the Fulton Formula. They would be quite
unnecessary without the sharp dichotomy of legislative powers
now in force.

Is there any reason to retain the exclusive nature of the
powers? It is a very rare case where it can be said vehemently and
with confidence that the worth-while arguments are all on one
side, but this is one of them. There is absolutely no value in
keeping the word, or the concept, in the law of the confederation. It is a snare, a delusion, a scandal, a completely unnecessary and futile intrusion.

In fact, anything useful that exclusive powers can do, the doctrine of paramountcy can do better. That is, there is no need of a traffic rule unless there is an actual clash of powers and in such case the rule determines which shall prevail. With all respect to Sir John A. Macdonald's hopes,[7] it is by now amply proved that exclusiveness does not prevent clashes. It merely makes it difficult (and often morally impossible) to achieve full self-government for Canada because of the intricate problems in meshing the enactments of the interested legislatures.

In sum, exclusiveness as a principle of law-making jurisdiction has too long been an obstacle to effective Canadian government, too long unnecessarily occupied the time of statutory draftsmen, too long engaged the attention and the talents of advocates, too long hobbled the lawmaker and the administrator. This projected beneficence, designed to protect us from Yankee habits and frailties, has been the curse of our legal structure. Let us cast it out.

The plan put forward in the Article is, at bottom, very much the same as the 1867 one with the evil spirit of exclusiveness exorcized and replaced by the paramountcy principle. It is designed to work in this way (and this would be the approach to interpretation):

In the case of a federal act, if it is made in relation to a matter within a class of subjects enumerated in Section 1 of the Article, it will prevail over any provincial enactment. If not in relation to such a matter it must be measured in respect to Section 2. If it is made in relation to a matter within an enumerated class of subjects in Section 2, it must give way if there is any conflicting provincial act in relation to that matter. And if it is not made in relation to such a matter but yet clashes with provincial legislation made in relation to matters dealt with in Section 2, it must yield; otherwise, however, it will be paramount.

On the other hand, in the case of a provincial act, if it is made in relation to a matter within the classes of Section 2, it will prevail over federal enactments except such as are paramount by virtue of Section 1. But provincial legislation otherwise is always subordinate to federal law.

Here there will arise no question of *ultra vires* and there will be no point in challenging an enactment under the provisions of this Article unless there is an enactment of another government that conflicts.

We have passed over as hardly worth consideration the idea that there is any virtue in trying to confine the provincial government to the subject-matters of legislation in Section 92 of the B.N.A. Act and the federal government to those in Section 91. This is abrupt and possibly foolish, for many people in 1867 thought there was virtue in the idea. Nevertheless, the parliamentary nature of all Canadian legislatures is now so embedded in our political economy that the concept of exclusive jurisdiction is a source of constant strain and frustration to the rational operation of the provincial bodies as well as the federal parliament. So, by removing the exclusive principle, no harm is done to any existing value and the Article is so balanced that no government will be able to usurp a field that has hitherto belonged to another; the principle that jurisdiction is dominant or paramount is quite as effective in that respect as the principle of exclusive jurisdiction. But the new approach will give greater freedom and scope to all Canadian governments and will make certain that the nation enjoys complete powers of self-government in fact as well as in legal concept – a consummation devoutly to be wished.

CHAPTER 17

The General Powers

The Dominion and the provinces were each given legislative powers of a residual nature in the Confederation scheme, or so the promoters and draftsmen thought. Because of this, the words 'residue' and 'residual' do not aptly express what they had in mind. A more suitable term is 'general'.

The general power of the provinces was conceived to be the concluding one of Section 92:

> 16. Generally all Matters of a merely local or private Nature in the Province.[1]

This is a rather meek little power with hardly any substantive content that is not more easily catalogued under some other class of Section 92.[2] Its main effect has been to give some colour to the views of Clement and O'Connor that all exercise of legislative authority in Canada should be determined by the grand criterion 'the cardinal principle of allotment':

> To this end the Act, as now authoritatively construed, assigns to the parliament of Canada all such matters only as are of common Canadian concern, while the provincial jurisdiction embraces in each province all such matters as are of merely provincial concern.[3]

Today the general power of the provinces is conceived to lie in the class of Section 92 that was understood, from the beginning, to be fundamentally important: that is, Class 13, 'Property and Civil Rights in the Province'.[4]

The general power of the Dominion, on the other hand, is the power stated at the outset of Section 91:

> . . . to make Laws for the Peace, Order, and good Government of Canada, in relation to all Matters not coming within the Classes of Subjects by this Act assigned exclusively to the Legislatures of the Provinces; . . .

This is a true residue and is so designated, for example, by Duff J. in the *Board of Commerce Case*.[5] That is, it gives the federal government all legislative authority in Canada not assigned to the provinces. This follows from the words 'Peace, Order and good Government of Canada', which, as O'Connor points out:

> . . . have been . . . used by Imperial draftsmen for hundreds of years to express the grant of full and general authority to enact except as expressly or necessarily in the circumstances restricted.[6]

It is likely that any new departure will be of national concern. Whether that is so or not, the principle of paramountcy will permit any legislature to deal with such a departure in its provincial aspect, and yet if it does become important to the whole country the parliament can deal with it. For these reasons, it is not proposed to change the present law whereby the central government holds the residue of power. The principle of paramountcy makes the location of the residue much less important than it now is.

Accordingly, Article 7 is drawn so as to give every Canadian legislature powers to make laws 'for the Peace, Order and good Government' of its territory. This gives full parliamentary scope to the statutes, subject only to the Articles and the rules respecting supremacy.

One point is important. Number 45 of the Quebec Resolutions proposed:

> In regard to all subjects over which jurisdiction belongs to both the General and Local Legislatures, the laws of the General Parliament shall control and supersede those made by the Local Legislature, and the latter shall be void as far as they are repugnant to or inconsistent with the former.[7]

The provision for avoidance (that is, rendering void) is unnecessary. Lawyers, draftsmen, and judges have a nasty habit of making things they don't approve of null and void. This is to be deprecated: the device of nullification should only be used to deal with a wilful breach of the law, such as the extortion of a confession. In the present case, avoidance is not needed to carry out the principle of paramountcy and it raises collateral problems. For example, what happens to the suppressed law of a subordinate legislature if the paramount one vacates the field: does the law revive? If a repugnant law is made void, the implication is that it is dead forever; if it merely becomes inoperative, it will revive on the withdrawal of the paramount law.

The paramountcy rule, as finally embodied in Section 95 of the B.N.A. Act in relation to the concurrent powers over Agriculture and Immigration, seems to imply that the suppressed law will be ineffective rather than void. This is all that is necessary, and it is not prudent to go beyond what is necessary in this case. But to make the result of any conflict clear, Article 7 spells out that the subordinate law shall be inoperative.

The chief purpose of the enumerated classes of Sections 1 and 2 of the Article is not to grant powers (as is the case in the B.N.A. Act) but rather to define the cases where the legislature concerned is paramount. The parliament and the legislatures will be equally competent to pass laws in any case, but if both do so, the Article determines which shall prevail in case of conflict. Another purpose of specifying the legislative powers in the Article is to make sure that they are recognized as proper topics for lawmaking and thus to discountenance the notion that the Articles themselves say all that is to be said by law about them.

These changes of purpose and effect in the sections, as reborn in Article 7, demand some changes in coverage and detail. First of all, since federal unenumerated powers in Section 1 are not superior to the enumerated provincial powers in Section 2, it will be necessary to specify all subjects of federal jurisdiction that are to be absolutely paramount. (This is probably the existing law although it is unlikely that it was intended to be.[8]) Again, it will be desirable to spell out powers to deal with topics that the Articles also deal with, because of the danger noted above, that the Articles might be given too restrictive an interpretation. And it will be good to gather in one place many powers that are scattered through the B.N.A. Acts so that their ordinal values, their places in the scheme of paramountcy, can be assigned to them.

CHAPTER 18

The Federal Paramount Powers

The scheme of Section 1 of Article 7 is a systematic progress from the structure of the federal government to the principal bodies with which it has relations and then on to its more particular field of operation. The section opens with classes dealing with the three chief functions of government – legislative, executive, and judicial – touches on the public service, goes on to provinces and territories, deals with citizens and certain denizens, moves to external relations, and then proceeds to the business of the central government. The first eight or nine classes are static and organizational; the rest are dynamic and operational.

CLASS 1

The Parliament

This states concisely the substance of several sections of the B.N.A. Act, 1867, including Sections 18, 35, 41, 47, 51, and 52. It does not contain all the detail of these sections but it gives a general and comprehensive power to deal with such detail. On the other hand, the specific powers in the B.N.A. Act do not have the scope of this clause, for the clause includes many subjects that were beyond the powers of the parliament until the 1949 (No. 2) Amendment or were in the residuary power. Since these powers deal with subjects over which the central government should be paramount and since the law should clearly say so, this is the place to put them.

This clause is complementary to Article 3 and in this respect makes manifest that the parliament, although subject to that Article, has the power to deal with itself and its constituent bodies and members, by law. It shows, as do the similar clauses that follow, that the limits and checks imposed on the legislatures in the Articles do not prohibit legislation within those limits but rather the contrary.

CLASS 2

The Governor General

This clause is to Article 4 as Class 1 is to Article 3. The B.N.A. Act is almost silent on the matters mentioned there. Section 12 of the Act is remotely related to Article 4, Section 3, and hence to this class, and Section 105 of the Act gives the parliament the power to fix the Governor General's salary.

The phrase 'Appointment or Election' of the Governor General gives a permissive power. It need not be exercised but it does give the government of Canada one more degree of freedom to develop the democratic alternative of an elected executive head if the two-party system of cabinet government should fail to function.

CLASS 3

The Federal Courts

Again, this class, dealing with the third great division of government, the judiciary, is related to Article 5 in the way Class 1 is to Article 3 and Class 2 is to Article 4. It is a moot point whether the phrase 'Courts of the Confederation' should not rather be expressed as 'federal Courts', as this is the intent. But the phrase used is more consistent with the language of Article 5, Section 4, which enables such courts to be set up. Moreover, an attempt has been made to avoid the adjective 'federal' in the Articles, except where any other term would be too awkward, because many people consider it an alien word and dislike it. The subjects of Class 3 are represented in Section 101 of the B.N.A. Act, but, for the reasons stated in the discussion of Article 5, the treatment is very different.

One minor point is of some importance. The explicit inclusion of 'Procedure' in the class makes it quite patent that the parliament can regulate the way in which the Supreme Court of Canada does business. In the absence of such a provision it would be arguable that the parliament could not do this because the Court is established by the Articles as a co-ordinate and independent division of the government.[1]

CLASS 4

The Federal Public Service

This clause is expressed in much more general and inclusive terms than Class 8 of Section 91 of the 1867 Act, to which it corresponds. The latter is, indeed, a very imperfect statement of the subjects in the field, and were it to be strictly construed (of which there is little danger), it could hardly support much in the way of legislation. Legal caution inspires the reference to corporations.

CLASS 5

Federal Public Property

This represents one division of Class 1A of Section 91 (formerly Class 1 of that section), 'The Public Debt and Property'. The slight expansion of the terms used is calculated to make it clear that it is *federal* public property that is in question, that the clause relates not only to existing property but to property to be acquired for the public service, and that land is explicitly included. Picayune considerations? Possibly, but courts and lawyers can become entangled in such minute questions.

The first five classes of Section 1 are so clearly linked to the nature and structure of the central government that they would probably be held to be excluded of their very essence from provincial dominant powers. The main purpose, then, of putting them in express terms in Section 1 is to make it crystal clear that the central government has such powers despite any implications to the contrary that the ingenious legal mind might discover in the Articles as a whole. In the remaining classes of Section 1, however, there are obvious instances of overlapping with classes of Section 2 or of genus-species relationships between the two, or of natural federal dominance being otherwise questionable.

CLASS 6

New Provinces and the Territories

The subject-matters in this class are dealt with to some extent by Sections 146 and 147 of the B.N.A. Act, 1867, and in a more comprehensive way by the 1871 Amendment. That Act does not speak of a province ceding territory but it provides that the consent of a province is a prerequisite to any alteration of its limits. In the result, where a province is affected by the federal power, the two governments must agree. Thus, this aspect of the subject is not a proper one for federal dominance, or provincial dominance either. It obviously is material for an agreement between them and is so dealt with in Section 3 of Article 9. For the rest, the federal management of the creation of new provinces and territories has proved reasonably satisfactory despite some recriminations over property provisions.[2]

CLASS 7

Citizenship and Naturalization

In 1867, citizenship was not an ordinary, familiar, everyday concept in British law; so Section 91, Class 25, of the B.N.A. Act corresponding to this class reads 'Naturalization and Aliens'. Now that we have developed a law of citizenship, citizenship should take first place in our category, and immigration, naturalization, and aliens will be implied as necessary but subordinate topics. This class will also make it clear that the content of

Article 2 is proper matter for legislation. The appropriate authority and the one that now governs the subject is the parliament, and the federal paramountcy in this field is so obvious and pre-empts so much of the field that it does not seem feasible to give the provinces an analogous paramountcy over provincial citizenship. They will be able to legislate in the field, because of the parliamentary principle incorporated in Article 7, but subject to Article 2 (especially Section 4) and to federal paramountcy.

CLASS 8

Aboriginal Inhabitants

When is an Eskimo not an Eskimo? When he is an Indian. Despite the antipathy that is said to exist between them, Eskimoes are classified as Indians for the purposes of Class 24 of Section 91 of the B.N.A. Act,[3] to which Class 8 corresponds. This was necessary because the Act does not mention Eskimoes in the subjects for legislation. But the judicial response cited applies only to the Eskimoes of Quebec; so it seems prudent to make the clause say what Class 24 means.

CLASS 9

External Affairs

This class might read simply 'External Affairs'[4] but there is some value in being a little more explicit because the inclusion of relations with international bodies other than states is not necessarily part of 'External Affairs' as a concept of international or domestic law.

Would the inclusion of this class change the existing legislative balance by bringing subjects ordinarily within the provincial supremacy into the field of federal dominance, for example as ancilliary legislation? The federal powers over external affairs do not permit the parliament to encroach on provincial legislative subjects because the federal powers are not legislative but executive.[5]

Section 132 of the B.N.A. Act, 1867, has the only explicit

grant of law-making powers concerning external relations. In fact, the parliament cannot do much with this section because it applies, in its terms, only to treaties between the British Empire and foreign nations.

This will have to be worked out. As far as external relations in themselves are concerned, the logic of the federal structure and responsibility requires that the central government should be the sole channel, and our history and traditions are in accord. On the other hand, a reasonable interpretation of the clause would limit it to external relations in a proper sense and would not permit a treaty to be used as a 'disguised' basis for a federal law designed to subvert provincial enactments that are entitled to paramountcy. This approach to interpretation is well established in criminal law.[6] The question is not without difficulty, however.

CLASS 10

Defence Against National Emergencies

The national parliament has legislative power to deal with defence, but the power is expressed in such limited, not to say parochial, terms that the courts have had to invent another head of jurisdiction called the 'emergency power' to give it some substance. The defence power is contained in Class 7 of Section 91 as 'Militia, Military and Naval Service, and Defence'. The emergency power lurks in the general words of Section 91 dealing with 'Peace, Order and good Government', and ordinarily it cannot override the explicit powers of Section 92.[7] In certain emergencies of a national importance the federal government will be permitted to use this power while the emergency continues; instances that have been considered acceptable are war and epidemics. A later judicial rationalization of the early case of *Russell* v. *The Queen* puts widespread intemperance in the same class. On the other hand, profiteering and labour-management contention failed to make the grade.[8]

The proposed Class 10 would enlarge the acknowledged class of emergencies to include civil war, famine, and such things as earthquakes and forest fires of national proportions. It would probably include a disaster such as would result from a rain of giant meteors. But it is difficult if not impossible to devise a formula defining social pathology, such as intemperance, profiteering, or class warfare, that, without being a proper subject for criminal legislation, at the same time would constitute a national peril. Any such proposal would inevitably sap the foundations of provincial supremacy. It thus appears better to omit the so-called perils of human provenance unless they can come under the canon of 'civil Strife'.

This class is one where it seems prudent to make the federal power explicit rather than rely on the general powers in the Article.

CLASS 11

The Criminal Law

This clause carries the theme of the protection of the state and the public into the domain of personal and private attacks on the peace of the realm. It does not differ in substance from Classes 27 and 28 of Section 91, but the wording is not the same because Class 28 was expressed in a trivial and hidebound way. Its message is incorporated in this class as 'the Punishment and Reformation of Criminals'. Class 28, coupled with Class 6 of Section 92 (dealing with Reformatories), affords some basis for the belief that there must be a hard and fast distinction between penitentiaries and reformatories and even between the length of sentence that may be served in each. This is great nonsense, even if it may be the law, and should be eradicated.

It should be noted that the class speaks of the *ordinary* courts of criminal jurisdiction in the province. That is the factual and legal situation now because of Section 101 of the B.N.A. Act. We have discussed this in Chapter 14.

The existing division of jurisdiction over the criminal law, whereby parliament creates it and the provinces enforce it, has worked quite well. It does away, for example, with all those questions of extradition that can arise between the states of the United

States. It guarantees, at least to a minimum extent, the local control of the police, which is a well-approved British device to forestall a nation-wide tyranny, and at the same time it hampers the excesses of legislation to which parochial lawmakers are prone.

The chief complaints against the present system are that nation-wide laws do not always meet local needs and that the courts of different provinces diverge in their construction of the law. The substitution of the principle of paramountcy for that of exclusiveness in law-making will enable the provinces to pass police measures to fill the gaps left by the Criminal Code without any question of exceeding their powers.

CLASS 12

Health, and the Prevention of Disease

This is the third great category of preventive powers. At present it is held to be a provincial power by construction of Class 7 of Section 92 of the 1867 Act, but the question does not appear to have been finally decided by either the Privy Council or the Supreme Court of Canada. Parliament has some legislation in the field such as the Food and Drugs Act and the Opium and Narcotic Drug Act, but it has to rely on other powers such as those relating to the criminal law, or trade and commerce, or on the general words of Section 91, to save the validity of these acts.[9] The central government has no express authority to deal with health or disease except in the narrow limits of Class 11 of Section 91 'Quarantine and the Establishment and Maintenance of Marine Hospitals'. These subjects relate to the law of the sea rather than to health in general. On the other hand, Class 7 of Section 92 was probably intended not to deal with health and disease legislation as we know it today, but with charitable institutions as a class.

Class 12 of Section 1 of the Article must be read together with Class 10 of Section 2. This division of the subject, while it recognizes federal dominance over the whole field, retains provincial paramountcy where it now exists.

The case for federal supremacy in this class of subjects is based on the single fact that disease observes no geographical or political boundaries. The central government spends immense sums both on fighting disease and on fostering good health. The purpose of this clause is to give it a clear and explicit mandate to do so. No doubt there are dangers in such a supposed transfer, but the proposal is more in accord with the economic, political, and legal facts than is the present constitutional theory.

This is a sound instance of the good effect of a change over to the paramountcy principle: all the governments concerned will have much more legal freedom to deal with the problems involved.

CLASS 13

Unemployment Insurance and Assistance

It is a short passage from public health to public welfare, and it is an equally short step from the protective nature of health legislation to the quasi-protective nature of welfare laws. At present the parliament has exclusive power over unemployment insurance[10] but only a shared power over old-age pensions: it cannot affect the operation of any provincial law on the subject and has therefore a subordinate jurisdiction.[11] In addition the federal government assists the provinces to provide disability assistance and other public welfare measures.[12] Unemployment insurance and family allowances are administered by the federal government alone. There is a mixture of authorities in the other programs and in some the provinces determine the nature of the operation. In most cases, however, the financial command of the federal government effectually dictates the purposes, conditions, and fundamental identity of these schemes across the land.[13]

Who the appropriate lawmaker should be is debatable. Since the central government has exclusive control in fact of two chief fields, unemployment insurance and family allowances, and provides the financial backbone of old-age pensions and many other welfare programs, Class 13 was first drafted to read

> 13. Public Welfare and Protection from Want through public Insurance and Assistance;

But in recent federal-provincial conferences the provinces have become almost unanimous that the central government, through its initiatives and ascendancy in the welfare field, is dictating objectives and priorities that are none of its constitutional business and making it hard for the provinces to cope with local needs and conditions. The Ontario and Quebec stands on the Canada Pension Plan illustrate this movement but most of the provinces have expressed similar views. Class 13 restates the present law. The paramountcy principle allows the federal government to play an important part in public welfare but the provinces will have the scope and power to act that is properly theirs. The principle makes the 1964 Amendment unnecessary.

The phrase 'Insurance and Assistance' is necessary as not all the money presently being handed out is properly called insurance. The unemployment-insurance scheme, for example, has had to be supplemented by extensions, beyond the prescribed period, in the nature of direct relief.

CLASS 14

Communications

With this class we pass from those topics that relate to the protective aspects of government to those impinging on production or dealing with adjuncts to the economy that governments commonly regulate and foster and often provide.

Class 14 deals with the transmission of written or spoken material. In each subject in the class there is a vast international network of facilities. The scale of these network organizations makes it almost self-evident that federal paramountcy alone can cope with the major questions likely to arise. On the other hand, the principle that every legislature will be competent to deal with the class means that existing provincial laws need not be disturbed except when necessary.

All the subjects in this class are within the field of federal jurisdiction now, either expressly under Section 91, Classes 5 and 29, and Section 92, Class 10, of the B.N.A. Act, 1867, or by judicial interpretation.[14] In the case of telephones and telegraphs, the provinces have a residual jurisdiction over purely intraprovincial systems, but this is subject to supersession through a parliamentary declaration that the work is for the general advantage of Canada.

CLASS 15

Transportation and Public Works

This class is substantially the same as the group of subjects provided by Section 91, Class 13 and Class 29, and Section 92, Class 10, of the B.N.A. Act, 1867. It is designed to catch up with the present ambit of the federal jurisdiction and to allow scope for future developments. This can be done only by generalization: it is hopeless to try to enumerate the things that might in future come under this canon. Who knows what may happen in the space age?

This class differs from the previous one in that there are transportation systems and public works that are not included in it whereas the terms of Class 14 are quite general. It is, in practical effect, the same as the present law and is based on the facts of life. Postal systems, telegraphs, telephone, radio, and television are, in fact, national and international in their structure and operation. There are, on the other hand, many transport systems and public works of wholly provincial or local concern. Public highways and ferries are examples of great importance, but there are also railways and other public works. Accordingly, there are sound practical reasons for the difference in approach between the two classes.

CLASS 16

Standards

The calendar is the only new subject in this class, which is otherwise the same as Class 17 of Section 91. It is probably already included as a measure of time, but as it is possible that calendar reform will prove feasible some day, even internationally, there is no harm in being explicit. At the moment the regulation of time is undertaken by the provinces. Clement writes of Class 17 of Section 91:

> The establishment of Canadian standards was apparently all that was contemplated by this class.[15]

Even if this is assumed to be so, it may be that provincial regulation of time-standards is *ultra vires*. It would not be, of course, under the Articles.

CLASS 17

Money

The genus *money* brings together Classes 14 and 20 with part of Class 15 of Section 91 of the B.N.A. Act, 1867. Although Alberta on one occasion tried to issue money substitutes,[16] it is probably a fair assumption that the majority of Canadians are quite satisfied that the central government shall have the final determination of what shall be money. That is the effect of the clause. It detaches the issue of paper money from the class dealing with banking. This is only proper as the private banks no longer issue their own paper money. The power was taken from them gradually, beginning in 1934 and ending January 1, 1945, as part of the process of establishing the Bank of Canada as the note-issuing body.[17]

CLASS 18

The Law Merchant

The species set out in this class are hard to sum up under any satisfactory generic title. 'The Law Merchant' is the nearest but it is not definite enough in its content to stand alone. Thus it may or may not include such topics as agency, partnerships, company law, carriage of goods, guarantee, insurance, etc., which are not now within federal jurisdiction and which it is not intended to transfer there. It is therefore necessary to limit the expression to the subjects set out in the class. They are all of special interest to commercial people and they all have a cosmopolitan flavour.[18]

The latter aspect is the most important reason for including most of them in the federal jurisdiction, as in most there is some need to conform to international standards.

It is conceivable that the federal power over 'The Regulation of Trade and Commerce' in Section 91, Class 2, of the B.N.A. Act, 1867, was intended to include the whole of commercial law.[19] If so, it has not worked out that way and it is not practicable now to try to reassert that intent. The proposed substitute for the content of Section 91, Class 2, is dealt with in Class 20 of this Article and section.

All the subjects in Class 18, other than Trading in Shares and Securities, are now within federal jurisdiction as Classes 18, 19, 21, 22, and 23 of Section 91 of the B.N.A. Act, 1867. The proposal to include Trading in Shares and Securities stems from the scandalous swindles that have been perpetrated in this line under provincial control. Every province has a system of regulation, but the high-pressure operators work across provincial limits and international boundaries with ease and considerable impunity. There are some economic advantages also in putting this subject under central control.

CLASS 19

Banking and Investment

The subjects in this class are grouped together because they are variants on the common theme, the need to regulate people and institutions that handle large masses of money supplied by other people. So vast is the extent of banking, insurance, and investment funds and so extensive are the effects of employing them, that only the federal government could have a hope of exercising adequate and necessary controls. Because of central control, the Canadian banking system is extremely stable and this stability should be imposed on the other subjects in the class. The proposed class is in accord with the recommendations of the Royal Commission on Dominion-Provincial Relations, 1940, Book II (pp. 59-62) except that the financial affairs of all insurers would be subject to federal supervision, leaving insurance contracts and

agents etc. to provincial jurisdiction. A like division of the investment field (except for trading in shares and securities) would
also seem to be in order.[20]

Class 19 is patently a large section of Class 18 that merits
separate treatment because of its importance.

CLASS 20

Trade and Commerce

The federal power in relation to 'The Regulation of Trade and
Commerce' is probably the most disputed and uncertain in the
B.N.A. Act, 1867. The words themselves, if not cut down by the
context, were thought by the Privy Council to be able

> . . . to include every regulation of trade ranging from political
> arrangements in regard to trade with foreign governments, requiring
> the sanction of parliament, down to minute rules for regulating
> particular trades.[21]

subjects set out in the Classes 15, 17, 18, 19, and 21 of Section
91. For this reason and others the Privy Council concluded that
if this were their meaning it would be unnecessary to mention the
Class 2 of Section 91, 'The Regulation of Trade and Commerce',
must be given a restricted meaning. It would still apply to (1)
'political arrangements in regard to trade requiring the sanction
of parliament' and (2) 'the regulation of trade in matters of interprovincial concern'. It might include (3) 'general regulation of
trade affecting the whole dominion'. Trade marks and trade
names probably come under the third category,[22] which also
covers the power to create and regulate companies with Canada-
wide objects,[23] although here the jurisdiction may be ancillary to
'a general power which the Dominion Parliament possessed independently of it'.[24]

But Class 2 of Section 91

> . . . does not comprehend the power to regulate by legislation the
> contracts of a particular business or trade, such as the business of
> fire insurance in a province.[25]

The actual incidence of any enactment is peculiarly uncertain.

The proposed Class 20 of this section will preserve the existing authority of the federal government while giving the enacting phrase a more exact meaning in the context. And expressing it in these terms will make it quite unnecessary to include in the Articles a counterpart to Section 121 of the B.N.A. Act, 1867. The federal government will have the final say on this subject, and history proves that it requires detailed legislation or much litigation to make sense of any summary expression of a right of interprovincial free trade.[26]

Trade and Commerce is the field where federal-provincial legislative co-operation has proved most difficult, not because of any unwillingness of the legislatures but because of the sharp division of powers required by the exclusive-jurisdiction device. It is in this field that the demands for 'delegation' of powers between the federal and provincial spheres are loudest.

All this rigidity, conflict, and confusion is dispelled when exclusive powers are done away with, and when each legislature is omnicompetent, the need for power to delegate vanishes without a sigh. The simplicity of the solution need not blind us to the fact that the new traffic rules, the rules of paramountcy, conceal problems of their own. Whatever frustrations those problems may bring, they can hardly compare with those inherent in the doctrine of exclusiveness. In fact the problems are not likely to be new, but the old ones in a lesser, less malignant form – the problems of determining whether an enactment is authorized by a head of jurisdiction and whether the acts of different bodies conflict.

In sum, the 'watertight compartments' of the ship of state serve no useful purpose: they only baffle communication and useful co-operation. It is time some other picture was substituted for this unfortunate and barren metaphor.

CLASS 21

Navigation and Shipping

This is another large division of the law merchant that has become a distinct subject-matter because of its ramifications. The subjects included, such as Marine Hospitals and Sable Island, indicate that it cannot be characterized as necessarily within the meaning of commercial law. Class 21 is a summary of Classes 9, 10, and 11 of Section 91 of the B.N.A. Act, 1867, but it explicitly extends its coverage to navigation and shipping 'through the Air'.

The present federal power over aeronautics depends on a much-criticized and hard-to-define doctrine that it is 'a class of subject which has attained such dimensions as to affect the body politic of the Dominion'.[27] The doctrine cannot rely on any enumerated class of Section 91 and so it is said to be an exercise of the power to make laws 'for the Peace, Order and good Government of Canada'. It is thus an example of the approach favoured by the O'Connor Report.

Obviously Aeronautics has the closest analogy in Navigation and Shipping: but in 1867, just as obviously, these terms did not apply to aircraft. The Supreme Court of Canada had no option but to cast aerial navigation into the general power, and the only basis for that was that it had become a subject of national interest and concern. But this is not a satisfactory canon because it imposes on the judges the duty of deciding what is essentially a political rather than a juridical question.

Two points remain: the wording is probably sufficient to apply to space travel; and there is probably no need to retain the subjects, such as Quarantine, that are set out as included in the general words of the class.

CLASS 22

Extraprovincial Fisheries and Migratory Birds

This class carries forward, with some changes, the only part of Section 91 of the B.N.A. Act, 1867, that deals with a natural resource. Despite the exclusive nature of the federal authority over all fisheries, this is a field that is thoroughly divided between the federal government and the provinces for administrative purposes, by arrangements between the governments.

> Specifically, all tidal or sea fisheries except those of the Province of Quebec are administered by the federal Department of Fisheries and the freshwater or non-tidal fisheries, with some exceptions, are administered by the provincial departments.[28]

Moreover the regulations promulgated by the federal department are made to suit local needs and situations. The job could be done at least as effectively with respect to intraprovincial fisheries by the provinces; there is no compelling reason for federal control in that aspect of the subject. Sea fisheries, however, do get involved in foreign relations and the case for federal paramountcy is clear as far as they are concerned.

Migratory birds are like fish in that they affect external relations. The Dominion exercises authority over them in much the same way as it first got it over Aeronautics, by means of a treaty. The Migratory Birds Treaty of 1916 was the source of the Migratory Birds Convention Act of 1917. For the same reasons that prevailed in the case of Aeronautics it seems better to be specific. It is merely a matter of paramountcy, however, not of the validity of the law.

CLASS 23

The Census and Statistics

The chief reason for this authority is to deal with the ten-year revision of membership in the House of Commons, but it has grown so that it is now a general and miscellaneous power that touches on the whole field of government in Canada, federal, provincial, and municipal, and in both public and private law. It might fit anywhere in Section 1 of Article 7 but it seems reasonably appropriate to wind up the purely and specifically federal powers with it. It is in the wording of Class 6 of Section 91 of the B.N.A. Act, 1867.

CLASS 24

Interprovincial Enforcement of Law

This is new. The actual recognition by one province of the laws and judgments of others depends on a juridical concept called *comity*; such recognition is subject to legislation of the several provinces. This is the field called *private international law* or *conflict of laws* and it is beginning to matter more and more. It is a field where uniformity is valuable because the status of an individual can be very different in different states owing to differences in law. It has its international aspects not only because of this but also because satisfactory solutions to various approaches based on nationality, domicile, race, or the like can depend on treaties. In the result there is a strong case for federal supremacy in the field.

Australia has a similar but not identical provision in Section 51, placitum (xxv), of its Constitution and also has, in Section 118, a copy of the 'Full faith and credit' clause contained in Section 1 of Article IV of the United States Constitution (which, however, gives the Congress a limited power of legislation). The clause has proved unsatisfactory, particularly in connection with divorce, because it attempts to state the substantive law in a concise form where the juridical background is extremely and necessarily complex. It is better to confer a power to override the local authority where it is expedient to do so than to attempt to sum up in a single sentence the core of a subtle, varied, and changing region of the law.

Moreover the Australian and United States formulae deal only with the states of the Commonwealth and the Union respectively and presumably leave international private law in its present tenuous position.

The power to deal with private international law is a genuine advance over the only similar class in Section 91, Class 26, Marriage and Divorce. Except for the unhealthy situation with respect to Quebec and Newfoundland divorces (where the parliament was so long acting as a divorce court[29]), federal action has been of the same type as it would be under a general power over private international law. It will clear the air and put things where they belong to restore ordinary jurisdiction over marriage and divorce to the provinces while instituting a federal control over conflicts in this and other fields.

Marriage and Divorce is the chief power in Section 91 that is omitted in this section. Constitutional amendment and taxation and fiscal powers are dealt with in other Articles. The main effect of Section 1 of Article 7 is to confirm federal supremacy where the parliament now has exclusive power, sometimes in more general terms and sometimes with a more restricted field. The language is intended to state more accurately the present and probable scope of the powers and to be explicit where the change in approach in the Articles makes it desirable to be explicit. But the great and hopeful change is in the replacement of exclusive authority with the principle of paramountcy and the consequent relaxation of all those juristic tensions and inhibitions that make the legal existence of Canadian governments so peculiarly cabin'd, cribb'd, confined, bound in.

CHAPTER 19

The Provincial Paramount Powers

The original division of powers between the federal and provincial governments was not expected to eliminate overlapping. Various approaches were suggested to avoid conflicts, and the test that has fitted the text most successfully is the one that assigns subjects of national importance to the federal government and subjects of only local importance to the provinces. This is more properly called the 'aspect' doctrine[1] and comes into play where each authority appears to have a legitimate power to act and it must be decided which shall prevail.

This is in explanation of the language of Section 2 of Article 7. It might have been drawn so as to give the provinces an absolute supremacy over classes in this section, akin to that enjoyed by the federal government under Section 1. To do so, however, would imply that the subject-matters in the two sections are completely distinct and that no question could arise involving a clash of absolutely paramount powers. Which is absurd. Even if it were understood that clashes would occur but that the courts would resolve them, they would have to do so between claimants of equal weight on some such principle as the 'aspect' doctrine.

So, it is fundamentally better to enact in this basic law that the central government will be absolutely dominant in relation to its specific powers and that, subject to that dominance, the provinces will be relatively paramount in relation to their specified powers. This is a political decision about the course the law

160

should take, and it should be decided in the Articles and not in the courts.

In other words, Section 1 of Article 7, to the extent that it may trench on subjects assigned to the provinces by Section 2, is an attempt to declare what aspects of the provincial subjects are of such national interest and importance that federal laws concerning them should be supreme. The Article also has the effect, however, of diminishing, if not getting rid of, any need to use the 'aspect' doctrine in the manner contemplated by the O'Connor Report.

CLASS 1

The Provincial Constitution

This corresponds to Class 1 of Section 92 of the B.N.A. Act, 1867, with the omission of the governing exception 'except as regards the Office of Lieutenant Governor'. The language of the clause parallels that of Class 1 of Section 1 to some extent, but there are certain necessary differences due to the fact that only Quebec has a two-chamber legislature. The wording of Section 92, especially the phrase 'notwithstanding anything in this Act', is not appropriate to the Articles, which impose limits on all governments in Canada. The proposed wording is more general than a power of amendment to which, however, it is probably equivalent as there seems no doubt that the provinces have very complete powers over their own constitutions subject to the B.N.A. Acts.[2]

CLASS 2

The Head of the Provincial Executive

It is astonishing what a determined and prolonged effort was made to diminish this office from the beginning. Party bias seems to have made no difference in the result although it certainly influenced the motives behind the attack. Sir John A. Macdonald, in his ardent desire for a legislative union rather than a federation, treated the governors as federal 'superintendents'[3] of what were little more than municipal governments. Provincial-rights advocates viewed them also as federal agents and accordingly tried to shut them out from any real influence or power. The Imperial government disparaged them as colonial appointees rather than officers of the Crown. Consequently the governors had a long struggle to obtain even such ceremonial recognition as a fifteen-gun salute or the right to wear a Windsor uniform.[4] Their salaries, as noted above, were not changed between 1872 and 1963.

The provinces cannot now legislate on the office and there is some opinion that the parliament cannot do so, although the power would appear to be within the terms of Class 29 of Section 91.[5] For the reasons suggested in Chapter 15 it is proposed that the provinces have legislative power over this office so that they can either make something of it or abolish it. It is not necessary to representative democracy.

CLASS 3

The Administration of Justice

The wording here is almost identical to that of Class 14 of Section 92 (the order of 'Organization' and 'Maintenance' being the only change – a matter of taste in the rationale of structure). The clause, besides enabling the provinces to have the chief say in the setting up of the ordinary courts, extends their paramountcy to the police, the prosecuting counsel, and to the Crown's prerogative in criminal matters (substantially, the right to take over control of a prosecution or even to stop it).[6] The division of function in this country respecting the courts, the criminal law, and the administration of justice has resulted in a balance of power very favourable to the liberty of the subject and devoid of the clashes between courts or governments that occur in some federal states. The administration of criminal justice, in particular, works quite well as far as the governments and their respective agents are concerned. There is, of course, scope for many improvements in detail. Our penology, for example, has been especially backward, but there are signs of radical change.

CLASSES 4 AND 5

Provincial Public Service and Property

These classes are parallel to Classes 4 and 5 of the first section of the Article and the notes on those clauses apply here. Class 4 is a more general expression of Class 4 of Section 92 of the B.N.A. Act, 1867, but Class 5 of this section differs from Class 5 of Section 92 which deals with lands and forests as natural resources rather than as involved in the public service. Class 5 of this section deals with the public-service aspect, Class 11 with natural resources.

CLASS 6

Provincial Penal Law

This class is designed to replace Classes 6 and 15 of Section 92 of the B.N.A. Act, 1867, with a more rational rule. The two classes in Section 92 are not in harness although they may have been intended to be. Under Class 6, the provinces may establish prisons and reformatories. Under the Quebec Resolutions (No. 43, cl. 9) the provinces were to be responsible for all penal institutions, no doubt as a specific part of the administration of justice, but in the London Resolutions, the penitentiaries were confined to the federal jurisdiction (No. 28, cl. 31). This was probably a device to relieve the provinces of some expenditure. In any case, that has been the substantial result. Provincial prisons have been used for federal offenders but penitentiaries are not used for provincial offenders. A prisoner cannot be sentenced to less than two years, all told, in a penitentiary.[7] There is no really sound reason for this. It is a manifestation of the 'watertight compartment' state of mind. Section 92, Class 6, is a substantive head of provincial power as part of the administration of justice, both federal and provincial. Class 15, on the other hand, which gives the provinces power to punish by 'Fine, Penalty or Imprisonment', is purely ancillary to the other classes of provincial power and does not itself found any substantive legislation: it merely provides the sanctions for other laws, if they are valid.

'Penalty' in Class 15 has been held to include a forfeiture[8] but it may be straining language to describe suspended sentence or parole as penalties. Class 15 of Section 92 speaks only of the 'Imposition of Punishment', and this wording is deficient because penal sanctions are imposed not only for punishment or retribution (a very necessary element) but also for such things as prevention, deterrence, restitution, reform, and public example. These may be generalized as punishment and reformation and, accordingly, Class 6 of Section 2 has been drawn in those terms.

There should, however, be some limit on provincial sanctions, as the serious crimes will be the business of the parliament still, but the proposal to withhold capital punishment is probably sufficient. There is, at present, no limit on the amount of fine or imprisonment that can be imposed by provincial law. It may be remarked that this class does not actually prohibit the provinces from imposing capital punishment, as it merely decides a question of paramountcy, but it is just as unlikely to be invoked by a legislature as a subordinate power as it is now as a possible 'Penalty'.

The first six classes of Section 2, like the first five of Section 1, form a group dealing with the government and public law of the provinces. There is a temptation to argue that here again, of their very essence, the matters in these classes would be held to be excluded from the classes of Section 1. But there are odd possibilities of overlapping. For example, there used to be a section in the Criminal Code inflicting a penalty for any offence against provincial law for which no penalty was otherwise provided.

CLASS 7

Public Works and Undertakings

All governments in Canada undertake public works, mostly in connection with their specific heads of jurisdiction. The great field of provincial enterprise unrelated to such heads is the public highway. This comes under Class 10 of Section 92, which contains exceptions of other means of transport in favour of parliament. The proposed Class 7, in conjunction with Class 15 of Section 1 of this Article, maintains the present division of the subjects in the class and there does not seem to be much more to say about it.

CLASS 8

Local Government

This is expressed in Class 8 of Section 92 as 'Municipal Institutions in the Province'. It is in the language of the mid nineteenth century. Class 8 of Section 2 of this Article says the same thing in the language of the twentieth century. It is debatable which is to be preferred. In any event, the phrase 'in the Province' is not needed.

CLASS 9

Education

This is a very important class which has two constitutional elements, also very important. The one is legislative authority, the other consists of educational rights. These are treated together in Section 93 of the B.N.A. Act, 1867, a section considered so fundamental that it was re-enacted, with variations, four times: on the entries of Manitoba, Alberta, Saskatchewan, and Newfoundland into the Confederation as provinces. The elements are distinct, however, and the scheme of the Articles requires that they be in separate parts. Accordingly, Class 9 deals only with legislative authority over education, and educational rights are treated in Article 11, on the limits of government. Section 93 gives exclusive authority over education to the provinces subject to certain remedial powers entrusted to the federal government and parliament to correct denials of constitutional rights by a province. Because of political pressures the federal powers have proved illusory, and so, when Newfoundland entered the union, she chose to rely on her own government to protect these rights, subject to the law and the courts. This is much more practical than the old approach: it is not wise to ask a political group to decide a disputed question of right and wrong with either alacrity or satisfaction when the electorate is divided on it to a serious extent. The judge, though he may be an ex-politician, is expected to answer such questions without regard to popular response and usually does so.

There may be some argument that this power, at least, should be exclusive. This must be resisted. The substitution of paramountcy for exclusiveness is so vital that no temporization should be considered. The principle of paramountcy is enough to deprive the subordinate legislature of the field completely *if the paramount legislature wishes to do so.* The federal government gives important help to universities and in technical education. If any province takes umbrage at this it can enact laws to prevent it in its own domain.

CLASS 10

Hospitals and Charities

The subjects in this class were not considered by the nineteenth-century promoters to be among 'the great subjects of legislation'.[9] This was fortunate because they are all subjects where the human touch is important. The management of any of the institutions referred to requires the interest and devotion of man to his fellow man, that unselfish love of another that is the proper meaning of charity. That is why it is reasonably said that charity begins at home: we cannot love what we do not know. Consequently it is usually easier to love our nearer neighbours than remote ones.

It is true that big institutions with government money to run them can often provide technically better services than small local or private ones. It is also true that health and welfare financing, either by way of insurance or assistance, is easier and more equitable if it is done on a national rather than a local scale: that is the justification for Classes 12 and 13 of Section 1. But the core of all charitable work is charity, a true fellow feeling with the sufferer, a desire to help him, an interest in his progress, a human concern for others. Reason and experience combine to show that these things cannot be provided merely by making a law and, while they are not absent from government institutions, a leaven of private, voluntary charities is essential to maintain a human level in this field. What the state provides becomes a matter of legal right, and love and devotion cannot be so coerced.

The existing complex of health and welfare institutions, based as it is mainly on local or private provenance and control with considerable assistance from the superior governments, would therefore appear to be soundly based. It is worth preserving, and that is the intent of this class, which corresponds to Class 7 of Section 92. The latter is much too limited in its expression, and the phrase 'in and for the Province' is absurd. It would inhibit Nova Scotia or Newfoundland, for example, from sending a hospital ship out to the fishing fleets on the Grand Banks.

CLASS 11

Natural Resources

In general, the ungranted lands in the provinces are owned by the provinces, although this was not originally the case with the Prairie provinces. Except for 'land covered with water' (as the lawyers call it), the atmosphere, and wild-bird life, the location of our natural resources is the land. Without any really clear mandate, the provinces, by virtue of their ownership of the public lands and minerals and with their legal claim over property and civil rights, have taken dominance over natural resources. The federal government, indeed, has departments of Agriculture, Forestry, Mines and Technical Surveys, Fisheries, and Northern Affairs and Natural Resources, and these departments provide important research and technical aid. There are also large federal money contributions in all fields.

Nevertheless the provinces have the chief interests here. Four of them have even established departments of fisheries by name and others intervene there in various disguises, although they are forbidden to intermeddle by the B.N.A. Act, Section 91, Class 12.

The federal government has a legal supremacy over agriculture under Section 95. It is hard to see any justification for this. No doubt there are national and even international aspects of this branch of the economy, such as wheat marketing and preventing the importation of pests, but the Articles give the central government ample authority to cope with these without any need for paramountcy over the whole field. The pursuits and problems of agriculture are generally regional and local, and are best administered at that stage. This, of course, means a change of legal emphasis only; the existing participation of the several governments would suffer no radical alteration.

As for the other natural resources, the subject of fisheries has already been noted under Class 22 of Section 1; there seems to be no reason to withdraw the others from provincial control and every reason why they should remain there.

CLASS 12

Private Law

Private law is that law 'applicable as between private persons'. O'Connor defines the distinction between public and private law as 'laws which in all countries prevail, as to public law between state and subject and, as to private law, between subject and subject'.[10] He points out that at the fall of Quebec and the capitulation of Montreal in 1759-60 the public law of England immediately applied in the conquered province but the private law then in force continued to exist until changed by the new régime. He ascribed to public law the laws relating to the constitution, allegiance, military and jury duty, crimes, and the creation and operation of the courts; also Magna Charta. On the other hand he equates private law in the main with 'property and civil rights'[11] or with 'civil rights'[12] alone, as understood by the eighteenth-century legislators. They included commercial matters in 'property and civil rights'.[13]

O'Connor's definition of private law is in general accord with other accepted ones. For example, in *Corpus Juris,* private law

> . . . means all that part of the law which is administered between citizen and citizen, or which is concerned with the definition, regulation, and enforcement of rights in cases where both the person in

whom the right inheres and the person upon whom the obligation is incident are private individuals.[14]

One might quibble with the use of 'citizen' instead of 'person' and with some other points, but this says fully what O'Connor says concisely. What is the content of the term?

The most satisfactory answer, for Canadian purposes, can be derived from the categories of the Quebec Civil Code for various reasons, of which two are important. Firstly, the Code was the only *complete* statement of the law of property and civil rights in the country before Confederation, although the statutory compilations in the other provinces dealt with most of the same matters. Secondly, the people of Quebec were determined to preserve their own system of property and civil rights and consequently the Code can be accepted as a rather emphatic definition.[15]

As a guide and a check, the Code can be compared with other codes (such as the provincial revised statutes) and with the topics dealt with in private international (international private) law. What emerges is, in substance, what is set forth in Class 12. Another statement might be the law of

1. *Persons* (including societies and corporations, and families)

2. *Property*

3. *Obligations*, whether contractual, delictual or otherwise.

But neither the term 'private law' nor the term 'property and civil rights' is so precise that it can control questions arising under it without more questions arising. Both are general terms and the limits are arguable. The fact that a leading exponent of the constitution such as O'Connor can mount a powerful and well-reasoned attack on the accepted scope of Section 92, Class 13, as enunciated by the Privy Council, should warn us to be somewhat more explicit than that clause is.

Accordingly Class 12 of Section 2 of this Article spells out, to some extent, the meaning of 'Private Law', and is careful to include as an undefined residuum the equivalent phrase 'Property, and Civil Rights'.

The effect of this is to make the province paramount in the whole of private law except those parts of it dealt with in the classes of Section 1 of the Article, and subject also to the federal power to affect civil rights in the exercise of its other powers under Section 1. This does not enlarge the legislative authority of the provinces (except on one point yet to be dealt with), but it does make it more certain *vis-à-vis* those who contend for a narrow meaning of 'Property, and Civil Rights'.

It was appreciated grudgingly in 1867 but is now fully established, that it is best for the happiness and development of Canadians and Canada that private law should be under provincial control. This has been already discussed rather fully. History justifies this stand.

Class 12 of Section 2 differs from Class 13 of Section 92 in one element, Marriage. This has been restored to private law, where it belongs with the rest of family law.[16] Marriage and divorce are bound up with the cultures, the ways and customs, the moral standards, of the peoples of the provinces of Canada, and the provinces differ markedly on these matters. Accordingly, if provincial autonomy means anything it means that control over marriage and divorce legislation is an appropriate provincial paramount power and is not a suitable field for federal law except to resolve interprovincial conflicts.

There is, of course, no need to include divorce expressly in Class 12 as it is a part of the general topic Marriage and the Domestic Relations.

Section 2 of Article 7 thus gives the provinces paramountcy in substantially the same classes of subjects where they now enjoy exclusive powers. The chief changes may be summed up:

(a) The head of the executive government becomes a purely provincial officer subject to its internal constitutional law.

(b) Agriculture becomes a paramount provincial power instead of a subordinate one and the provinces acquire legal as well as *de facto* power over fisheries within their own limits.

(c) Marriage (and divorce) are restored to the field of private law under provincial paramountcy.

Since Confederation no amendment of the legislative powers in Sections 91 to 95 of the B.N.A. Act has favoured the provinces or given them any new powers. On the contrary three federal powers have been added, two of them trenching on the provincial field of Property and Civil Rights and, in some form or another, those powers will remain as allocated. It is, therefore, neither premature nor rash to expect that the provincial authority in relation to natural resources and private law will be recognized and rounded out to its full and proper scope by the allocation of Agriculture, Fisheries, and Marriage to the provincial legislative fields where they belong.

The major topics dealt with in Sections 91 and 92 that are not included in some way in Article 7 are Taxation and the Public Debt. These form the subjects of the next Article.

CHAPTER 20

Fiscal Powers and Institutions

PART 1 : THE BACKGROUND

Fixed Dominion grants to the provinces, provided by Section 118 of the British North America Act, 1867, were intended to take the place of the taxes (mainly customs and excise) that the provinces were giving up, and to form the chief source of provincial revenue in addition to 'Shop, Saloon, Tavern, Auctioneer, and other Licences' and revenue from natural resources. Direct taxation was to be available to both Dominion and provinces but, in 1867, nobody expected that any government would dare do much with it, it was so unpopular.[1] The grants were set at $50,000 for New Brunswick, $60,000 for Nova Scotia, $70,000 for Quebec, and $80,000 for Ontario, but each province was entitled to 80¢ more a head. As this was the current price of a sheepskin, anti-Confederates were able to taunt the elector with the slogan that he had been sold into Confederation for the price of a sheepskin.

The print on the 1867 Act was not dry before the provinces started to agitate for better financial terms. The Canadian parliament, beginning in 1869, made changes in the scheme of grants without benefit of amending the B.N.A. Act, and this has continued ever since despite the protests of the constitutionalists. The agitation has never ceased nor is it ever likely to; so there is something comic in the expression 'final and unalterable settlement' with which Sir Wilfrid Laurier sent the 1907 Amendment[2] to London. The elusive concepts behind the various schemes adopted prior to 1940 were described by the Rowell-Sirois Commission Report:

> The subsidies have been based on no clear principles and it has been impossible to say whether or not different provinces have received equal treatment. Specious reasons have been advanced, and not infrequently accepted, in support of readjustments, in order to avoid the full implications of genuine reasons, and negotiations between the Dominion and the provinces have lacked the candour which is desirable in a democracy.[3]

In contrast, the Commission set down quite definite fiscal principles for Canada:[4]

1. The Dominion should be responsible for the maintenance of the employable unemployed and for disaster help to primary producers.

2. The Dominion should take over the dead-weight cost of servicing provincial debts, and future provincial borrowings should be under control.

3. The provinces should surrender to the Dominion the present subsidies, and income taxes, corporation taxes, and succession duties.

4. The Dominion should 'refrain from competing with the Provinces in respect of sources of revenue left to them and should leave the provinces free to collect these revenues in whatever way appears most efficient even if the method of indirect taxation should be involved'.[5]

5. 'Each individual province should receive from the Dominion annually "a sum sufficient" to enable it to provide normal Canadian services with no more than normal Canadian taxation.'[6]

6. The grants would be reviewable every five years but would be irreducible. Special provisions should be made for special emergencies.

7. All grants should be determined as scientifically and objectively as possible, and this should be done by a small permanent finance commission with an adequate technical staff.

8. The Dominion-Provincial Conference should have an adequate, permanent secretariat and should meet regularly, say every year.

The Report was a turning-point. People had begun to realize, in a subliminal way, the need for a more rational fiscal pattern in Canada, but this very important Royal Commission digested the then current ideas and produced a clear statement of the problems and their ramifications. Although not many of the specific proposals have been implemented since it was tabled in the House of Commons on May 16, 1940, the Report inspired much of the thinking leading to the ensuing changes in public finances.

During the summer of 1940, the federal government, with the agreement of the provinces, acquired jurisdiction over unemployment insurance, part of the first proposal.[7]

Next, Prime Minister Mackenzie King called a Dominion-Provincial Conference for January 1941 to discuss the Report. The Dominion was quite strongly in favour of it but the provinces split three ways. Manitoba, New Brunswick, and Saskatchewan were for it. Nova Scotia, Prince Edward Island, and Quebec were on the fence, although quite willing to discuss it. Alberta, British Columbia, and Ontario were strongly opposed. Mr. Hepburn would not talk about it because of the war. The three dissenting provinces prepared to leave; so Mr. King promptly wound up the proceedings, asking the delegates to sing the national anthem.

Mr. Hepburn founded his dissent on provincial autonomy and on the ability of Ontario to fend for itself if the Dominion did not invade its tax fields.[8] Mr. Aberhart of Alberta shared with Mr. Hepburn a fear of centralization and of the 'money powers'.[9] Alberta and Ontario thus did not find the third recommendation acceptable.

Mr. Patullo, premier of British Columbia, was against the principle of equalization grants. He pointed out:

> It may be accepted as axiomatic that there are five economic and social units comprising the confederation of the Dominion of Canada. . . .
> Each of these units is distinctive and there is nothing to be gained and much to be lost in attempting to bring them to a common level.

> Everyone desires to see Canada strong and united, but this object cannot be achieved by way of a mechanization to establish a general Canadian average.[10]

Such a point of view is tenable. It is held not on any bases of argument but as an article of faith, just as the concept that it denies, that all Canadians should have the right to normal public services at normal rates of taxation, is held in its turn as an article of a fairer faith. No doubt there are collateral arguments for and against, but the core of the doctrine is spiritual, a political inspiration.

Although the 1941 Dominion-Provincial Conference did not achieve anything, the war gave a very forceful boost to fiscal co-operation by abating the needs of the provinces somewhat and enormously increasing those of the Dominion. The period has been described authoritatively as 'one of unprecedented prosperity for the Provinces'[11] due to the decline of capital expenditures and relief costs. The Dominion, on the other hand, under the pressure of the demand for money, commenced to levy succession duties and gasoline tax (previously provincial tax sources only) in 1941. In that year, all the provinces agreed to get out of the income-tax and corporation-tax fields for the duration of the war in return for compensation from the Dominion.[12]

The compensation was computed by two alternative methods designed to make good the losses resulting from the 'rental' of the tax sources and from the curtailment of gasoline-tax revenue, but subsidies were also included although the principle of equalization payments (i.e., to provide 'normal' services with 'normal' taxation) was neither accepted nor applied as such.[13] The subsidies were based on proof of 'fiscal need': that is, the provinces getting them needed an amount over and above the tax-rental moneys to maintain services. But Finance Minister Ilsley made a strong suggestion of things to come, in his statement to the 1941 Dominion-Provincial Conference[14] in favour of adopting Plan 1 of the Rowell-Sirois Report:

> The third reason is the desirability of establishing and maintaining under present conditions minimum national standards – minimum standards of decency and justice in all parts of Canada.

> This is a war aim in itself, I submit. People ask us what kind of country is it that we are fighting for? . . .

At the Dominion-Provincial Conference on Reconstruction of 1945-1946, called to discuss, among other things, a renewal of the 1942 agreements that would lapse in 1947, Mr. Ilsley was more explicit:

> The third requirement of post-war financial arrangements is that they should make possible at least an adequate minimum standard of services in all provinces while not denying to any province the advantages which its resources give to it nor the freedom to establish its own standards.[15]

The Dominion proposal was that the provinces should forgo income and corporation taxes and succession duties in return for increased federal grants 'which would ensure stable revenues and provide for their growth in proportion to increases in population and per capita national production'.[16]

The 1945-1946 conference lasted longer than the 1941 one, but eventually foundered on the same shoals as its predecessor – a conflict between the federal proposals and the claim of Ontario and Quebec to prior constitutional rights to the direct-tax field. The federal government proceeded to divide and conquer, and came to separate agreements with all provinces other than Quebec and Ontario. The agreements enlarged on the wartime ones to take in succession duties but were on much the same lines. The Atlantic provinces got additional grants in aid.

The tax-rental system continued with variations until March 31, 1962, through a series of five-year agreements. Two years before each was to terminate there was a Federal-Provincial Conference to discuss generally the terms of the subsequent agreements, which were then negotiated individually with each province. Quebec remained out of the 1952 agreements but Ontario took part, reserving succession duties, however. The 1955 conference inaugurated a change in the tax-rental formula that made explicit the distinction between equalization payments and the advantages of having the federal government as the one central tax-collector.

In 1955, even before the conference, the federal government recognized by legislation that some provinces preferred to impose their own direct taxes rather than receive them as subsidies, and federal taxes were reduced in those provinces by standard rates: ten per cent of the income tax; nine per cent of corporate taxable income; and fifty per cent of federal succession duties. This was the '10-9-50 formula'.

Equalization became distinct from tax rental under these proposals. It was payable to the eligible provinces whether they rented their tax fields or not, whereas the tax-rental payments followed only after agreements. In the result, equalization became a primary federal responsibility while the imposing and collecting of provincial direct taxes became an optional one. All the provinces except Quebec took up the 1957 tax agreements, but Ontario kept the corporate-income-tax and succession-duty sources.

On June 21, 1957, the twenty-two-year Liberal régime at Ottawa came to an end and the new prime minister, Mr. Diefenbaker, called a conference for November of that year, 'to listen and to learn'.

Premier Frost promptly asked that the federal tax abatements be raised to more realistic rates in view of the shift of peacetime burdens to the provinces. He wanted fifteen per cent of the federal income tax instead of ten per cent, fifteen per cent of corporate taxable income instead of nine, and succession duties to remain at fifty per cent of the federal; this was the '15-15-50 formula' instead of the '10-9-50 formula'. It was supported by other provinces. In the result, the income-tax allowance was raised to thirteen per cent of the federal tax.

Mr. Diefenbaker called a conference to renew the agreements in July 1960, the customary two years before the 1957 agreements were due to lapse. Some provinces, he said, had indicated a desire to resume the collection of their own taxes but, whatever the ultimate decision on that should be, 'the principle of equalization must be preserved'.[17]

Premier Frost began: 'The soundest principle is for Governments to levy taxation for the money that they spend', but while saying that, he recognized the justice of fiscal-need payments. He then went on to urge four points: (1) that the provinces were entitled to one-half the yield of the direct-tax fields; (2) that only one government should collect each form of tax and remit the other government its share; (3) in the alternative a constitutional amendment should permit the provinces to levy an indirect retail-sales tax; and (4) fiscal-need payments to maintain adequate standards of public service should be provided to the provinces that needed them. He also proposed that funds should be provided to stimulate economic development through exploration and research.[18]

The new premier of Quebec, Mr. Lesage, made a profound impression on the conference and the public by the scope of his proposals – for a permanent federal-provincial secretariat akin to the Rowell-Sirois recommendation, for an interprovincial conference, for a constitutional bill of rights, and for repatriation of the constitution.[19] He also proposed a variation of the Ontario 15-15-50 formula: that is, the federal abatement should be twenty-five per cent of income tax, twenty-five per cent of corporate income tax, and one hundred per cent of succession duties (i.e., the federal government should quit the last field). This was a 25-25-100 formula. Premier Lesage also favoured federal equalization payments – a marked departure from Mr. Duplessis's view.[20]

The Federal-Provincial Conference met again in October and was followed by an interprovincial conference at Quebec in December, at Premier Lesage's invitation. It turned out that the provinces preferred to deal with the federal government individually rather than by collective bargaining. Party differences were more prominent at the Quebec affair than at Ottawa, but the premiers have continued to meet yearly.

Meanwhile the Federal-Provincial Conference reconvened in February 1961, amid forebodings of unwelcome change. Mr. Diefenbaker had hinted pretty strongly in October of 1960 that the provinces would have to impose their own taxes, and many provinces did not like this. Premier Stanfield expressed disapproval of the freezing of equalization grants that appeared to be proposed, and was not satisfied with the stabilization formula.

So, when the conference met February 23 in private,[21] there was an air of more than usual tension which the event justified. Mr. Diefenbaker proposed:[22]

(a) To discontinue the tax-rental system March 31, 1962, leaving the provinces free to impose their own taxes in the jointly occupied fields.

(b) To have the federal agencies collect the provincial taxes free of charge if they were assessable by the same method as the federal tax, and if the province agreed.

(c) To pay half the yield of the federal estate tax from a province to that province if it did not impose succession duties, and to abate fifty per cent of the estate tax with respect to provinces levying succession duties.

(d) To reduce federal income taxes over five years by sixteen, seventeen, eighteen, nineteen, and twenty per cent in the successive years.

(e) To reduce federal corporation income tax by nine per cent of taxable income.

The foregoing was in lieu of tax-rental payments. The legal effect was to make the provinces responsible for imposing taxes to which, as a result, they would be absolutely entitled as of right. The chief practical effect would be to allow them to get a larger share of the income tax raised without raising over-all rates.

The changes in the equalization payments went two ways. Instead of the average of the top two provinces, the national average per-capita yield of the three major direct taxes at the standard rates in (c), (d), and (e) above would be the measure, a lower measure. But, in addition, one-half of the three-year moving average of gross natural-resources revenue would be included; this was new. The Atlantic Provinces Adjustment Grants would be raised by forty per cent to $35,000,000 a year to be divided by the four provinces by agreement. Moreover, as the result of a royal commission, special provisions were made for Newfoundland.

Stabilizing provisions guaranteed that no province entitled to equalization grants would be worse off than for the 1961/62 fiscal year, and every province was guaranteed ninety-five percent of parity as determined by a moving two-year average.

Comments on these proposals ranged from 'nice', by Premier Smallwood, to 'smokescreen' and 'window dressing' from Quebec and Saskatchewan. Half of the provinces expressed active dissatisfaction and only three, Nova Scotia, Prince Edward Island, and Newfoundland, any pleasure. Public opinion was largely adverse. The provincial criticism was largely due to the lowering of the standard of equalization to the national average; the public, on the other hand, viewed with distaste a double-taxation system. Mr. Diefenbaker and Mr. Fleming were unmoved. The prime minister said, 'The proposal is as presented', and it was, in fact, modified on one or two minor points only. Mr. Fleming told the press that the proposal was 'so good and so sound' that it would commend itself to a majority of the provinces.[23]

And why not? Without attempting to justify Mr. Diefenbaker, it must be admitted that he had achieved a synthesis of the two rather contrary principles of fiscal responsibility and equalization over which the several federal-provincial conferences since the Rowell-Sirois Report had contended. What more could one ask?

What more indeed? Mr. Pearson's government found out in the summer and fall of 1963. The Federal-Provincial Conference of November 1963 was very conscious of the tensions arising from Quebec separatism, but almost all the provinces demanded more autonomy. This demand focused particularly on the joint programs: in these, the federal government provides part of the money for a public service on condition that the province should pay the rest and keep to the federal plan for the service. It was generally agreed that 'mature' joint programs should be handed over to the provinces and that the related grants should become more general in purpose or be transformed into federal tax abatements.

But provincial ambitions went much further. Premier Lesage, after pointing out that economic expansion is the problem now demanding priority and that it is, constitutionally, a provincial responsibility, proposed that the federal government should consult and co-operate with the provinces in economic policy, both fiscal and monetary, and should not confront them with unilateral action. He did not, however, go beyond his 25-25-100 formula of 1960 (except in relation to the joint programs). Nor did he deny what most admitted, that the federal government had the ultimate responsibility for financial stability in Canada.

Premier Bennett of British Columbia mounted an attack on equalization reminiscent of Premier Patullo's. In fact, his presentation was far more forceful in tone than Quebec's and quite as strong for provincial independence. Despite this, the federal government returned to the higher standard of equalization of 1956 but agreed to increase the estate-tax abatement from fifty per cent to seventy-five per cent.

The federal government was very co-operative. Still, the chief defect in the present approach is a want of mutuality. All of the agreements to date have been dictated, in essentials and with more or less particularity, by the federal administrations. These have shown conspicuous good will and a desire to do equity over the past two decades, but the federal principle should not need federal good will to be operative. It is time we had constitutional machinery capable of allocating taxes and determining grants.

CHAPTER 21

Fiscal Powers and Institutions

PART 2: THE PROPOSALS

The time is indeed ripe for a rational restatement of our fiscal principles. All of the developments of the years since 1940 have pointed towards three objectives:

1. Every government in Canada should be primarily responsible for imposing the taxes that it spends.
2. There should be a constitutional method or means of allocating the tax fields.
3. The Confederation should provide the supplementary funds required so that every province will be able to provide normal Canadian services.

1. Fiscal Responsibility

The first objective goes by the name 'fiscal responsibility' and has had such diverse supporters as Premier Drew of Ontario and Premier Macdonald of Nova Scotia. The premiers of Alberta contended for it when the province had refused to pay its bond interest and again when they were floating in oil royalties. Premier Duplessis used a rather amusing touch to emphasize his attachment to the concept; at the 1945-46 conference, where Prime Minister Mackenzie King was chairman, the Quebec premier quoted his own words to him, as the successor of Laurier:

> When on a previous occasion we were discussing this matter of grants from one treasury to another, I said I thought it was an unsound principle; in fact, I think I used the expression that it was a vicious principle to have one body raise the taxes and another body spend the people's money thus raised.[1]

On the same occasion Premier Drew quoted Sir Wilfrid Laurier himself:

> It is a completely false principle that one government should impose the taxes and another government spend them. This will always lead to extravagance.[2]

Since the principle of fiscal responsibility has such bipartisan backing and was accepted, rather grudgingly, as the point of departure of the 1960 agreements, one can admit it to a fundamental and proper place in the Canadian scheme of taxation if it can be reconciled with the other principles. There is no conflict, of course, with the idea of allocation of taxes, but there appears to be some with the idea of equalization grants. Nevertheless this has been anticipated, and the solution was well expressed by Mr. Garson as premier of Manitoba at the 1945-46 conference:

> This raises the question of whether the provinces would retain their financial responsibility if they get a large percentage of their revenue requirements from the Dominion treasury rather than from provincial taxation. If the moneys provided by the Dominion government were in excess of provincial needs, they would not. If, on the contrary, the normal provision by the Dominion government were measurably less than provincial needs, financial responsibility would be retained. Financial responsibility is marginal in character in the sense that it arises in connection with that margin of the provincial budget which is not taken care of by existing estimated revenues.[3]

Obviously, the larger the margin possible, the larger would be the province's responsibility and liberty. Mr. Garson went on to show that a government would have to weigh its own tax sources carefully when considering any extension of spending beyond its existing revenues. But to be able to do that, as he emphasized, the province must have a field of taxation *under its control,* to which it can resort to finance any unusual expenditure.[4] And this brings us to the second objective.

2. Allocation of Tax Fields

The conferences have voiced unceasingly the need to redivide the sources of taxation between the central and provincial governments. However well suited the 1867 division was for that day, it did not contemplate either the growth of public services or the radical switch to a preponderance of direct taxes. In 1867, personal and corporate income taxes and succession duties were not levied in this country. The chief general taxes were customs and excise and the main local ones were royalties, licences, tolls, legal fees and fines, and such petty grafts.[5]

In 1866, the total current-account revenue of the three confederating provinces was $13,776,000. In 1874, federal revenue was $21,601,000 and provincial revenue $6,665,000, of which subsidies made up $3,842,000.[6] In 1958, federal revenue was $5,065,524,000 and provincial revenue was $2,178,869,000, including $60,197,000 in subsidies and $399,100,000 tax-rental moneys. In 1958 also, municipal revenue was $1,379,453,000 of which $62,885,000 consisted of subsidies. In view of the masking effect of the tax-rental system the figure for subsidies to the provinces is meaningless. At least fifty-two per cent of the tax sources are of the direct-tax type.[7]

The drastic changes since 1867 leave not the least doubt that it is grossly imprudent to try to divide the sources of taxation among the several governments by kind, type, or species or even by so general a formula as the distinction between direct and indirect taxes. Our history shows that such a pattern is difficult to devise for five years, let alone fifty. Certain principles can be established:

(a) Interprovincial free trade must be maintained. There are arguments against it, no doubt, but the sentiment and the entire complex of the national economy both favour it.

(b) But the distinction between direct and indirect taxes has now no useful function to perform in the constitution and should be abolished. Free trade can be otherwise provided for.[8]

(c) All tax fields, consequently, other than customs, should be open to the provinces. The *incidence* of taxation should be determined by the ability of the province to collect the tax by its own means. This is a traditional concept (now sadly undermined): that the courts of one country will not enforce the tax laws of another. The rule need not prevent federal collection of provincial taxes on an agency basis. The rule only affects the lawfulness of the tax, not the method of collection.

(d) Tax allocation should be, not by formula, but by agreement between the governments concerned. What is needed is not so much a law as an *institution*. Every attempt to fix a formula has proven ephemeral. An allocation law is too rigid; the institution of the federal-provincial conference has worked well for twenty years. But it has two weaknesses: it lacks status, and the federal government dominates the results unduly. These can be corrected by writing it into the fundamental law[9] and by imposing equality between the parties. Equality follows largely from equal access to the tax sources, but it might be wise to impose a system of collective bargaining so that the provinces would speak with one voice. The federal government has too much bargaining weight for each individually.

(e) No tax allocation should be permanent, as then our last state will be worse than our present. A limit, say ten years, should be placed on any allocation agreement.

The draft Article, as will appear, is designed to embody most of these principles. It also contains an equalization provision and that should now be considered.

3. Equalization

Equalization of provincial revenues so that every province can provide normal Canadian services with no more than normal Canadian taxation has been recognized, as previously noted, as a political end in itself and a main motif of the reconstruction period. Every national political party professes it as an ideal. It was recognized as a necessary ideal by the Rowell-Sirois Commission, and any opposition has been sporadic and incoherent. It is not an inevitable ideal, as not all federal states adhere to it, but large inequalities in the conditions of the member states seems incompatible with the concept of a federal union: one reason for creating and maintaining a federation is to avoid such large disparities.

It cannot be argued that the promoters of the Confederation accepted this wholeheartedly, although they held some imprecise ideas in favour of equalization, complicated by the Upper Canadian demand for representation by population (one of the conflicts with Lower Canada that led to the larger union). Thus, the Rowell-Sirois Report:

> The total amount of the agreed subsidies was sufficient to bridge the estimated gaps but the current conception of equity which required calculation of subsidies on a per capita basis glossed over real differences in need arising from disparate circumstances, unconnected with differences in population. The result of the settlement was that Ontario and Quebec got subsidies greater than their needs at the time. For several years, Ontario had considered surpluses while the position of Nova Scotia became intolerable as early as 1868.[10]

Some such result was foreseen before the union: it was apparent that while the Province of Canada would retain about 11.7 per cent of its former revenue, Nova Scotia and New Brunswick would keep only 7.2 per cent and 7.1 per cent of theirs, because the latter provinces relied so heavily on customs duties.[11] Pre-Confederation per capita revenues were approximately equal in the Province of Canada ($4.17), Nova Scotia ($4.04), and New Brunswick ($4.63),[12] but quite unequal after 1867.

This means that the Maritime provinces yielded more in proportion to the union than did the Canadas, providing the basis of a long-waged contention that equalization grants are called for not only by the propriety of giving all Canadians similar public services but also by simple justice to the provinces that need them. It is doubtful, however, that this argument would be valid in every case. A more cogent reason for treating equalization grants as debts of justice arises from the results of the National Policy. This maintained a protective tariff of considerable force to build up Canadian manufactures. As a consequence the heavily populated market areas in the country prospered but the areas such as the Maritimes, the Prairies, and British Columbia, where the economy required favourable export conditions, did not.[13]

A collateral ground is that urged by Norman McL. Rogers:

> . . . a federation defeats its primary purpose if through its constitutional arrangements or through policies instituted by the national government it accomplishes the gradual debilitation of one or more of the provincial communities of which it is composed.[14]

This combines the two bases of the claim for equalization in phrases hardly to be improved upon.

British Columbia has opposed equalization fairly consistently, although admitting the need for occasional fiscal aid to a hard-up province. Ontario also opposed it in Mr. Drew's time. He suggested a national adjustment fund, a ten-per-cent levy on the direct-tax revenues of each province, which would be used to relieve needy provinces.[15] Mr. Duplessis later favoured a similar but less concrete scheme.[16] Mr. Manning of Alberta was at first against fiscal-need grants as they were 'in effect, applying a means test' to the provinces,[17] but he later recognized them as legitimate.[18]

On the other hand, Maritime premiers have continually stressed the need and the justice of such grants, although Premier A. L. Macdonald of Nova Scotia regretted that they were necessary as he strongly favoured fiscal autonomy. He and his successors, Mr. Hicks and Mr. Stanfield, have continued to point out that per-capita grants based on the main direct taxes only cannot and do not result in equalization.[19] This is because provincial revenues are largely composed of other kinds of taxes and payments, and in the needy provinces these are just as unproductive as the standard taxes, if not more so.

In fact, provincial administrations, despite changes in the party in power, tend to take consistent stands not only on equalization but on most of the other questions that persist through the years.

The changes that occur, such as that from Mr. Drew's attitude to Mr. Frost's or Mr. Duplessis's to Mr. Lesage's, usually result from a more willing recognition of the rights and necessities of other provinces.

4. The Article

An advantage of the rather long approach to the proposed Article is that the need to justify the text is largely eliminated. Some comments are called for.

SECTION 1

Section 1 combines part of Class 1A with Class 3 of Section 91 of the B.N.A. Act, 1867. The change of language is required by the nature of the context, which in the 1867 Act is a list of titles, but in the Article is sentences expressing powers. The insertion of the word 'Kind' may not add much except to the mind of the pedant, but here it has the advantage of showing that 'by any Mode or System' applies only to taxation. The phrase 'raising of Money' in Class 3 has been deleted, as it might be used to imply that taxation for other economic purposes is not lawful. No doubt this argument has not succeeded yet, but who can fix the bounds of legal ingenuity or judicial gullibility?

SECTION 2

Section 2 represents Classes 2, 3, and 9 of Section 92, and Sections 121 to 124 of the 1867 Act, and uses the same terms in the general part as Section 1. This shows that the powers of the governments are intended to be equally general and at the same time emphasizes the denial of customs duties to the provinces. The ability of the provinces to collect taxation will be circumscribed by the traditional rule, above mentioned, against one state enforcing another state's tax laws, even if the federal parliament exercises its powers under Class 24 of Article 7, Section 1. Indeed, the attitude of the courts to tax statutes, and a doctrine that denies extraterritorial effect to provincial laws, will probably be even more formidable obstacles to enforcement outside the province.

To include a specific clause about this would only provide a rich field for barren legal argument.[20]

Interprovincial free trade could be, as it has been, expressed in many ways. That chosen is probably the most concrete, as it deals specifically with import, export, and trans-provincial taxes. There seems to be no special value in incorporating the exception for inspection fees in the second clause of Article 1, Section 10, of the United States Constitution, but it would be more manageable than Section 92 of the Australian Constitution which requires that interstate commerce 'shall be absolutely free'. Of this, H. S. Nicholas writes:

> No section in the Constitution has given rise to so much litigation or to so many and such persistent differences of judicial opinion. No other section is so obviously in need of alteration.[21]

Every statement of the law, of course, can be litigated, but a more modest statement should lead to more modest litigation.

SECTION 3

This section is the same as Section 125 of the B.N.A. Act, 1867. It has a reasonably well understood meaning that is adequate. An analogous doctrine, known by the uncouth term 'immunity of instrumentalities' was invented in the United States, following the famous case of *McCulloch* v. *Maryland*,[22] to suggest that officers and agencies of the central government could not be taxed by the states and vice versa. The dictum of Chief Justice Marshall, 'The power to tax involves the power to destroy', is often quoted. After some vicissitudes, the scope of this doctrine has been narrowed to cases where the contested tax affects a truly governmental operation and does not apply to cases of non-discriminatory taxation of incomes from governmental sources.[23] It is desirable to say something clearly on the subject so as to fend off the wilder vagaries of the 'immunity of instrumentalities' doctrine.

SECTION 4

This section is designed to take the place of Section 118 of the B.N.A. Act, 1867, and its successor enactments. It is not a mathematical formula but a statement of the legal groundwork of a solution to the problem of equalization; therefore it requires an instrument to make it work. It is not just a matter of filling in gaps with current population figures or other figures and then multiplying. The section implies that the average standard of services can be determined, and this is work for the economist and statistician – as is the answer to the question 'Is this province using its power to tax and borrow prudently and efficiently?' The rule enunciated in this section could not be operated by a political body; the problems are not political ones, and the mixture of justice and expediency that is the usual outcome of political decisions has failed to settle this question and has no prospect of doing so. The rule requires an independent commission of technical experts in law and economics.[24]

The word 'average' is not exact in meaning, and other words such as 'normal' or 'standard' have been used in the discussions. If the average were taken as the arithmetic average representing the whole population it would be considerably higher than an average taken by provinces as units (i.e., an average of provincial averages). This is so because the more populous provinces are also the more prosperous.

The exclusion of grants in aid from the revenues used to determine the standard is necessary if the rule is to be simple and if the cumulative effect of grants on grants is to be avoided. But such a solution means that the tax-rental scheme does not suit as well as the idea of provinces imposing their own taxes. Tax-rental moneys are payable under a formula that is not immediately connected to the results of provincial taxation and confuses the assessment of those results. And there is some question whether the rental moneys would count as products of the efficient use of the province's powers to tax and borrow. No doubt the tax-rental concept could be adapted but at the sacrifice of some simplicity.

It is perhaps a delusion to hope that the idea of Section 4 can be expressed in simple terms. The expression must be exact enough to be administered by a quasi-judicial body and yet must take into account a great number of elements entering into the provision of 'normal services with normal taxation'.

The main concern is not to deprive the richer provinces of all the advantages that they enjoy but to make sure that the remainder do not lag too far behind and that the public services provided by the weaker members are compatible with membership in the same nation. It is apparent that the content of the section will have to be well worked over before it can guarantee these consequences.

SECTION 5

In contrast to Section 4, Section 5 proposes a political device for the allocation of the tax powers. Time has proved that a statutory allocation quickly gets out of joint with the needs of the day. Agreement between the governments concerned is the only way that has worked.

The purpose of the Section 5 is to ensure that the governments will meet to bargain and that, when they do, the parties will have a bargaining equality. For this purpose, the provinces have collective bargaining thrust on them. It may be necessary to provide for a qualified majority, such as is used in the amendment proposal in Article 12, Section 1.

There is a weakness in the scheme proposed in this section. The Rowell-Sirois Report and other studies were very strongly of the opinion that federal control over the total incidence of direct taxation was very essential to national economic survival and progress. This control would not exist – it would be impossible, for example, to use the 'cycle' theory of budgeting – if the provinces rushed to take over percentage points of taxation vacated by the central government.

It may be desirable to give the federal government paramount power over the total rates and incidence of the direct taxes. On the other hand, it does not appear to be necessary to do so. The fiscal power of the central government is so great that it outweighs even the collective power of all the provinces. Its primacy, the lack of limits on its authority to tax, the disparate interests of the provinces and their restricted jurisdiction, would seem to mean that the central government can veto any bargain it does not want, while the provinces, if they want an agreement, must accommodate it.

The Senate might perform the function for which the Federal Council is designed, but it is unlikely that the idea would be acceptable to the governments concerned. A well-balanced, efficient institution, especially made for the task, is what is required.

It remains only to review the five sections of this Article in the light of our three criteria. It is not essential to state the powers to tax and borrow of any of the governments explicitly, but it is necessary to do so in view of the historical limitations placed on our provinces. It is essential to provide some means of allocating tax sources between the central and member states of a federation; the bargaining table has worked well for us and it is therefore desirable to give it legal sanction. It is not essential that there should be any provision for bringing the services of the states to any standard, but it is necessary for the kind of federation that we have and want and it is desirable that this form part of the fundamental law. It is prudent, and therefore desirable, but it is not essential or necessary to provide that the property of a government should not be taxable by the others.

CHAPTER 22

Intergovernment Relations

The capacity of the provinces to make agreements with each other and with the federal government seems certain, and they have constantly exercised the power to do so. This is in contrast to the United States where interstate agreements and compacts without the consent of the Congress are forbidden by the Constitution. This prohibition was found impractical and it has been reduced to an innocuous condition by judicial interpretation.[1]

Our 1867 constitution was equally silent about agreements between the governments and the means of resolving conflicts arising out of them. The common-law principles applicable do not give the clearest answers in the world. The Crown may sue in any court but may be sued only in the court of its choice if any. When the Crown achieves the split personality required by a federal constitution this can lead to the dilemma of the irresistible force meeting an immovable object.

In an effort to deal with the problem, the parliament of Canada gave the exchequer court jurisdiction over controversies between the Dominion and a province or provinces, or between provinces that adhere to the jurisdiction. Six provinces have enabling statutes; four, as far as can be determined, have not.[2] Quebec has a characteristic comment in Section 3 of its Courts of Justice Act, R.S.Q. 1941, ch. 15:

> The Exchequer Court of Canada is a Federal Court, over which the Legislature has no control. . . .

193

The four provinces that have declined the invitation to accept the jurisdiction of the exchequer court can thus be sued, if at all, only in their own courts; this is so also with the federal government. A tripartite agreement, for example, between the federal government, Ontario, and Quebec would provide some tricky hurdles to leap before getting a question involving all three parties before a court of competent jurisdiction, if Quebec were a defendant.

The only case commonly cited on the federal legislation does not comment on the problems of jurisdiction but lays it down that the judge must decide the controversy on principles of law and not on his own ideas of justice. It is *Dominion of Canada* v. *Province of Ontario* [1910] A.C. 637, affirming (1909) 42 S.C.R. 1. The case does not say what law the judge shall apply and dismisses the problem rather airily, thus:

> It may be that, in questions between a dominion comprising various provinces of which the laws are not in all respects identical on the one hand, and a particular province with laws of its own on the other hand, difficulty will arise as to the legal principle which is to be applied. Such conflicts may always arise in the case of States or provinces within a union. But the conflict is between one set of legal principles and another. In the present case it does not appear to their Lordships that the claim of the Dominion can be sustained on any principle of law that can be invoked as applicable.[3]

There is no need to become concerned with the problem. It is not serious. The courts have evolved techniques for selecting the proper law for deciding cases arising out of agreements between individuals of different states and can do so in the case of agreements between states or governments. Because agreements between governments in Canada are subject to the fundamental sovereign power in the Confederation and responsive to judicial decision, the principles of private international law would seem to be more relevant than those applied to treaties.[4] There are, and would be, problems of enforcement, but the courts and scholars are more likely to arrive at satisfactory solutions of these problems than are parliaments or constitutional conventions. Courts and scholars can give the problems the attention, the informed criticism, and the time required, to work out methods and limits of enforcement. Even to the extent that the solutions express policy rather than ways and means, judicial and professorial discussion should produce more satisfactory results in this area of delicate relations than any other approach.

There are dangers, however, in leaving the matter of enforcement completely in the air. There is a possibility that the courts, without the guidance of an enactment of some kind, would allow judgments in cases between governments to be declaratory only. There are strong reasons favouring such a policy: it ensures the complete independence of the principal branches of the government. The heads of the executive government should not be subject to judicial coercion if the division of the government into legislative, executive, and judicial branches is to be preserved. But the need for the supremacy of law is even stronger than the need for independence, so that there are overriding reasons for making the judgments enforceable, at least against inferior officials. The sanction used would be punishment for contempt of the order or prohibition of the court, as officials are not personally liable on governmental obligations. Consequently, the executive head could defy the courts by any act that he could do by himself alone, but not by anything that required the help of others.

Should governmental money or property be exigible? This is extremely debatable. It would not be a happy situation if the sheriff could put a post office on the auction block to satisfy an award of damages against the federal government in favour of a province. The same objection would apply to the seizure in execution of any property employed in the public service. That is, with the exception of money or bank credit: these could be attached without interrupting government action. Execution is an extreme remedy against a government and should prove unnecessary in almost all cases. Still, there is always a chance that some administration will not bow to a judicial declaration of indebtedness. It may be better to leave the problem unresolved, a sanction to be evoked by the courts in threat rather than in practice.

SECTION 1: JURISDICTION IN CONTROVERSIES

This provision has no equivalent in the B.N.A. Act. It goes beyond the rather limited scope of Section 30 of the Exchequer Court Act and the related provincial statutes to make sure that some court has effective jurisdiction over every government. The section allows for additional jurisdiction in the terms of the present law but does not directly lay down a way out of the three-party problem. A suit against Nova Scotia and Quebec by the federal government would have to be fought in the courts of both provinces. On the other hand it is doubtful that it could be started in either at present.

SECTION 2: POWERS OF ENFORCEMENT

This attempts to outline what the courts should be permitted to do to enforce judgments in controversies between governments. The expression 'award Damages' is inconclusive and is left that way in line with the previous discussion. The special mention of the provincial executive heads is necessary because their privileges are within the dominant powers of the provinces and are not explicit in the Articles.

SECTION 3: ALTERATION OF PROVINCIAL LIMITS

This says concisely what Section 3 of The British North America Act, 1871, says verbosely, and adds a power for provinces to change a border that they share, by agreement. Parliament has exercised the power on several occasions but future changes could be made more conveniently by agreement between the provinces concerned. There does not seem to be any overriding federal concern in adjustments of boundaries between provinces and hence no great reason for federal supervision of the subject such as is now the case.

The subject-matter of Article 9, relations between the governments, consists chiefly of agreements. There does not seem to be any need to deal directly with the power to contract, to prescribe any bounds to it, or even to concede it expressly. The only apparent needs are those that have been dealt with, but the scattered nature of the result suggests that a more coherent and comprehensive Article is possible.

CHAPTER 23

Impeachment

Impeachment, which has a long history in Great Britain, has become obsolete there. The last successful impeachment was that of Lord Melville in 1806, although one was attempted in 1848. No doubt the power to impeach remains in the parliament and could be revived if the occasion presented itself, but the process does not suit the taste of the times.

On the other hand, impeachment is an integral element of the United States Constitution and people are quite conscious of its existence, especially since the John Birch Society proposed the impeachment of Chief Justice Warren.

The processes in each country are similar but the sanction in the United States is limited to deprivation of office, disqualification to hold office, and liability to the ordinary processes of the criminal law.[1] Only executive and judicial officers may be impeached. In the United Kingdom, on the other hand, the House of Commons may impeach anyone for any crime, and the judgment is of the same nature as that for any other criminal conviction.[2]

The process of impeachment is necessary in the United States and not only unnecessary but undesirable in Great Britain. The British constitution does not provide that strict separation of legislative, executive, and judicial powers that prevails in the United States. Neither does the United Kingdom have an entrenched body of constitutional rights. Consequently it is eminently desirable that the rights of the subject be dealt with by the ordinary courts, especially in criminal cases, and that extraordinary courts, particularly those of an openly partisan composition, be discountenanced.

The dangers hinted at are, of course, present in the United States, but the independence of the executive and judicial magistrates demands that their 'good behaviour' be triable only by an extraordinary tribunal. Canada, because of its federal form of government, inevitably shares the needs of the United States in this respect despite the fact that individual Canadian governments imitate the British pattern. It seems an essential element of the federal state.

It might be sufficient to mention impeachment, where necessary, in the other Articles without trying to lay down the ground rules for it. There is a considerable body of law on it that could be applied with reasonable facility. But the rules that would apply in that case would be the English ones, which allow any person to be impeached for any crime and under which the upper house of parliament imposes the ordinary penalty. Under the Articles, the persons who might be impeached would be politicians, the charges would be political, and the managers of the prosecution would be political opponents of the accused. A sense of decency and caution suggests that this necessary but dangerous system of trial should be limited. It should be limited to charges against public persons with respect to their conduct in office. It should also be limited in its penal consequences. In these respects, the United States model is to be preferred.

SECTION 1: PREFERRING THE BILL

The content of this section conforms to the principle that the popular house of parliament has the sole right to initiate an impeachment. It makes it clear that impeachment is available for provincial prosecutions also. The phrase 'in relation to the Government' is wide enough to encompass any public conduct, while it implies that the questioned conduct must have some relation

to a government. There does not seem to be any advantage in
being more precise.

SECTION 2: TRYING IMPEACHMENT

This section also conforms to the existing law that makes the
upper house the judge and jury on impeachments. But in this
instance the second chambers of the provinces are passed over
in favour of the Senate. The Senate is clearly to be preferred, as
its country-wide recruitment and superior position guarantee that
it will ordinarily be more detached from the controversy and
more inclined to be judically impartial than a local body could
hope to be.

SECTION 3: PROCEDURE AND PENALTIES

This section opts for the United States principle that the effect
of a conviction should be limited. The limitation proposed is even
more stringent as it does not extend to disqualification from holding office but only to removal from office and loss of immunity.
This directs impeachment to its true function in its modern
form, which is not to punish an evil-doer but to remove from
office a person who is a danger to the peace, prestige, or security
of the state and to submit him to the ordinary processes of the
law. In this way the vindictive drives of partisans are to a great
extent curbed, and though they may oust an opponent from his
position, in order to impose a penalty they must further convince
a court of law of his guilt.

Since impeachment is intended as a means of discharging an
official, of firing him, the grounds should include at least the
grosser forms of misconduct for which a person can be dismissed.
These are, in general, crimes, bad conduct not amounting to
crime, and neglect of duty.

The terms selected for this section are chosen with some care.
Thus, 'wilful or wanton Crime' is intended to extend only to
those crimes that require a blameworthy mind, i.e., *mens rea*;
'wilful' ordinarily means that a man intends to do what he does
(without necessarily intending all of the consequences), while

'wanton' denotes a state of mind in which 'ought to know' and 'I don't care' are usually apposite.

Infamous conduct is not necessarily limited to crimes. A habitual seducer might qualify although he always made sure to avoid criminal seductions, as might a malicious and persistent slanderer.

The phrase 'culpable Neglect of Duty' is reasonably clear and precise. Under this phrase a Canadian counterpart of President Woodrow Wilson could not be impeached because he became too ill to exercise his office properly.

The present section goes on to permit liability not only for crimes but for 'Wrongs'. This is probably wide enough to cover a breach of contract if it should be dishonourable enough to form the ground of a conviction on impeachment.

The purposes of the sections of this Article are not to spell out the content of the impeachment procedure but to impose certain essential bounds upon it. The procedure is not a stranger to our law, but it exists, at least in potentiality, in a dangerous form. The Article changes it from an arbitrary form of criminal procedure into a necessary check and rein upon the major independent Canadian public officers.

CHAPTER 24

The Limits of Government

A community of mind and will, the moral condition precedent of true liberty, cannot survive in a state where the will of a majority carries every question. The tyranny of a majority is the most absolute of all tyrannies. To get something like the desired unanimity, the basic interests of the several minorities must, if possible, be out of bounds to the will of the majority and hence to the action of ordinary law. This is in addition to the intrinsic merits of placing some rights beyond the pale of ordinary legislation as peculiarly sacred and fundamental. Here there are some absolutes, for example: the direct and intentional taking of innocent human life is always wrong; no man can be forced to act against his conscience; a good end does not justify an intrinsically evil means. If we add to these the practical principles of freedom dictated by our history, we arrive at quite a formidable body of limitations upon the governments, the legislatures, and the courts.

Political liberty forms the means by which we assert and maintain our physical and social liberty. It rests upon an extremely complex balance of laws and institutions. The establishment of independent legislative, executive, and judicial branches of the government is part of that balance, as is the federal structure itself. But the institutions need to be told, with authority, that they are not the whole of that balance, that they are expected to operate in conformity to the idea of freedom and to share the world with other non-political institutions, such as the family, without destroying them or usurping their functions. In short, liberty requires that all political institutions be subject to law.

SECTION 1: THE SUPREMACY OF THE ARTICLES

This asserts that the Articles are the supreme law of the land. There is no corresponding provision of the B.N.A. Acts, its place being supplied by the political theory of the supremacy of the Imperial parliament. The same theory applies to Australia, but the Commonwealth of Australia Constitution Act[1] by section 5 supplements the theory. The Constitution of the United States in a single clause[2] provides not only for its own supremacy but for the dominant effect of treaties and of valid federal laws over state laws.

But this makes it all the more conspicuous that we have retained the danger to every law of being held *ultra vires,* while ousting the idea in conflicts between federal and provincial law. There is no contradiction here. Putting a fence around the legislatures is not the same as putting one between them. The internal fence establishes useless corrals that have seriously curbed the effectiveness of our governments. The outer fence is a necessary safeguard for our freedom.

Section 1 is thus a statement of the essential principle of the supremacy of the constitution, that is, the Articles. It is not necessary to be explicit about it, but it is desirable to state it, because of the interpretive customs of our judiciary.

SECTION 2: PROMULGATION

Our criminal law, in common with that of many other countries, holds that ignorance of the law is not an excuse for breaking it.[3] A person has a duty to know the law that is applicable to his conduct before he ventures it; he cannot use his failure to know as an excuse. This would be a monstrous injustice unless ignorance of the law were somehow culpable, unless the person accused had a chance to know the law and neglected to inform himself and thus acted at his peril. To accommodate justice on this question (and for various other reasons) the traditional philosophers of the law have always treated *promulgation* as an integral part of the making of every law. Law is conceived as a command, which obviously cannot be expected to be obeyed until it is uttered and heard. In the theory of the common law, the sovereign or chief of state promulgates (that is, formally publishes) a law when he signifies his assent to an act of the legislature. Consequently we have no theory of the need to make the law available and known throughout its domain, as a condition of its efficacy.[4]

In the case of statutes this is good enough. They are printed and made available to lawyers and others who need the texts. Important acts are discussed in the press. The public comes to have an appreciation of the statute law by a process of osmosis, assimilating the common understanding (or misunderstanding) through the skin, as it were. In some countries such as France, where enactments are blessed with a reasonably concise and readable text, the public are considered to be more familiar with the exact language of the law.

A vast mass of law is enacted in secret by order in council or ministerial regulations. Regulations are generally required to be tabled in the legislature but they can go into effect long before that and there is no requirement that they be published. During World War II, the number of unpublished federal orders in council having the force of law was a subject of grave concern to those attentive to liberty.

Local governments commonly fail to keep their printed by-laws up to date or even reasonably available. This can be a great hardship on people dealing with them, especially when, as is not infrequent, local officials are unable to give an accurate statement of their laws. To obtain a complete set of by-laws, amended to date, of any local government can be very difficult.

Judicial law is contained in tens of thousands of decisions not all of which are reported, and even those that are reported are not accessible to the layman. Of course, if the layman needs to know a point of law that has to be derived from the decisions, it is obscure enough to justify consulting a lawyer. The accessibility of law reports is not an important practical question, but there is a fairly weighty theoretical point to be made. Judge-made law is just as much law as any other, and it follows that the public authorities should be obliged to make all of it available at public expense. The obvious device would be to publish a judicial gazette and put it in the stacks of the chief public libraries of every region.

What, then, is the effect of the section? It does not require that everyone be advised of the content of a statute before it can be enforced nor does it oblige the government to publish acts or regulations free of charge. It requires no more than what the federal government does now with respect to statutes, but it would require the government concerned to do likewise with all acts, regulations, or orders that have the force of law.

As an example, if the Minister of Fisheries made regulations applicable only to the Atlantic coast, he would be required to have them printed so that they could be sold to persons on the Atlantic coast. But he would have no need or duty to have them for persons on the Pacific coast or anywhere where they did not apply.

The section asserts merely that no one should be penalized for breaking a law that he could not by any reasonable means find out about. This should be a reasonable and sufficient safeguard for both the legislator and the subject. There would be no need of any other sanction than the one mentioned in the section, the suspension of the law until it becomes knowable. The substance of this provision would appear to be essential to freedom.

SECTION 3: THE RULE OF LAW

The memorable words of the great medieval jurist Bracton were used in the thirteenth century to mean the supremacy of the natural and divine laws.

> But the King himself ought not to be subject to man but subject to God and to the law, for the law makes the King. Let the King, then, attribute to the law what the law attributes to him, namely, dominion and power, for there is no king where the will and not the law has dominion.[5]

The revival of the maxim in the seventeenth century by Sir Edward Coke gave it a rather different tone. It then began to mean that the king, being only a part of the parliament, was subject to the laws made by the king in parliament. This is now accepted as a legal platitude. The more apt modern paraphrase would be 'The king is subject to the law'. Against this we must place the principle 'The king can do no wrong', which guarantees the personal immunity of the sovereign. Both ideas are important to efficient government in a free society, and it is therefore also important to restate them in terms suitable to a representative democracy and to reconcile them.

Logic and common sense suggest that if the courts can effectively order the executive head of the government or the legislature or its chief parts to do or abstain from doing something, the courts become the actual sovereign power in the state. This would be a usurpation. On the other hand the courts must have power to restrain all unlawful conduct in relation to the members of the body politic. The method of achieving these objectives that has evolved both in Great Britain and in the United States is this:

(a) The courts do not attempt to exert any power over the person of the head of state or over any legislature or house of the legislature.

(b) The courts will maintain the law by declaring any illegal act to be *ultra vires* and by restraining subordinate executive officers or by ordering done what should be done.

Thus the courts in the United States have no power of mandamus to compel a legislature to redistribute seats but will appoint a master to do it in place of the legislature where the failure to do so constitutes a denial of constitutional rights.[6] In England, the courts will determine the law under which parliament and its houses act but will stop short of interfering with the internal proceedings of either house.[7] Because the courts in England are now the creatures of the parliament there is no need to bar them from ordering it about. But since we have determined that it is essential to our federal state to have the courts independent, and hence co-ordinate with the other branches of the government, the independence of the other co-ordinate branches must be safeguarded.

These would be the parliament, the legislatures, and the heads of government (i.e. the Governor General and lieutenant-governors). But the courts could go far to constrain the parliament by action on the individual houses; so these also ought to be excluded by law from court control.

The only other persons excluded by law from the jurisdiction of the courts are foreign sovereigns and their ambassadors. It is common to include the ambassador's suite in this privilege and the privilege has been extended to rather extreme limits. An analogous situation is that enacted by the Visiting Forces Acts[8] which provide that foreign troops on Canadian soil are subject to their own tribunals.

It may seem the height of imprudence to grant constitutional exemptions to foreign nationals rather than leaving these to the operation of ordinary law. Indeed, there are dangers; but to devise a constitutional provision that allows such exceptions to be made by ordinary statutes without unduly weakening the constitutionally entrenched rule of law has proved extremely difficult and may be impossible, because of the inherent contradictions of the two ideas. It therefore seems wiser, in the long run, to parade the exempt persons in the proposed section. And, in the end, the phrase 'recognized Representatives' is probably ample to enable the federal government to keep the problem within bounds.

Section 3 of this Article, although it is a fair and considered attempt to render the foregoing ideas, will pose problems. But this stems from the ideas themselves: it will always be difficult to resolve conflicts between the independent branches of the government, just as it is hard to state a complete reconciliation between that independence and the rule of law.

For example, it would seem rational to extend the independence of the legislature to shield its committees or even its members, but the jurisdiction of the courts, on the other hand, must begin to attach somewhere down the line, and the higher the better, for freedom's sake. It is possible, of course, that the legislature can confer privileges, as contemplated in Article 7, that would prevent judicial control.

It is a problem of interpretation. Not everyone is subject to
every law. Infants under seven, for example, are not governed
by the criminal law.[9] There are very many instances of classes
of people being excluded from the operation of a law. It simply
does not apply to them. It is unlikely that the proposed section
would be interpreted to change that, in view of the known habits
and outlook of the courts.

Accordingly it should be possible to enact exemptions for legislators and committees that would rely on the same approach.
On the other hand, ordinary law is not made so that people can
escape the control of the courts, and parliamentary privileges
would thus differ in intention and in kind from other statutes.
In the circumstances, a compromise is the likely outcome.

The limited immunities that the Articles secure for legislators,
the Censor General, and judges would not prevent the courts,
when necessary, from ordering them to act or to abstain from
acting. This seems reasonable. The rule of law demands an equal
law and the only exceptions permitted should be those essential
to the legitimate operations of the government.

It should be emphasized that while the executive heads are
not subject to the ordinary courts, they are subject to the law
by means of the extraordinary court of parliament through the
process of impeachment. And though the parliament and legislatures are not subject to the law in this way, their acts are. The
law of the constitution thus binds them under sanction of in-
validity. The scope of the rule of law is made as wide as can be.[10]

SECTION 4: THE EQUAL PROTECTION OF THE LAWS

Many modern constitutional instruments are quite definite and
explicit about equality before the law. The most famous statement of it is in the United States Declaration of Independence:

> We hold these Truths to be self-evident, that all Men are created
> equal; . . .

The force of this affirmative having been dissipated in the compromises dictated by self-interest that were incorporated in and

perpetuated by the Constitution of 1787, that nation found itself driven to reassert the principle in a more concrete legal form as a result of the immense and fratricidal conflict, unique in history, that erupted in 1861. Of the many causes that led to that conflict, popular opinion has justly given the prime place to slavery and the reaction to it of men who could read and believe and breathe 'that all Men are created equal'. The restatement was the Fourteenth Amendment which, among other things, forbids any State to 'deny to any person within its jurisdiction the equal protection of the laws'.

These, the most pregnant words in an inspired document, were originally adopted to protect Negroes from the legal harassments that resurgent Southern governments might inflict on them in a desperate fight to preserve white ascendency. The intent of the amendment was thwarted by many stratagems and for decades the judiciary favoured a policy of gradualism, countenancing 'equal but separate' public facilities for Negroes.[11] In other respects the law was administered with firm prudence from the beginning. In the 1940s the fact that the separate facilities provided for Negroes were in fact unequal became apparent to the United States Supreme Court,[12] and this culminated in the famous case of *Brown* v. *Board of Education of Topeka,*[13] in which the court held that despite the physical equality of segregated schools, they were inherently unequal because of intangible factors, and the 'separate but equal' doctrine had no place in public education.

Absolute equality of all persons is impractical, if not impossible. All laws cannot in fact be made to apply equally to everyone. Special provisions are usually made for large classes of persons, such as married women, infants, lunatics, inebriates, seamen, etc. But much narrower classifications have been held to be capable of special legislative consideration without denying equal protection. Examples are chain stores[14] and river pilots.[15] The court has justified these cases, not as exceptions to equality, but because the 'equal protection' clause was not intended to apply to any legal classification upon 'a reasonable distinction'.[16]

'Reasonable' is the key word here and it is not a very good word in the context. In law, it usually means what a jury thinks reasonable, but in this department it means what the judges think reasonable, a very different thing. And what the U. S. judges seem to mean is that a distinction is unreasonable if it amounts to unjust discrimination.

Because of the truly profound cleavage in the United States, as, in fact, in all the Western World, between the pragmatists and the exponents of natural law, on the meaning of justice, we can give no certain content to such a phrase as 'unjust discrimination'; the Supreme Court of the United States, in common with many other bodies, has shown notable variations of approach on even so elementary an injustice as the colour bar. Thus, 'equal but separate' train compartments were held in 1896 to be reasonable to preserve the public peace, but 'separate but equal' schools were held unreasonable in 1954, despite an equal threat to the public peace (in Little Rock and elsewhere), because the colour line was at bottom an unjust distinction.

Equality before the law is a universal problem with varied shadings in different places, and many constitutions have something to say about it. Some treat it as a right of all persons,[17] some restrict it to citizens.[18] In most cases, as in the Universal Declaration of Human Rights,[19] the expression is as general as in the 'equal protection' clause, but the statements of two nations are worth a closer look.

Article 40 of the Irish constitution of 1937 enacts, as Section 1:

> All citizens shall, as human persons, be held equal before the law. This shall not be held to mean that the State shall not in its enactments have due regard to differences of capacity, physical and moral, and of social function.

The draftsman saw the difficulties implicit in the absolute terms of the first sentence and tried to formulate the usual and necessary qualifications. The section is drawn to go much further than the 'equal protection' clause. It establishes a régime of equality with exceptions rather than merely safeguarding against unjust discrimination. The very exceptions can be viewed as means of achieving equality, although the draftsman has not expressed this.

The Italian constitution is more explicit and complete on this point. Article 3 provides:

> All citizens have equal social dignity and are equal before the law, without distinction of sex, of race, of language, of religion, of political opinion, of personal and social condition.
>
> It is the task of the Republic to remove the obstacles of an economic and social order which, limiting in fact the liberty and equality of citizens, prevent the full development of the human personality and the effective participation by all workers in the political, economic, and social organization of the country.

An example of how this is probably intended to work will make the point clearer. A contract of labour between an individual workman and an employer, if governed by a rule of strict legal equality, becomes in many instances a very unequal thing. The average workman, whose chief resources are his energy and his skill, is not evenly matched with the average employer. The latter has a much greater field of choice, more staying power, because of his capital, and more formidable backing from his associates. And the trend to limited liability means that the average employer is now a corporation with special legal privileges.

The natural remedy is to form associations of workmen to deal collectively with employers. But this did not, by itself, achieve equality in fact. These associations were weakened by the nature of their members, generally less educated, less prudent, less wealthy than the employers, quite apart from the fact that in the beginning they were liable to prosecution as conspiracies or combinations in restraint of trade and were long in existence before they attained the easy legal recognition given to trading companies. The associations rarely included enough of the labour force to prevent strike-breaking, and the persistent fact of unemployment meant that the economic laws of supply and demand cheapened labour as a commodity. Capital, of course, if in a fixed form, can also suffer unemployment.

It is clear, then, that the collective-bargaining laws, which require an employer to deal with the recognized agent of his employees, have brought the parties more on a par at the sacrifice of some part of the field of choice of each. They have, in effect, legislated the employees into a labour company with restricted objects and obliged the employer to deal with it. This is the core of the laws; the related matters, such as the closed or union shop, picketing rights, and injunctions against strikes, are subordinate and much more debatable.

Similarly, minimum-wage laws, workmen's compensation acts, industrial-safety laws, and full-employment measures work to make the bargaining positions of capital and labour more equal. Some would say that the balance has been reversed and, no doubt, this has happened on occasion. Where it has happened it has been due, largely, not to the law, but to intimidation under cover of the law, blinked at by the police authority and the courts. This makes it all the more urgent to insist that the laws give equal protection. It follows that the more powerful a corporation or a union becomes the stronger should be the power of the law over it.

The Italian law seems to be made in contemplation of this kind of equalization. It is designed to allow and even require that the poor, the weak, and the lowly be brought up to the plane of the strong, the rich, and the well placed in their social and economic dealings.

The Italian text is rather verbose and does not suit our legal tradition. Moreover it is part of a complex that bases the republic on labour, imposes a duty on everyone to produce, and in this very article speaks of the workers as if they alone were significant. It is not a practical proposal for Canada.

Section 4 of our Article 11, therefore, while it tries to capture the idea of helping people up to a community level, is differently and more concisely expressed. It incorporates the expression 'the equal Protection of the Laws' because, with all its dangers, it is the best suited to express the idea and has a reasonably satisfactory jurisprudence to build on. (One would hope to have it persuasive rather than binding.) We can summarize the effect as follows:

1. By Section 3, everyone is subject to the law.
2. By the 'equal protection' clause, everyone is entitled to the

benefit of the law equally, without unjust discrimination based, for example, on race, speech, religion, political opinion, family background, etc.

3. The proviso for offsetting inequalities shows that the aim of the section is to encourage equality.

The fact that we have little or no legal discrimination in Canada, although we have our share of social discrimination, means that there is no substantial vested interest opposed to this section, while the vagaries and imperfections of human nature and the pride of old Adam, ever ready to be puffed up, suggest the wisdom of adopting it.

SECTION 5: NO HEREDITARY TITLES

In theory, titles of honour are compatible with democracy. That is to say, it does not detract from essential equality before the law to commend some citizens for conduct that the nation thinks worthy. If the citizen is allowed to keep the commendation before the public by adding it to his name in some way, we have a title of honour, at least in embryo. In our day we favour a string of letters after the name, such as D.S.O., O.B.E., or the like, but very few would refuse a knighthood or a peerage. In the past, the more prudent and far-sighted aristocracies recruited fresh blood from among the people of achievement (and others), and in this way what were chiefly titles of political or economic superiority became, to some extent, titles of honour.

Here lies the danger to legal equality. To confuse public honour with the marks of wealth or office by attaching privileges or substantial public functions to a title, or by giving the same title to the merely rich or powerful as well as to the worthy, undermines equality and is an affront to democracy. The Canadian instinct has been, on the whole, to shun titles or to be content with simple knighthoods. We have had several baronets and a lord or two, but the politicians have sensed that the hereditary principle contradicted the only basis on which the people would tolerate honours in this country – that they be for honour's sake. Even the rather feeble and inoffensive inequality of the British House of Lords would be unthinkable here. The subject of honours at one time figured in political controversy but it is now dormant, if not dead.[20]

Many nations outlaw titles of honour and permit their citizens to accept them from foreign states only with government consent. This is more than we need. Section 5 is enough to keep the question within the bounds set by our history and tradition. One might question whether we need such a provision at all. It is true it is not essential to our federal form of government, nor is it necessary to our political approach to things. But it is desirable to give this question its quietus. However trivial it may seem to some, its further injection into practical politics can only cause very unnecessary division and distress.

SECTION 6: PERSONS AND CAPACITY

A person is anyone who is the subject of legal rights and duties. In the past, the law has refused recognition as persons to large numbers of human beings. This was the case with most slaves and is largely the case with slaves today. Some slaves were admitted to partial personality, and in this respect the later Roman law was more liberal than that of the Southern states. Not all persons are admitted by the law to have the same capacity for rights and duties. Such are infants, lunatics, and, to some small extent, married women. On the other hand, a group of people are sometimes treated as a single person, distinct from the members of the group, by a fiction of the law. This is a corporation. Or an individual may exercise some office, such as the Crown, a bishopric of the Church of England, or official trustee, and will have a split legal personality. The rights, duties, property, and course of devolution of the individual and of the office may be quite distinct.

Not many modern constitutions explicitly state that every human being is to be accounted a person, although most of them provide phrases and clauses from which a conclusion to that effect might be drawn. It may, for instance, be a valid and necessary implication of the 'equal protection' clause and its counterparts, at least those that are not limited to the citizens.

The Universal Declaration of Human Rights, having in mind conditions around the world that include slavery and similar oppressions, is plain and forthright in Article 6:

> Everyone has the right to recognition everywhere as a person before the law.

From the point of view of ordinary language this is quite satisfactory. From the legal draftsman's point of view it is possible to quibble. Who, for instance is 'everyone'? Does it literally mean every human being or just us (whoever we are) as opposed to the lesser breeds without the law? Again, does the 'right to recognition' imply, by the illogical but prevalent exclusion rule, that the duty to be a person can be avoided, to avoid the obligations of that status? And does recognition as a person mean as a complete person in every case? Surely not, or the laws made for the protection of incompetent persons would go by the board.

Our Section 6 is drawn so as to answer these questions.

The exceptions are those where it is now considered proper, in at least some jurisdictions, to take a person's property and affairs out of his hands and commit them to a parent, guardian, trustee, or representative. Profligacy is a rather unusual cause for putting a person under tutelage but it exists in some jurisdictions.[21] Habitual drunkenness is not expressly mentioned, but it would fall under Insanity or Profligacy in any case where a guardianship would be proper.

Coverture, the suppressed personality formerly imposed on married women, is the one common disability not mentioned. This is in accord with the almost universal direction of the law, not only the common law but those systems based on the Roman law also. The revision of the Quebec Civil Code now in train is likely to bring changes that will march with this principle.

Section 6 may be compared and contrasted with Section 5 of Article 2, dealing with the permissible limitations on citizens' rights as compared with the rights of persons. Those in Section 5 are much narrower and rightly so. It is clearly of ultimate importance that the vote and public office should only be denied for very real and pertinent reasons. The reasons are naturally much broader in the case of personal rights.

This section is not essential to the federal form of government but it is necessary for the kind of democracy we have and want in Canada.

SECTION 7: FREEDOM OF CONSCIENCE

Freedom of conscience connotes many things to us, the chief of which are contained in Article 18 of the Universal Declaration of Human Rights:

> Everyone has the right to freedom of thought, conscience and religion; this right includes freedom to change his religion or belief and freedom, either alone or in community with others and in public or private, to manifest his religion or belief in teaching, practice, worship and observance.[22]

This article is good, and might, as Senator Roebuck proposed, form the basis of our own text. Our religious history, our proximity to the United States, and some lack of precision in the article combine to suggest a different treatment.

The 'right to freedom of thought, conscience and religion' is not specific enough. It can be analysed into freedom to believe and freedom to say and do what we believe to be right. Obviously, different limitations will apply to these two freedoms, of their very nature.

Belief — not only the expression of belief, but the very action of the mind itself — can be coerced and sometimes should be. Thus we have no qualms in sending criminals to reformatories to convince them that crime does not pay. The expression of belief in word and action is regulated by every state by what is conceived to be the public good. In some the bounds are very narrow, in others, broad enough. Some declare freedom to exercise religious belief in the most absolute terms, as, for example, in the First Amendment of the United States Constitution:

> Congress shall make no law respecting an establishment of religion, or prohibiting the free exercise thereof.

This has been held to give the expression of religion such a preferred position, that a religious propagandist may trespass on private property in defiance of the owner, in the exercise of this right.[23] The right to persuade so far outweighs the right to privacy and the right to resist persuasion! This absurd extreme has not prevented the federal government from suppressing religiously inspired polygamy or any other conduct considered criminal, and this must be considered an implied limitation of the freedom of religious practice as effective as the explicit one in Article 44, Section 2, of the Irish constitution,

> 1. Freedom of conscience and the free profession and practice of religion are, subject to public order and morality, guaranteed to every citizen.

The only difference between this and the First Amendment is the difference between the views of the courts concerned with them on what is public order and morality. Neither court will suppress a religious activity unless it is otherwise illegal. The content of the two views may be very different because the Irish will no doubt take the traditional attitude, which is also the British legal and political attitude, that a religious motive, however worthy, will not excuse an act that is in fact unlawful.[24]

Is there, in fact, any need touching liberty to extend the free expression of religion beyond our ordinary civil rights to think, to do, to persuade? Should a religious motive alter the political character of an act? The accepted liberties of speech are enough, except on one point. Freedom of speech is a citizen's right, and experience shows that the State must be restrained from imposing a religious creed on individuals. Accordingly, this section deals with state action on the individual's rights and conscience, and provides that no law shall impose the beliefs or practices of any particular religion. This clearly implies a right to change one's religion, as otherwise the law would be imposing the previous religion. The section also prohibits any religious test for the exercise of any civil right or public function, because this prohibition is not clearly implied in the first clause although a religious test for public office is the classic means of upholding the official religion. These are concrete measures adequate to guarantee the first part of Article 18 of the Universal Declaration of Human Rights.

There is one religious freedom that has been neglected in liberal thought: the freedom of a religious people to do honour to God publicly and through their public instruments. The constitutions of Ireland and of the Federal Republic of Germany show that it is possible to give God his due in public life while maintaining a high degree of freedom of religion. In particular, it can be done without establishing a state church or curbing freedom of conscience. There are difficulties, no doubt, but they are never as great as the difficulties that the State has in divorcing religion from public affairs without showing active hostility to it. There can be no injustice in permitting the majority to pray in whatever unison they can achieve if the minority are not compelled to join in or to support it.

Section 7, then, prevents the imposition of an official creed and the use of religious tests to discriminate between persons or to compel conformity. It does not guarantee absolute freedom of conscience but only that degree of freedom that civilized states have found possible.

Strictly speaking, the proposed section does not prevent an establishment of religion. The situation could be like that in England where the Church of England is still established. Religious tests are applied to the Crown and one or two officials,[25] but these could be abolished without affecting the case. Religious freedom in England is quite as real as in any secular state. The American colonists who thought that freedom of religion consisted in disestablishing the Church of England were thus mistaken, although hardly blameworthy, considering the times and the then prevailing attitude and powers of the established church. But forbidding an establishment of religion is not the same thing as forbidding the State to compel everyone to worship in the same way.

Freedom of religion is essential to the Canadian federation because of the religious nature of the population and the distribution of the different faiths. It is also an added dimension to the political balance achieved by federation.

SECTION 8: PROHIBITION OF SLAVERY

Slavery still exists in Arabia, Central Africa, and one or two other places, and it is perhaps for this reason that some of the newer constitutions, such as those of Italy, Germany, and Japan,[26] prohibit it, either expressly or by immediate inference. Of course, all three former Axis powers were under strong American influence when their governments were reconstituted after World War II, and had the example of the Thirteenth Amendment of the United States Constitution before them.

> Section 1. Neither slavery nor involuntary servitude, except as punishment for crime whereof the party shall have been duly convicted, shall exist in the United States, or any place subject to their jurisdiction.

The wording is preferable to Article 4 of the Universal Declaration of Human Rights, although less explicit:

> No one shall be held in slavery or servitude: slavery and the slave trade shall be prohibited in all their forms.

This was Article 2 of the Bill of Rights proposed by Senator Roebuck for Canada. The Canadian Bill of Rights provides that in Canada there has existed and will continue to exist

> ... the right of the individual to life, liberty, security of the person and enjoyment of property, and the right not to be deprived thereof except by due process of law; ...

The best word for slavery is 'slavery'. To make doubly sure, the proposed section includes a definition of slavery couched as an added prohibition, and there is a further clause to ensure that even voluntary servitude can be ended at will. As to this, in the jurisprudence under the Thirteenth Amendment in the United States, a presumption of fraud in a statute designed to be used as a threat to enforce labour contracts was held unconstitutional.[27]

The necessity of Section 8 is that of most of the sections of this Article, the need to found the Confederation on the enduring elements of human dignity.

The theme common to the foregoing sections of this Article is equality before the law. This tone of universality pervades them from the opening note – the supremacy over all of the Articles, through the demand that the law be knowable by all bound by it and that it bind all, to the sections that outlaw the historical forms of discrimination. All are implied by the requirement for the equal protection of the laws, but the implication is not strong enough to rely on. Or, rather, the human obstacles to drawing the implication – the vested interests, legislative lethargy, executive inertia, and judicial caution – are too obvious. Far better risk wasting a few words than risk liberty.

The civil liberties under the United States Constitution, so often mentioned in these pages, are largely the elaboration wrought by the courts of that country on a few simple phrases. Of these, the two most important, summing up most of the others, are 'the equal protection of the laws' and 'due process of law'. We have dealt at some length with the first phrase. We now come to a group of sections more directly related to the second.

CHAPTER 25

Due Process of Law

The eight sections next to be considered are all concerned with
the relations of the individual to the courts and legal procedures.
The gist of them is best summed up, in our tradition, in the words
'due process of law'. This phrase, while probably most familiar
to us as a prominent element in the United States Constitution,
used in both the Fifth and Fourteenth Amendments, has also an
important historical connection with the constitutional struggles
for liberty in England. It is said to have its roots in Magna Charta[1]
and was used in the Petition of Right of 1628 to translate a statute
of Edward III as follows:

> . . . in the eighth-and-twentieth year of the reign of King Edward III
> it was declared and enacted by authority of parliament that no man,
> of what estate or condition that he be, should be put out of his land
> or tenements, nor taken, nor imprisoned, nor disinherited, nor put to
> death, without being brought to answer by due process of law. . . .[2]

The detailed provisions of the sections, while they deal with
matters intimately connected with the courts and the administration of justice, are as much directed to the executive and the legislature as to the judiciary. Indeed the courts have an honourable
record, on the whole, when it comes to individual liberty, and it
was the failure of parliament and the ministries to provide the
legislative and financial bases for the freedoms in question that
hampered justice in the past and prompted the judges to provide

221

some means to attain them. In this way, many of the procedural and evidential safeguards that are found in the United States Constitution have evolved in Great Britain and the Commonwealth as 'principles of fundamental justice',[3] embedded in the common law. Indeed, Mr. Diefenbaker's Canadian Bill of Rights is largely a codification of the law upon which the judges act in supervising the conduct of inferior courts and officers. This ingenious idea of an interpretative code has much to commend it, but it is only a half-way house to constitutionally guaranteed rights. It binds the courts but not the legislators, who need it more.

The development of the doctrine of substantive due process in the United States is a strong obstacle to the use of the words in Canada.[4] The persuasive effect of the United States case law would be too strong and hence too dangerous to our own more moderate and balanced idea of liberty under law.

Our 'due process' sections are aimed at spelling out in concrete terms the safeguards in the administration of justice that have some universal backing or some special place in Canadian legal practice. The requirement of an impartial tribunal is of the first kind; our own solution of the 'incriminating question' problem ('taking the Fifth') is an example of the second. Some may find the wording too concrete. This is regrettable but necessary in most cases to avoid the extremes to which more general expressions have led.

The 'due process' sections were originally drafted with a general eye to the provisions of the Universal Declaration of Human Rights and the United States Constitution with such modifications as the Canadian and British experience suggested. Much later they were reviewed and revised in the light of a group of constitutions, including those of the two Germanies, Italy, Ireland, Japan, Switzerland, and the U.S.S.R., and the Canadian Bill of Rights. The Australian Constitution on this point more nearly resembles the B.N.A. Acts than its more usual inspiration, the United States Constitution, in that it has no 'due process' provisions other than a requirement that federal crimes be tried by jury.[5] The East German and Soviet constitutions did not offer anything new or particularly helpful but they were in agreement with the Western ones on many points. Some would contend, of course, that this proves written constitutions to be of little value, and this is so where they have not achieved a national popular canonization. But the East German and Soviet concurrences show the universality of the notions involved and, since these are largely propaganda papers, the value of these rights in the eyes of people everywhere.

The sources cited show that there is widespread support for most of the ideas in Sections 9 to 16. In these sections the amount of detail dictates a more itemized and minute consideration than in the first group. Indeed the first four of these are really each a number of safeguards rolled into one. Each section deals with a broad topic in the administration of justice. Each also includes aspects not closely connected with the general theme, such as the provision against retroactive taxation in Section 14 and the impact of Section 13 on health and sanitation measures. Section 9 also has a much wider scope than merely to regulate police procedures, as it lays down general norms respecting privacy.

SECTION 9: PERSONAL PRIVACY

This originated in the Fourth Amendment of the United States Constitution designed to protect the people and their property from unreasonable searches and seizures. The expression 'the people' is ambiguous: it may apply only to citizens but may also include denizens. It did not extend to Negro slaves: this is a fair inference from the Dred Scott case.[6]

Since 1789 the idea of privacy at law has expanded to cover not only persons and houses (including offices and garages), letters, papers, and personal property, but also other personal communications such as telegrams and telephone calls. The individual's honour and reputation are also included at law, and this is recognized in many modern statements of rights including the Universal Declaration of Human Rights, Article 12. It is hard to see how an individual's honour, apart from his reputation, can be legally protected. A good reputation should not be destroyed out of malice. For example, a convict who has been rehabilitated should not be subject to having his past raked up. This is a valuable aspect of personal privacy very suitable for fundamental protection.

No right of privacy is even approximately absolute. The Fourth Amendment is directed against 'unreasonable searches and seizures', and the resultant case law on the meaning of 'unreasonable' exhibits all the weaknesses of judicial law-making. The main weakness, of course, is that it requires the ordinary policeman to anticipate, in the heat of action, the refined and subtle reasoning of the courts. The main sanction used by the courts in the United States is to deny the prosecution the use of evidence that is obtained illegally. This results in absurdities. By hiding behind the protections designed for honest men, obvious criminals go free.

'Unreasonable' means what the judges say it means, rather than what a jury might consider to be unreasonable, and it does not mean 'unfounded', although an unfounded search would be unreasonable. It seems to mean something like 'uncalled for', 'undue', or 'excessive'. This is an almost mystical idea depending upon a nearly substantial Spirit of Moderation that broods over and breathes life into these dry legal bones. A thing is unreasonable if it lowers the dignity of the individual below this standard. This is a notion that should be plainly stated with some attempt to establish the standard rather than be let rest on the interpretation or misinterpretation of such a word as 'unreasonable'. We have therefore used 'unfounded' as more exactly expressing what should be the limits here.

In Canada, we do not have the rule that illegally obtained evidence is inadmissible,[7] although every court has the right to reject evidence if its probative value is little and its prejudicial effect great.[8] This, of course, concerns the quality of the evidence rather than the way in which it was obtained, but the latter aspect may effect its trustworthiness, as in some confessions. There was an attempt to adapt this rule to the case of illegally obtained evidence, under the concept of fairness, but this is treacherous ground and should be avoided.

In fact, everyone who is the subject of an illegal search and seizure can sue the perpetrator. It is argued that this right is illusory because it is usually a case of a poor, uneducated individual, often with an unsavoury reputation, against the combined powers of the police and their public employers. But this does not bear analysis. The plaintiff is no worse off than in the case of an individual against a corporation (possibly a situation to be corrected as a measure of equal protection). In most cases of technical illegality there is no substantial basis for a claim. The would-be plaintiff knows that no jury would award him even nominal damages. This is not so where the interruption is substantial.[9]

What search or seizure would be unfounded? Rather, what foundation should there be for an arrest or a forcible entry without a warrant? Obviously and rationally the foundation should be the same as for an arrest or entry with a warrant with the added consideration that to require a warrant in the circumstances would not be sensible, either because some harm could happen while getting it or because the case clearly calls for intervention immediately.

In Canada, the rules of arrest are not very satisfactory, being based mainly on distinctions between peace officers and other people and between indictable offences and those punishable on summary convictions. In general, a peace officer may act on reasonable and probable grounds but a civilian must be right when he makes an arrest. The policy of the law is against citizens' arrests except in extreme cases. The distinction between the two classes of offences is only remotely related to the true reasons for an arrest and is complicated by the fact that some offences can be prosecuted in either way.[10]

Why should any man be arrested? One obvious reason is that he is doing or about to do something unlawful and should be stopped. Another is that he appears to have done something unlawful and unless he is taken into custody he may escape or conceal the offence or some evidence of it or dispose of stolen property or the like. A third, which in Canada would also be included in the first, is that he is about to commit suicide.[11] If there are any other exceptions to the rule requiring a warrant 'they do not now occur to us'.[12] They cannot occur frequently.

Section 9 spells out these exceptions in its second clause and thus sets out some idea of what constitutes a foundation for an interruption of privacy. But it deals in that clause only with arrests; searches and other breaches of security are left to the ordinary law. Except for pure breaches of privacy (for example, where a school board publishes its teachers' salaries in a salary dispute) the general lines of the law are reasonably well understood. In this clause, arrests and searches are equated on the principle that the sanctity of the dwelling should be no greater than the sanctity of the person. It should probably be equally as great because it is a protection and guarantee of the sanctity of the person. The section by the word 'Houses' covers more than dwelling houses, of course.

Some things in the clause call for comment. The right is limited to adult persons because those not fully competent, such as infants, lunatics, and inebriates, are in the custody of their parents, guardians, or tutors. Guardians have the authority of a judicial order, but parents do not. The rights of infants are better dealt with by ordinary law. Section 9 does not prevent a more stringent rule respecting arrests and searches.

The clause requires a reasonable belief. The word 'reasonable' haunts us, but here it is quite safe because it is the word used in the Criminal Code in this kind of context. Practically, here, it means with sound and objective reasons for the belief. The same considerations apply to the use of 'reasonable Cause' in the third clause in the section. The words 'reasonable grounds' are used in the Code in precisely the same connotation. The Fourth Amendment uses 'probable Cause' and the Code in Section 435 (a) uses 'reasonable and probable grounds', but the word 'probable', if it adds anything to 'reasonable' here, calls for too high a standard. It is probably meaningless when combined with 'reasonable', and since sound and objective reason is the standard we wish to set up, 'probable' can and should be left out.

Belief is required and it is sufficient. The person acting does not have to be right if he acted on sound grounds, but he must believe that it is necessary to act. This means that the exceptions can only be invoked in urgent cases, which is as it should be. There are, of course, a great number of urgent cases happening all the time.

If a warrant is used it must be the order of an independent magistrate of the judicial order and he must act judicially, that is, on grounds proved for each occasion. The third clause of the section specifies some of the conditions of a judicial warrant. This uses the words 'reasonable Cause' instead of the 'probable Cause' of the Fourth Amendment, as already noted, and 'sufficiently' instead of 'particularly' to apply to the description of the objects of the warrant. The purpose of putting a description in the warrant is to limit it to the persons, places, and things described, and a description sufficient to do that, that is, sufficient to identify them, should be enough.

The requirement that a warrant be judicial would involve quite a change in the policy of some legislation in Canada. Under most provincial liquor-control acts a minister is authorized to issue a blanket warrant to the officers charged with enforcing the act, giving them the right to enter any place to search for evidence of infractions. Such powers would not subsist under Section 9, but it is doubtful if they would be really necessary since the section is drawn to except the cases to which the powers apply. The blanket warrants are sometimes used for purposes for which they were not intended and are capable of abuse. It must not be forgotten, also, that much of the seventeenth- and eighteenth-century agitation was directed against such warrants.

Investigators under the federal taxation statutes[13] have even more alarming powers. They can be used to maintain a system of 'spot checking', but they are mostly invoked to get at suspected violators. The public revenue would probably survive some curtailment of these powers.

The necessity for Section 9 is the necessity for fundamental protection of the right of privacy. This right has suffered much attrition in Canada, the more so because the excessive powers adopted have, on the whole, been used moderately. With increase in population the right will be under greater pressures and it should be asserted now while we can consider it calmly.

SECTION 10: RIGHTS ON DETENTION

What should happen to a person who is arrested? The classical bills of rights are silent on the subject and the rights to counsel and bail have had to be extracted from clauses dealing with trial or punishment. Modern documents are more articulate and none more so than the Canadian Bill of Rights. On this aspect it is concrete, detailed, and adequate, in marked contrast to most of its other provisions. Mr. Diefenbaker and Mr. Fulton, as distinguished defence counsel, were conscious of the problems arising and of the inadequacy of the law at this stage.

In Canada a person making an arrest has the duty to tell the person arrested the process or warrant under which he makes the arrest or the reason for it, if it is feasible to do so.[14] This must be done promptly.[15] The prisoner must be taken before a justice of the peace within twenty-four hours if one is available; otherwise as soon as possible.[16] He must be permitted to retain and instruct counsel promptly. Once before a justice he must not be denied reasonable bail without just cause.[17] He also has the right to have his imprisonment challenged by habeas corpus. These particular provisions apply only to imprisonment under federal law and are subject to change at any time by the parliament.

Section 10 restates these rights (except for habeas corpus, which is incorporated in Section 6 of Article 5). In doing so it drops the twenty-four-hour rule, and this seemingly inconsequential change, coupled with the right of prompt access to counsel, would probably initiate a searching re-examination of the bases of criminal investigation in this country. Because the law allows the police twenty-four hours before they must bring a prisoner before a justice, they firmly believe that they have the right, in investigating a crime, to detain anyone who seems to be connected with it for twenty-four hours without charging him or arraigning him. It is a debatable point whether a justice has the right to intervene in such case and order the detainee brought before him.[18] The law may have been meant to give the police a day to determine whether or not the grounds of the arrest are valid. (Because the section applies also to arrests on warrant, this view is difficult to maintain. The true reason for the day's delay was probably to enable justices to keep regular office hours.)

Be that as it may, the twenty-four-hour rule is a fixed part of police lore and it is used extensively. A great deal of information is obtained by detective officers from suspects who are invited in or detained for questioning. Quite a lot can be done to crack a hard shell simply by questioning over the course of a morning and afternoon.

If the police are deprived of the benefits, real or fanciful, of the twenty-four-hour rule, it will be a serious blow to their investigative techniques. But it should go. The purpose of arrest or detention is not to enable the police to determine whether a crime has been committed: with proper legal authority and backing they should be able to do that anyway. Arrest is for the purposes mentioned in Section 9 and these imply prompt arraignment and a judicial decision on bail. That is, the present practice involves the police in a judicial function that is not properly theirs. If after an arrest they decide that the charges cannot be supported, the courts can always permit them to be dropped.

Apart from its infringement of personal liberty and its obvious incidence on ex-convicts and less favoured people, the twenty-four-hour rule encourages the police to rely unduly on confessions. Confessions, while useful evidence, involve too many dangers of falsehood and of official bullying to be allowed by the courts to be the main stock-in-trade of the detective officer.

But if the rule is to go, there must be something to take its place; for without it, the police do not have sufficient legal authority and backing in the detection and prevention of crime. The straightforward solution is to require more real investigation by those magistrates who now have powers, while investigating crimes, to compel answers *before charges are made*. These powers should be, as they are, subject to protection against self-crimination and subject also to the control of the courts. The coroner is such a magistrate and so, originally, was the justice of the peace.[19] Section 440 of the Criminal Code retains a little-used remnant of a justice's powers to hear evidence before an accused person is brought before him. He holds such a hearing to determine whether to issue a summons or warrant or to act on the complaint at all. To do so, he should find out whether a crime was committed and, if so, who committed it.

A more frequent use of such powers would have several advantages. It would compel recalcitrant witnesses to tell what they knew. By a quirk of the law, while it is an offence to dissuade people from giving the police information about crimes, it is not criminal, except for accessories after the fact, to refuse to give such information.[20] Again, the oath would tend to make accusers and witnesses more accurate and careful than they are in ordinary police statements. Thirdly, the statements would be available to the accused as of right. Moreover, such statements would make it possible to waive preliminary inquiry, a procedure that is not desirable under the present practice. Above all, many ill-founded prosecutions would be stopped at the outset without putting accused persons to any indignity or expense. It is now only too easy to launch a prosecution. But if the hearing is to have any value as an investigation the justice must go and see for himself, as well as listen. He should try to find out the truth rather than merely review the evidence, as is the practice on preliminary inquiries.

There are strong suggestions here of the examining magistrate familiar to European systems. This is not to be disparaged. If our trial system is better (and, on the whole it is, because the adversarial process is better for weighing disputed questions), their preliminary inquiry is more effective. In fact, we would require little or no change in our law to have the advantages of both procedures. The most radical would be to authorize a justice to take evidence when the perpetrator of a crime was unknown. This is not a new idea to our law. Not only do we have the coroner's inquest, the oldest of the common-law courts, but there are other inquiries of the same nature such as those conducted by fire marshalls or mine examiners.

This is a necessary parenthesis to explain the conditions under which the twenty-four-hour rule could be dropped.

The necessity of Section 10 is that of imposing constitutional controls and safeguards on that stage of a criminal prosecution, the detention before trial, where there is most danger of abuse of official powers and where the most scandals have arisen on this continent. On the other hand, the safeguards should not be such that they cripple police investigation or encourage that impudent and seemingly nation-wide conspiracy of criminals and hooligans that is in such a strong position in the United States. The safeguards should not prevent those charged with the safety of the public from getting at the truth and tearing up the roots of crime.

SECTION 11: TRIAL RIGHTS

A speedy and public trial, however important it may be to the litigant, is even more important to the people, who are entitled to know the quality and energy of their judges and the way in which justice is administered. That is why this section is expressed as a mandate to the courts rather than as a right of the plaintiff or defendant or, as in the United States, of the accused in a criminal trial. When King John promised, in Magna Charta, 'to none will we . . . delay right or justice', it is most probable that the suitors in mind were on the civil side. Criminal justice in those days was likely to be swift and sharp; though the criminal law has since become softened and refined, it is not usual for the accused or his counsel to desire a speedy trial. The law's delays work almost invariably for the defence. Witnesses die, go away, lose their wits or memory; the prosecutor's determination becomes dulled and the healing hand of time ameliorates the outrage of the crime and leaves room only for pity for the plight of the accused. This is unjust to the people and to those who have been injured, and it is evident that speedy justice is necessary for the fair administration of the criminal law, within reasonable limits. Nor should the accused be kept dangling.

But in civil matters also, justice delayed is justice undone. Delay leads to forced and unworthy compromises, to despair, cynicism, and a disrespect for the law and its ministers. Delays arise from many causes. In some places there is a dearth of judges, in others an excess. Procedure can be useless and time-wasting or there may be a lack of competent help for the courts. What sanction can be applied in such situations? Do you nonsuit the plaintiff or the defendant? That is hardly just, even if the plaintiff is the state. One major cause of delays is the inability of some judges to come to a decision. This is regulated by law in some places but the law has no teeth in it.[21] So the provision for speedy trials may be only a pious expression of hope, but it should stand, if only as a reminder to all of the need.

The need for public trials goes hand in hand with the right of the citizen to watch and criticize the processes of government. There is some, but very little, of the element of private right in it, to the extent that publicity helps to keep the courts on an even keel. In many cases the accused would be more than happy to have his trial in private, but it is in the public interest that justice be seen to be done, if only that wrongdoers be deterred. The accepted occasions in this country for trials in private are when children are on trial,[22] where the evidence will concern indecencies,[23] or where state security requires that some of the material be kept secret. These are the usual exceptions even in the United States where the right to a speedy and public trial is quite absolute in terms.[24]

The courts exist not only for defendants and accused persons but even more particularly for plaintiffs and others seeking redress. Even-handed justice requires that suitors should not be omitted in any constitutional guarantee of rights that are as important to them as to the respondent parties. So, the second clause deals with the rights of litigants generally, both plaintiff and defendant, civil and criminal, while the third clause declares those rights that experience indicates are more particularly important to defendants.

All litigants deserve an independent and impartial tribunal. As far as the public courts are concerned, independence is based on political arrangements, which it is the aim of Article 5 to ensure. The independence of the domestic tribunals of clubs, unions, trade associations, and the like cannot be so readily provided for, but it is implied in the command for impartiality. Some judicature laws make express provision against partiality,[25] but whether they do or not, it is understood that partiality may deprive a court or judge of jurisdiction and, if there is even a reasonable suspicion of partiality, the judge should take himself out of the case.[26] The mention of domestic tribunals points up the wording of the clause under consideration, which, with the exception of the provision for compulsory attendance of witnesses, can apply equally to both private and public courts.

Many constitutions forbid 'extraordinary' courts, and others stipulate that the court of trial is to be that of a prescribed district, or that no one is to be deprived of his natural judge. The idea behind these expressions is not easy to express concisely and clearly but, in general, it is that the court should not be one invented or set up especially for the case, as it is so easy to rig or pack it against one of the parties. This means that every case should come before its ordinary court, but this way of saying it is again so loose as to permit extremes both of laxity and rigour in its applications. It is difficult to say where the exchequer court, courts martial, and similar courts would fit, under this expression, or what would be the place of arbitration or the well-established system in Canada by which, in the majority of indictable offences, the accused has the right to choose one of three or four trial courts. The expression used is intended to prohibit courts of the *ad hoc* Star Chamber type, and it is probably as effective as any other.

The Sixth Amendment to the United States Constitution gives the accused in federal cases the right 'to have the assistance of counsel for his defence'. This is ambiguous. It might mean merely that he has the right to be heard by counsel, but it has been interpreted to mean that if he is unable to hire a lawyer the court must provide him with legal assistance.[27] This is a very one-sided guarantee. If the idea of state-provided legal aid is to prevail it should apply to the poor plaintiff also. We are not prepared to propose so radical a provision as part of the constitution.

But every litigant should have the right to plead by counsel. On the other hand, lawyers should not have such a monopoly of the right of audience in any court that a party may not appear for himself. It is often said that anyone who acts as his own lawyer has a fool for a client, but this is not always so. Some experienced criminals seem to have an intuition for the cases and courts where they can fare better without counsel. In any case, whether he is acting wisely or foolishly, a man should have the right to plead his own cause if he wishes.

Witnesses in civil cases are usually willing to come to give evidence for the side calling them, which means that compulsory process is needed in such cases only for the reluctant witness. But it is needed; and it is still more necessary in criminal cases because people on the whole have a strong dislike of any entanglement, however innocent, with the criminal law. There seems to be no reason why this safeguard should be limited to accused persons when it is so fundamental to all cases.

The like considerations apply to the right to interpreters. The Canadian Bill of Rights gives not only parties, but witnesses, the right to an interpreter. This is sound enough as a rule of law but there is no need to make constitutional provision for it. After all, if a party is anxious to get across what his witness has to say he can exercise his right to call for an interpreter. Section 11 is probably wide enough to give witnesses the right to an interpreter, but it would not likely be construed in that sense unless the witness were a quasi-party, or in other extraordinary cases.

The third clause of Section 11 catalogues the elements of a just trial as they particularly concern the defendant. The phrase 'Life, Liberty, or Property' derives from the Fifth Amendment to the Constitution of the United States and is repeated in the Fourteenth Amendment. It is a concise summary of the items in the statute of Edward III quoted from the Petition of Right at the opening of this chapter. The Canadian Bill of Rights[28] has a similar but more diffuse phrase which includes 'security of the person' in addition to life, liberty, and enjoyment of property. The addition has no particular value in the context of Section 11 and is not used.

The section uses the word 'Opportunity' because otherwise a default judgment would not be legally possible. The majority of judgments are, in fact, entered in default of contest. What justice requires is that the defendant get adequate notice of the claim and the legal way to fight it if he wants to. The ordinary legal procedures are usually sufficient to give this, although some of the writ forms need to be rewritten to the common understanding. Here again the word 'reasonable' gets into the text, and in this instance it is more closely related to the 'unreasonable' of the searches and seizures banned by the Fourth Amendment of the United States Constitution. It is safe to use in this instance and is, indeed, the only adequate word.

To tell the nature of a claim or charge is to give its legal category with sufficient particulars to identify the transactions in question. It does not require that every legal element of the claim be stated nor that all the particulars be given, but only that there should be enough to let the defendant know the kind and magnitude of the thing he has to face so that, if he decides to contest it, he will be able to prepare properly for the contest and, if he decides not to dispute it, he will be able to know the possible results.[29] The opportunity to prepare is a counterpoise, in favour of the defence, of the 'speedy trial' clause. A trial can be too speedy. The prosecution can usually choose its time so as to be ready, but the defence, especially in criminal cases, often has difficulty in locating witnesses, and there are other valid reasons to avoid rushing into trials.

The right of confrontation and especially of cross-examination of opposition witnesses is essential to our adversarial method of trial. There are some cross-examiners, it is true, who can make a witness deny his own parentage, but cross-examination is the best way to get a witness to qualify too extreme a statement or to expose bias, malice, carelessness, defect of faculties, or other things that affect the value of evidence. Cross-examination is least effective in dealing with an intelligent but moderate liar (of which there exist not a few) and strongest against an honest but biased witness.

The right to the opportunity to make a full answer and defence, borrowed from Sections 557 (3) and 709 (1) of the Criminal Code, is a residual clause designed to include any safeguards that are commonly accepted but not expressly mentioned in Section 11. This might include, for example, the right to take evidence abroad on commission or even appeals against errors in law made at the trial.[30]

The need for Section 11 is the need for guarantees of just process in trials and other hearings.

SECTION 12: RIGHTS OF THE ACCUSED

It need hardly be said that the rights specially provided for persons accused of crime are not intended to protect the guilty but the innocent. It follows from this point of view that no safeguard need be included that would not be required by an innocent man. There are other considerations, however, and one of them is our political tradition against torture, the Star Chamber oath, and, as a consequence, any form of self-crimination.

The presumption of innocence is, on the whole, needed for the protection of the innocent. There are not-guilty people whose characters, abilities, and histories could not stand the burden of proving themselves innocent, and there are perfectly honest people who could not do so in some circumstances.

The presumption of innocence, in one aspect, is merely the ordinary burden on the party putting forth a claim of proving it. It becomes more stringent, however, when the proof must be 'according to law', because the criminal law requires proof beyond a reasonable doubt to rebut this presumption. There is this qualification: while the Crown must prove its case beyond a reasonable doubt it does not have to disprove every defence (and, in particular, the defence of insanity) beyond a reasonable doubt.[31] And it may take advantage of certain *prima facie* and other presumptions if it introduces the evidence that gives rise to them. So, the rule of proof beyond a reasonable doubt cannot be made absolute without subverting the present law. To subvert that law would be unjust in many instances, such as the defence of insanity, because the existing rule represents a sound and prudent approach to the problems involved.

Short of making the presumption absolute, however, it can be made universal by constitutional guarantee, and this could be a welcome change. It would at least give the courts a means of discouraging the other branches of government from loading undue burdens on the defence. In particular, it would give a good basis for the contention that the law of presumptions cannot be arbitrary: there must be some foundation in practical reason for the presumption, or it becomes a deprivation of the right to be presumed innocent. This might involve some recasting of the liquor laws but probably not to the extent some think should be done.

It should not be necessary to enact, for example, that a court may infer that whisky is intoxicating. Many such rules were put in the liquor laws because magistrates disliked the laws and interpreted them with absurd strictness.

The right of jury trial stated in Section 12 is as close an approximation to our present law as can be made in a concise statement, and is sufficient for constitutional purposes. In Canada, there is a small group of indictable offences, including petty thefts and frauds, some assaults, and some disorderly-conduct crimes, where the accused usually is not entitled to a jury trial.[32] The jury, on the whole, is a good institution, although in ordinary criminal cases judges give a consistently higher standard of justice simply because of knowledge and experience. But in any case involving the common feeling of mankind, the collective reaction of twelve is usually more reliable than that of any judge. And in a trial with any political overtones, the jury offers an indispensable bulwark against any improper enforcement of the law. That is the main reason for putting trial by jury into a constitutional guarantee. There are other cases, such as libels and homicides, where the courts should have the views of a random sample of the community to guide them. The formula in Section 12 tries to sum up these various thoughts, and the wording includes attempts and conspiracies as well as the complete crimes.

The grand jury is a different matter. In the United States it is guaranteed in the case of any federal indictable offence by the Fifth Amendment. In that country, the grand jury has earned an honourable place in life and politics by challenging crime and corruption, and it deserves its constitutional position. But it was accepted long since that the Canadian counterpart could make no presentment on its own but must take or reject what the prosecution offered.[33] It plays no political part, high or low, and only a lingering judicial one. Only Newfoundland, Nova Scotia, Ontario, and Prince Edward Island retain it, and there seems to be no virtue in trying to restore it where it has been abolished.

In every case, whether civil or criminal, it is possible to raise the plea of *res judicata,* that is, that the issue has already been decided between the parties by a competent court. This is a defence. The only cases that cause difficulty are those where the charge is phrased differently or laid under a different law; but the jurisprudence on the question is adequate. In the United States this is known as protection against double jeopardy and is provided in federal cases by the Fifth Amendment. The wording is construed to prevent appeals by the prosecution. We have not followed it in the ordinary application of the principle. In Canada, the prosecution is entitled to appeal against errors in law, and the word 'lawfully' in the draft would preserve this right. The principle as drafted is limited to indictable offences and expresses the law as it is. In summary conviction cases, either party can obtain a new trial before a slightly higher judge by a routine procedure. Our appeal system works well and is actually beneficial to the accused, because trial judges know that any errors they make in favour of the accused can be corrected and are not so prone to determine questions in favour of the prosecution as, it is said, English judges are inclined to be.

Protection against self-crimination is not an inherent and necessary part of due process. The reason for the rule is not fairness to the witness or any fundamental right to be silent, but it exists to prevent the abuse of official powers by torture or harsh treatment, and the resultant danger of falsehood.[34]

The privilege against self-crimination was developed by the courts as a protest and a safeguard against the habits of the executive in Tudor and Stuart times. It was the privilege of a witness and did not apply to the accused until, late in the last century, he was permitted to be a witness at his trial. In Canada, we have a further provision that, if the accused does not give evidence, the court or prosecution counsel may not comment on that.[35]

Parallel to the witness's privilege, there grew up the law on confessions, which is essentially another stage of the same problem but has become a different and much more elaborate law. There is a current fancy that an accused person should not be required to do anything that might provide evidence against him, such as walking a straight line, attending an identification parade, giving samples of his handwriting, or the like. That is not the law and there is no reason why it should be. On the contrary, everyone may justly be obliged to help in the administration of justice so long as the methods do not involve dangers of secret bullying or improper official pressures resulting in falsehoods.

Accordingly, Section 12 contains a concise summary of our law, which is a satisfactory law and differs from that in the United States. The privilege against compulsion is limited to accused persons and is not available to witnesses generally, but the latter are given protection against prosecution if they are compelled to answer, unless they commit perjury. No attempt has been made to extend the exception to the offence of giving contradictory evidence.

The need for the clauses of Section 12 seems to be fairly obvious.

SECTION 13: MENTAL AND PHYSICAL INTEGRITY

We are a lot more tender-hearted in handing out punishment than were our fathers, and there should be no difficulty in securing a constitutional ban on torture. But we have lost a lot of the respect for the individual that our ancestors had: we find acceptable, not in the name of punishment, but for the sake of health and sanitation, things they would count as enormities.[36]

A human being is entitled to remain whole, both mentally and physically, at least while he is legally innocent. And even those punishments that involve the taking of life or members must be regulated by the ends, the aims, of punishment, which, in addition to retribution and deterrence, include reformation. There is no valid reason in a modern society to dock a man's ear or nose or chop off his hands. If he is to live, he will need all his parts and faculties to get by. It can be safely urged that such things have no place in wise penal practice. Very few will dissent.

On the non-penal side of the picture, there are three or four problems, such as compulsory vaccination, fluoridation, blood transfusion, and surgical operations, that nag the public conscience. The opponents of such practices further compound the difficulties by disseminating practical doubts as to their efficacy, but these doubts have little to do with the political morality of the practices, whatever weight they may have on the policy of the laws. A reasonable interpretation of Section 13 would permit some compulsory medication, such as vaccination to prevent the spread of disease, but would forbid it in most other cases.

While the protection of bodily integrity would invalidate any law authorizing the forcible taking of blood samples to test for alcoholic impairment, there is no reason why the Saskatchewan statute[37] that requires a motorist to submit to testing or have his driving licence suspended should not stand. The compulsion of the statute is a just and reasonable one and is directly related to the purpose of the test.[38]

Section 13 does not employ the phrase 'cruel and unusual punishments'. This goes back to the British Bill of Rights of 1689, whence it was incorporated verbatim as part of the Eighth Amendment of the United States Constitution, proposed in 1789. It is the obvious source of Article 5 of the Universal Declaration of Human Rights, which reads:

> No one shall be subjected to torture or to cruel, inhuman or degrading treatment or punishment.

This clearly influenced clause (b) of Section 2 of the Canadian Bill of Rights, which is, in essence:

> 2. . . . no law of Canada shall be construed or applied so as to . . .
> (b) impose or authorize the imposition of cruel and unusual treatment or punishment. . . .

This is very hard to get your teeth into. In the United States, the phrase 'cruel and unusual punishments' has been mainly directed against torture and disproportionate penalties, such as

ten years' imprisonment for petty theft. 'Treatment' may add
something to the phrase: modern penology has tended to emphasize treatment rather than punishment. But it is not wise to try
to straitjacket the courts in dealing with offenders when we consider all the elements that enter into a sentence. A constitutional
rule of proportion between sentences could easily make them
subject to a régime of mere pedantry. There is, however, a real
need for a ban on torture. The vicious devil that lurks in us all
requires such an ever-present curb.

Is there any better word for torture than 'torture' itself? Despite
the age of the phrase 'cruel and unusual punishments', there is
no certain jurisprudence upon it. It is vague and general and its
content is entirely up to the courts. There is no virtue in using
it, if it is meant to restrain the judiciary with the rest of the government. The constitution-makers abroad have not been any
more successful or precise. Germany enacts that 'Detained persons may be subjected neither to mental nor to physical ill-treat-
ment.'[39] Italy's constitution says, 'Any physical or moral violence
to persons who are in any way subject to restrictions of liberty
is punished',[40] and again, 'Penalties may not consist of treatment
contrary to humane feeling and must be directed towards the re-
education of the condemned.'[41] Japan's constitution (drafted by
the American Military Government) gives, 'The infliction of torture by any public officer and cruel punishments are absolutely
forbidden',[42] and this brings us back to our original terms. Of
these, the word 'torture' is preferable.

Thus, Sir Edward Coke knew well enough what he meant by
torture when he boasted that it was not part of the law of England. It was true that warrants for torture were not issued by
the common-law courts or judges and were not part of the common-law judicial processes, but Coke himself had signed them
as a member of the Privy Council and was well aware of the executive use of torture from his work as a prosecutor. Indeed, the
phrase quoted from the 1689 Bill of Rights was not an idle one,
as official torture was in use not too long before.[43]

Section 13 is intended to apply not only to courts and officials
but to everybody. It is designed to prevent a person being

chopped up or misused, and it is careful to include mental torture within the ban. It will not prevent lawful searches, seizures, and imprisonments, and even corporal punishment. On a fair reading, of course, they do not come within the terms, but in any case they are patent and obvious exceptions, analogous to those the courts have found to the 'equal protection' clause.

Here again, Section 13 is not essential to the federative idea but it is necessary for our concept of freedom. Recent history makes it all the more pertinent and important to include it.

SECTION 14: NO 'EX POST FACTO' LAW

The Canadian Bill of Rights does not contain any phrase that could be construed, without great ingenuity, as forbidding retro-active criminal law. This is one more indication that the Bill was aimed at the courts, which did not need its admonitions, rather than at the legislatures and the executive governments, which did. In contrast, the Constitution of the United States, even before the enactment of that country's Bill of Rights, was careful to provide curbs of the Congress and the executive. One of them is Clause 3 of Article I, Section 9, which reads:

> No bill of attainder or *ex post facto* law shall be passed.

Section 10 of the same article applies the same law to the states. We do not need to consider bills of attainder, which would be outlawed by Sections 4 and 11 of this Article. *Ex post facto* law has been defined in the United States[44] as every law that:

1. Makes criminal an action done before the passing of the law, which was innocent when done, and punishes such an action.

2. Aggravates a crime, or makes it greater than it was, when committed.

3. Changes punishment, and inflicts a greater punishment, than the law annexed to the crime when committed.

4. Alters the legal rules of evidence, and receives less or different testimony than the law required at the time of the commission of the offence in order to convict the offender.

Ex post facto laws are thus restricted to criminal laws, and retroactive civil or tax statutes are not included.

The first three classes listed are the same in substance as the provisions of our Section 14. The fourth class should not be accepted as a valid one. It differs in kind from the other three, which are obviously dictated by justice to the accused. That is, a man is entitled to do anything not forbidden by law and should not be thereafter penalized for doing it, even if it is an immoral act. And a penalty increased beyond what the offender could look forward to when considering the offence does not satisfy any of the criteria of a proper penalty.

But criminal procedure and evidence can be made retrospective without injustice. To do so merely puts better tools in the hands of the prosecution and is thus strictly analogous to an improvement in the science of detection taking place after the offence. The only argument against retrospective procedural and evidential rules is the one derived from the 'sporting theory' of the administration of justice: i.e., since the accused based his chances of escaping detection and punishment on the rules existing at the time of the offence it would be unfair and unsporting to change them. This is patent nonsense. The other rules concerning the definition of crimes and punishment protect the legally innocent or, at least, the comparatively innocent, but the 'sporting' rule protects the guilty. Accordingly, the 'sporting theory' has not been accepted. Section 14 has been made explicit so that we will not have to rely on judicial interpretation of an uncertain Latin phrase for this freedom.

Most interpretation acts require statutes to be construed in the spirit of this section and so as not to affect vested civil rights; but the only aspect of the matter that is essential to liberty is the prohibition against the retroactive enactment of crimes and penalties.

SECTION 15: NO WRONG WITHOUT A REMEDY

It is curious that there is no explicit statement in any of the constitutions we have considered that every wrong shall have a remedy. There are expressions from which it can be gathered, and it is probably implied in most 'due process' clauses, but the closest to the idea itself is that contained in Article 8 of the Universal Declaration of Human Rights:

> Everyone has the right to an effective remedy by the competent national tribunals for acts violating the fundamental rights granted him by the constitution or by law.

This might be criticized on several points. For example, in the view of the law every remedy is designed to be effective, but in fact a lot depends on the status, wealth, and disposition of the person against whom the remedy is directed. Nor is there any apparent reason why it should be directed to fundamental rights only. But it is good and fills a gap.

Section 15 may be implied by Section 11, but the latter does not make any express provision for enforcement of the rights and obligations determined under it. Section 15, therefore, completes the judicial process by ensuring that it come to a practical conclusion. Cases of wrongs without remedy have existed in the past.[45] In any case, the provisions of Section 15 are so obviously essential to complete the order of due process that it needs no apology.

SECTION 16: COMPENSATION FOR EXPROPRIATION

This must be important because most written constitutions have something to say about it. The Canadian Bill of Rights is not explicit on the subject, but the right to just or due compensation is probably implied in the right not to be deprived of the enjoyment of property except by due process of law in clause (a) of Section 1.

The first part of Section 16 is a full restatement of the dictate of the Fifth Amendment of the United States Constitution that private property shall not 'be taken for public use without just compensation'. The second part of the section is intended to lay down the method of computing compensation justly. The latter seems to be desirable because the various and somewhat contrary opinions in the case law under the existing expropriation statutes are likely to subvert this safeguard otherwise. These opinions, of course, are based on the wording of the statutes, but there is a considerable body of general law on compensation of this type that has, unfortunately, been somewhat warped by the standards of the dominant statutes, the Exchequer Court Act and the Expropriation Act, both federal laws.[46]

These have, somehow, firmly established the idea that it is the price or value that the courts have to determine by substituting the opinions of a reasonable buyer and a reasonable seller for the obstinate minds of the state and the owner. Thus, the courts will say, the test to be applied is what the owner, as a prudent buyer, would be prepared to pay for the property rather than be deprived of it.[47] However useful this is, it is not fundamental enough. This is emphasized by another test used by the courts, the price that a willing buyer and a willing seller would agree on. This smacks even more of the market-place and the market-place may have little to do with the loss in question. For it is the loss to the owner that is truly in issue in all these cases.

As commonly used in relation to loss of property, 'compensation' is the more usual word where the taking is lawful, and 'damages' where the taking is unlawful.[48] The terms are really equivalent, however. Where property is taken unlawfully, in trespass to goods or trespass to land, punitive or exemplary damages may be awarded to the owner as compensation for the malice, the illegality, and the outrage of the wrong, and as punishment against the wrongdoer for the same reasons. These are in addition to the actual pecuniary loss. Apart from such damages, the object in both expropriation cases and in tort law is to assess the actual loss suffered by the claimant, and it is obvious that the same principles of assessment will apply and should apply. This may well work out in a similar way to what we now have, but it will tend to discourage the fanciful and misleading idea that the courts should try to play buyer and seller. The buyer-and-seller technique works substantial justice in dealing with properties of a common, numerous class, such as the ordinary dwelling, but it is little or no help with unique-purpose properties, such as a steel-rolling mill. It also can cope with consequential damages, such as business disruption, only by the further fiction that the seller would take that into consideration in setting his price. By such dodges, the market-value test, the willing-buyer-seller test, the owner's-fair-estimate test, and other tests arrive at approximately just and similar results, but always in a second-hand way and with an ever-present danger of overlooking the purpose of the assessment – to make a full compensation in money to the owner not only for the property taken but for whatever values he has lost by the taking.

Our eight 'due process' sections form a reasonably complete code for the just administration of the law. As in every other case their value would lie in the way they are construed, respected, and upheld. A too-pedantic reading, under the influence of generous but unbalanced pity for the oppressed, would be just as useless in the end as a tendency to ignore or override them. They have been so drawn, in most cases, that each is a balance of law and of limitation, or of a rule containing its own exceptions. That is, the implications from common sense that are generally read into the seemingly absolute commands of the United States Bill of Rights and other such documents are stated here in the text itself, although in a general way, so that the law says all that it means and means all that it says. This is an act of faith, perhaps. No law in such general terms exists, but the ingenuity of the ungodly can read into it things never intended.

No law is perfect as no human thing is perfect. Perhaps we should be glad of this. Professor Parkinson warns us that when any human institution attains perfection it immediately suffers a complete and catastrophic decline.[49] This contains both truth and poetry. Let us rejoice that in Canada we have not only the urge to improve things but room enough for improvement to keep us busy for a long time to come.

CHAPTER 26

Economic and Social Rights

In the classical constitutional instruments of the seventeenth and eighteenth centuries, the individual is paramount. We see each citizen as an atom of a rarefied society, alone and untouchable, with his property, his houses, his family, his slaves, sharing with him the benefit of the protecting law. His traffic with his neighbours, if it was peaceable, was not the concern of the state, except to protect and enforce the obligation of his contracts. The law existed to prevent others from interfering in his sphere and not to inhibit him from doing what he would within it. Even a state with the absolute parliamentary supremacy of Great Britain would not dream of exercising its powers in any general scheme to control life in business, the family, or other associations. Restraints there were indeed, relics of the very different medieval and Renaissance outlooks, but the spirit of the age was individual liberty, and it ruled political and legal thought until well into the nineteenth century.

But the seeds of change were already sown, or, a juster metaphor, the perennial flowers of justice and compassion, with other, ranker, weeds, again came to the surface. It is impossible to give a complete and balanced account of the change, so many and varied were its causes, but in due course a powerful political and social movement, culminating in the extremes of collectivism, came to dominate the minds of men, even those minds that opposed it.

In the old society, practically everyone had a status, a claim on some firm place in the world – property, a craft, a fixed abode. The industrial revolution began to undermine this but the social framework was not shattered until the political revolutions.

The new constitutions take these changed social conditions for granted and prescribe certain rights and duties respecting them. This is a theme common to both the Marxist statutes (such as the 1936 constitution of the U.S.S.R. and that of East Germany) and the democratic post-war laws of Italy, Germany, and Japan. And that of Eire, although anything but Marxist in its content, is vitally concerned with the social relationships.

Any constitution made with an eye to the future must, therefore, take into consideration not only the social rights and obligations that we have come to accept as necessary but also some individual rights, formerly taken for granted, that are in peril in our collectivist-minded world. Capitalism itself is now dominated by the Organization Man.

The sections considered in this chapter try to achieve a balance between the needs of the modern world, even the Welfare State, and the survival of individual freedom and integrity. This is in the hope that our system will attain a balance in the economic field analogous to the balanced political structure that Aristotle called a polity.

SECTION 17: THE RIGHT TO WORK

To plagiarize the Scriptures, man was not made for the economy but the economy for man. We do not exist to feed the furnaces of Mammon. On the contrary, any economy that does not serve the human needs of all of its constituents is not a sound one and wants correction. No doubt even those who propose unchecked competition as the sure guide to a prosperous economy are human and profess that their remedy is the best for everyone, at least in the long run. The trouble is that men live and die very often in the short run and the readjustments imposed by unregulated economic forces are too drastic.

The ordinary man wants to work, either to support himself or because he cannot bear idleness beyond a certain point. The strength and duration of this appetite shows how firmly based is the right to work. Unfortunately, the phrase 'right to work' has acquired in the United States, and to some extent in this country, an evil aura because in the former it was applied to state constitutional amendments of a kind that organized labour considered anti-union. The proponents claimed, of course, that they were designed only to cut the unions down to size and much of the contention took the form of name-calling. We are not concerned with these questions here (they arise under Section 19) except to the extent that occupational associations attempt to get legal backing for a monopoly of any trade or profession.

More and more, associations begin to come between man and man.[1] Are you being sued for an automobile accident? Your insurer will insist on defending or settling the case for you. Are you giving to charity? United Appeal will distribute it for you. Do you want to see a teacher about your children? The Home and School Association arranges a night to queue up. And do you belong to a union? It makes your contract of employment for you, takes up grievances, collects for and pays out sick benefits, and probably operates other welfare plans.

The non-associated man in this world of ours is a veritable midget, almost a nonentity. To survive in the new feudalism, the individual must be fixed with certain rights of which the most important is the right to practise his trade or profession without lawful denial unless he is a bad workman.

This applies to barristers as well as bricklayers, to plasterers as well as physicians. If a man in the legal or medical profession commits a serious crime, such as rape or theft, even though it does not happen in any professional circumstances, he is usually barred from practice. This would be conduct unbecoming a barrister or physician. Would the section permit this? The problem is more verbal than real. The public has to trust things of high personal or monetary value to professional people, and anyone with a criminal character would be incompetent to accept or exercise these trusts. But, with all just respect for them, moral incompetency should be harder to establish in other trades and occupations. Thus they might not, because of the section, be able to exclude convicts from their ranks. A dishonest carpenter is a nuisance but a dishonest lawyer is an abomination.

The section will not prevent occupational associations from having police powers over their own members or from setting proper standards of competence. It will bar arbitrary exclusions, such as some trades are suspected of applying, on account of race, colour, lack of family connection, or the like.

The right to work does not impose on anyone the duty of providing work but merely the duty of not preventing it.

What about the right not to work? This usually conjures up a picture of the idle rich. Some states forbid idleness. The Stalin constitution of the U.S.S.R., in Article 12, quotes St. Paul (without acknowledgment): 'He who does not work, neither let him eat.'[2] The Italian Constitution also, in Article 5, declares the duty of every citizen, according to his own capacities and choice, to develop an activity or function that contributes to the material or spiritual progress of society. The 1946 French Constitution states that everyone has the obligation to work and the right to obtain employment. This appears to be the beginning of a consensus.

But the right to withhold labour is surely as basic as the right to work. Exercised in concert it becomes the right to strike, which is generally accepted as a human right, at least in the West.[3] Should this be available only to groups? Is it not, in fact, another aspect of the protection from slavery and legally enforced servitude that is made unlawful by Section 8 of this Article?

In sum, Section 17 does three things: (1) it declares the right to work and so ensures that no one may be forbidden by law to work; (2) it prevents a professional society that has, in law or in fact, the control of the profession or trade from denying practice to anyone except for incompetence or misconduct in the trade; (3) it entrenches the right to quit and to strike. It is a little hard to guess how it would be construed with respect to public employees.

The need for this section is the need to safeguard the individual against the gigantic pressures of modern life that tend to squeeze him out of the field of his chosen work or even any work.

SECTION 18: THE RIGHT TO PRODUCTIVE PROPERTY

Labour is not the only means of making a living. Land, and labour applied to land, are the primary sources of wealth, but without capital, land and labour yield very meagre results. No one disputes the fact that capital – wealth capable of being used to produce more wealth – represents the result of applying labour, in some cases generations of labour, to land, but the lawful owner of the capital rightfully represents that labour. Marx's idea that there is a surplus value that the capitalist somehow withholds from the wages due to labour has been completely discredited by the practice of the Marxist economies. Indeed, the chief economic dogma of Marxism is the necessity for public ownership of the bulk of productive property, that is, capital. It is in this sense that the U.S.S.R. declares itself to be a socialist state,[4] although it permits 'the small private economy of individual peasants and handicraftsmen'.[5] That is, socialism, even in this formal sense, does not preclude private ownership of some productive property and, of course, it does not demand public ownership of non-productive property, such as houses and consumer goods.

The public ownership of the bulk of productive property, of capital, denies human rights and liberties. It says 'No!' to one of the chief functions of mankind. It substitutes for the normal way of exercising that function the spirit and customs of the hive, the commune, the megalopolis. It deprives a man of an essential means of expressing and developing his personality and turns him into a worker bee.

There are a myriad reasons for the right to private productive property. Certainly the most appealing is that property and the means of production are essential for our liberty. Productive property secures liberty in two chief ways. It furnishes a means of exercising the creative appetite free of the bounds imposed by the directions or interference of others. It also enables an individual to subsist and resist, to live on his own, as it were, in circumstances where society, or some part of it, is adverse to him. No one, of course, can live entirely to himself, but even a small amount of property can support a decent independence, not complete but enough, from contumely or outrageous fortune, from economic dictation as well as social oppression.

It is not inconsistent with true liberty that the man of property is more legally vulnerable and hence more responsible than the proletarian. The latter has more ability to do harm and to go wrong with impunity, but these are no real part of freedom. The ability and means of the proletarian to do what he wishes within the limits of true liberty are much less than those of the proprietor.

Property, although it requires the protection and hence the recognition and definition of the law, is not a legal institution but a natural one. That is, the law did not create the régime of property but found it existing. It is probable, in fact, that law enforcement came into being as much to safeguard property as to repress personal violence.

Most modern constitutions, including that of the U.S.S.R., recognize the fundamental right to property and inheritance.[6] The spirit of most of them is similar to Article 17 of the Universal Declaration of Human Rights:

> 1. Everyone has the right to own property alone as well as in association with others.
> 2. No one shall be arbitrarily deprived of his property.

But very few of these charters specify the right to own productive property. Curiously, East Germany makes provision for the rights of authors, inventors, and artists,[7] but the only constitution among those we have considered that is at all definite about private enterprise is that of Eire. Even there the provision (Article 45, Section 2) is phrased as a direction to the *Oireachtas* (Parliament) and is not cognizable by the courts. Moreover, the right is stated in very carefully balanced terms, worth considering:

> 2. The State shall, in particular, direct its policy towards securing
> (i) That the citizens (all of whom, men and women equally, have the right to an adequate means of livelihood) may through their occupations find the means of making reasonable provisions for their domestic needs.
> (ii) That the ownership and control of the material resources of the community may be so distributed amongst private indi-

viduals and the various classes as best to subserve the common good.

(iii) That, especially the operation of free competition shall not be allowed so to develop as to result in the concentration of the ownership or control of essential commodities in a few individuals to the common detriment.

(iv) That in what pertains to the control of credit the constant and predominant aim shall be the welfare of the people as a whole.

(v) That there may be established on the land in economic security as many families as in the circumstances shall be practicable.

The section is a rather definite example of how present-day statements on property are likely to be qualified, in contrast, for example, to Article 17 of the French Revolutionary *Déclaration des droits de l'homme et du citoyen:*

Property being an inviolable and sacred right, no one can be deprived of it, except when public necessity, lawfully established, clearly requires it, and under the condition of a just and previous indemnity.

Our draft section does not attempt to express all the social purposes of the Irish text but it is based on like principles. It does not, of course, go beyond saying that a man is entitled to acquire property *if he can,* but the kind and quantity of property is strongly indicated. It is productive property that is specified and the section thus rejects doctrinaire socialism. On the other hand it would not prevent a large degree of public ownership.

The phrase 'proper Support' is akin to the phrase 'proper maintenance' used in the Testator's Family Maintenance Acts and might be construed in the same way. It should be given a more liberal interpretation, however, as the purpose of the law is different. The draft section would not bar the curbs that our society thinks fit to put on the accumulation of great wealth.

It might be argued that the provision for transfer by will would undermine the Testator's Family Maintenance Acts just mentioned. These acts interfere with the effect of wills if the testator has not made provision for the proper maintenance of his dependants. Such a construction is hardly likely in view of the express condition of the section that the property be for the support of the owner and his dependants. Nevertheless, it is a point to be considered. A similar argument with respect to deeds and dower (where it remains to plague the conveyancer) would meet a similar reply.

The section is necessary in an orderly structure of fundamental freedoms.

SECTION 19: FREEDOM OF ASSOCIATION

Freedom of association is one of the most ancient liberties noted in the law. For this we have the testimony of the Twelve Tables of Rome (*c.* 454 B.C.), which declare:

> *Ut sodalibus legem sibi ferre liceat.*[8]

This was expounded by Gaius to mean that the law gives power to associates to make any pact for themselves that they please so long as they do not breach the limits of public law.[9] This is quite in tune with our own approach and is remarkable, considering the importance of status in the ancient world and the lesser importance of contract. It may be that this latitude of action explains why we feel more at home in Roman society than we do in the Greek world, despite the inspiration that the latter has given to our mental life and despite the remaining very great impact of its literature. The Greeks were, in fact, more totalitarian in their view of the relationship of man to society, no doubt because of their strong sense of membership in the state.

Article 20 of the Universal Declaration of Human Rights is a modern echo of the ancient text:

> 1. Everyone has the right to freedom of peaceful assembly and association.
> 2. No one can be compelled to belong to an association.[10]

This might be criticized for more than one reason. It confuses freedom of assembly, a citizens' right that we have incorporated in Section 6 of Article 2,[11] with freedom of association, which has long been recognized as a human right. The right of assembly exists for political purposes but the right of association for economic, religious, and other social ends.

The draft section takes the word 'peaceable' from the First Amendment to the United States Constitution. The interpretation in that country gives the word a very wide extension: conduct is peaceable unless the circumstances are such as 'to create a clear and present danger' of things the legislature rightfully prohibits.[12] In *Boucher* v. *R.*,[13] the Supreme Court of Canada came to a rather similar conclusion about sedition. They held that an intention 'to promote feelings of ill-will and hostility between different classes of subjects' cannot be seditious unless the 'intended, or natural and probable consequences of such promotion of ill-will and hostility is to produce disturbance of or resistance to the authority of lawfully constituted government'.[14] One would hope, however, that when the right is not exercised and challenged on political grounds, the ambit of what is peaceable would be determined by the ordinary criminal law. In fact, the ordinary legal sense of 'peaceable' is 'not contrary to the criminal law'.

Although the laws of the United States against cartels and monopolies, the Anti-Trust laws, are valid, the legal history of the word 'peaceable' below the border makes it prudent to insert in our Section 19 the provision for forbidding or curbing associations that are too powerful for the good of the people. No loophole should be left in the law that would permit such powers to contend that they may not be trammelled.

There are certain associations that exercise public functions, including police powers over their members, for the general benefit. Such are the law societies to which lawyers are compelled to belong. Because these corporations are created for public purposes their constitutions are usually more directly regulated by governments. In these points, they differ from those private societies that try to coerce people to belong, mostly employers' and labour groups. There seems to be no just reason, in principle, against compelling an individual to belong to a public body, created for public purposes and administered on our accepted political principles, whether it is a school district, a regiment, a civil-defence squad, or a professional society. On the other hand, to yield to private bodies, formed by individuals for private ends and governed by their own compacts, the right to compel the

unwilling to become members is, both in theory and as a matter
of practical experience, to submit the weak to a new and repulsive
bondage.

It should be emphasized that the prohibition against compulsory membership does not do certain things. It does not ban compulsory collective bargaining nor does it prevent the check-off
of union dues for all employees, non-union as well as union (the
Rand formula). It may not even prevent the closed or union
shop, although it is arguable that it should where the circumstances constitute a labour monopoly. On the other hand, 'compelled' would not be limited in meaning to compulsion of law
but should apply to any intentional effort to force a non-member
to join an association.

The justification of this section is the justification of freedom
itself. Freedom is nothing if it cannot be exerted in co-operation
with others. On the other hand, the justification for the two
provisos is the preservation of the freedom of the state, the people, and the individual from the great combinations of our era.
For, however benevolent their purposes and beneficent their
works, they cannot operate on the same scale as the individual
or on an equal plane with him, unless his position is fortified or
they are suitably handicapped. The section is not put forward
to destroy corporations and unions. Far from it. It is designed
to give everyone greater freedom of association while ensuring
that the increasing complexity of social structure does not warp
human nature or snuff out freedom. This very complexity is a
means to greater achievement and hence to greater liberty, if we
can only keep its engine on the right track.

SECTION 20: FREEDOM OF MARRIAGE

The most natural, the most necessary, and the primary association formed by man is the family, and it is formed by marriage.
The primacy, necessity, and naturalness give the family and marriage a strong claim to independence, an independence from the
state that is not absolute but that applies to certain vital elements,
especially the formation of the bond, its character, and its immediate purpose. But the property and other civil rights that

depend on marriage are established and maintained by the law, which can rightly demand that the fact and the conditions of marriage be made known and certain. The independence of marriage, although liable to be thus qualified, is none the less necessary and real.

Freedom of marriage obviously implies the right to marry. But it does not imply the right to marry at any age, although here we have a possible conflict between civil regulations and the provisions of Section 20. Such conflict need never occur in fact, however.

Freedom of marriage is not limited to the right to marry. It includes the right to have children, a right that has been accepted to date and that should be stoutly maintained until we are ready to concede that human breeding should be conducted on stud-farm principles.

Freedom of marriage also means that 'marriage shall be entered into only with the free and full consent of the intending spouses'.[15] But the right to refuse a marriage means more than that. If a man or woman cannot be forced to choose any particular partner it follows that he or she cannot be forced to choose any partner. So, the right to refuse a marriage involves the right to refuse to marry, the right not only to be single but to make the single state a vocation, a career. This is not a popular notion at some times and places. That is all the more reason why it needs to be affirmed. Indeed, there is some aspect of nearly every basic right that on occasion collides head on with popular feeling. That is why such rights cannot be entrusted to the will of a bare majority for their security.

In the Western tradition, which is that of both Jews and Christians, marriage is monogamous. That is, it is what Lord Russell, one of its chief critics, calls a one-to-one relationship. Monogamy is the norm, the standard pattern, and polygamy a complexity that arises in special circumstances, such as a large and persistent excess of one sex over the other, or else in exceptional cultures, such as those of the higher hunters or pastoral nomads.[16]

We are fortunate indeed that monogamous marriage is the accepted basis of our society, and the section states the existing law. It is also the existing law that every marriage is made until death parts the spouses. As far as the law is concerned, people do not marry 'until divorce do us part', because divorce is not an incident of a normal marriage, not something contemplated at the wedding, but an exceptional and radical remedy for breaches not considered then at all. That is, the premises of the divorce laws include the principle that marriage is intended to be life-long. The validity of divorce is denied, not by reference to that principle, but by denying that a breach of the marital obliga-tions frustrates the contract or warrants rescinding it, or by denying the competence of the state and the courts to legislate or adjudicate upon the subject.

It is full time that this last denial was made on the authority of a constitutional act, to save the institution of marriage from the mire in which state intervention has trapped it. No one is satisfied today with the laws on divorce: a large party would do away with it altogether and another large party would enlarge the grounds of suit to a radical extent. There is no consensus on the subject except that the present law is bad. The legislature and the courts are, in fact, continually enforcing an idea of ma-trimony that belongs to no one's morality. It is a compromise between civil and religious ideas and one that most people find repugnant in some aspects.

There are two alternatives to the ungainly straitjacket of state control of marriage. In the more radical, the state would not legislate upon marriage at all. The marital relations of the part-ners would be regulated not by law but by their consciences, and their civil obligations by whatever contract they might choose to make. With respect to the care of offspring, the law would impose exactly the same obligations on the married and the un-married. Such a separation of the family and the state would be quite analogous to the separation of church and state that exists under secular constitutions, such as that of the United States, France, or the U.S.S.R. A major objection to such a solu-tion is that, while feasible, it would be unjust and disruptive of society. The state owes the family its protection and support because the family is the natural basis of a decent community.

Liberty demands high moral standards and these are not widely attainable without a good and stable family life. To try to ignore the family, which is what the solution amounts to, is in itself to down-grade it in the popular view.

The other solution is to give the family its rightful independence while legally recognizing the fact that most marriages are made in relation to some religious pattern and sustaining them on the basis of that pattern. There are differences, for example, between the Catholic and Orthodox views, the Jewish view, and the many Protestant views, although the last named have a great deal in common.

Such a solution is neither extreme nor unworkable. It is designated a 'personal law' and is in effect in many countries with people of different cultures or religions, such as India, Israel, and Nigeria. It is the obvious answer to the impasse now existing in this country because of the profoundly different moral convictions of the main religious groups. Paradoxically, it is most likely to meet opposition among the more conservative confessions, because it would allow laxer views on matrimony to prevail on occasion. For those to whom it is an indissoluble sacrament, this would be an objective evil that they might tolerate but could never commend. To others, not so concerned, but upholding strict views, such a change would threaten to drive the unstable into the more indulgent churches. While these notions are entitled to some weight, the latter outcome is unlikely: it would be a strange couple that would deliberately pick out a divorce-minded church to be married in. On the contrary, most men, most of the time, want stability in their circumstances. It is more likely that the proposed law would fix some churches with a greater responsibility for the sanctity of marriages than they have been willing to admit. This would be good for society.

The remaining parts of Section 20 exist to permit civil marriages and to take care of cases made under the auspices of churches without matrimonial canons.

The necessity for this section is double: not only to eradicate from this country one of the chief scandals of our time but to ensure to the family a true and decent independence from public meddling.

SECTION 21: THE INDEPENDENCE OF THE FAMILY

The natural independence of the family, beginning with freedom of marriage, extends also to the usual consequences of marriage and, in particular, to the raising of a family. The intrusion of the state into family life is a sombre and deadly enormity of the twentieth century. Our times have seen in very fact the soulless fictions depicted in *Brave New World* and *Nineteen Eighty-Four*. Do we need to go to Russia or Nazi Germany to see examples of children deprived of family life by a social policy calculated to mould them in the image of the state? This is a very great wrong and is the kind of thing described by a leading intellect of the century in the following passage:

> ... it is an injustice, a grave evil and a disturbance of right order for a larger and higher organization to arrogate to itself functions which can be performed efficiently by smaller and lower bodies. . . .[17]

This is the now well-known *principle of subsidiarity*.[18]

But family unity and independence are based on more than efficiency, although that is important. It is the natural thing to do for parents to raise their children. It is always possible to cite vagaries, but that is the normal arrangement. Moreover, only family life can give the child the attention, intimacy, and affection that every human being needs if he is to become a whole man, able to fit into society. Even a brief practical experience with the products of broken homes or of institutions who come before the criminal courts will confirm this conclusion. As in all things human, the rule admits of very wide variation but it remains valid in essence.

There are families that cannot or will not fulfil their functions. In such cases the state obviously must step in, to help or even to coerce. But the intervention should be limited to the necessities of the case. The terms of Section 21 are aimed at the least standard of intervention and may clash with some child-welfare legislation that gives a broad meaning to 'neglect'.[19] This suggests that such statutes may give improper powers to welfare agencies and family courts. A more important question is whether the section would interfere with adoptions. This unfortunate, though unlikely, outcome should be guarded against. In the common case, an unmarried mother consents to the adoption of the child or, with her assent, the child is made a ward of a welfare body on grounds of 'neglect', by a court order. There is an interpretation of Section 21 that would outlaw both processes, but such an interpretation is improbable. Adoption, of course, gives a family to a child who lacks one and is fully within the spirit of family freedom and unity.

Our ideal of humane living demands Section 21. Without it, despite the other entrenched rights, our society could be subverted drastically and its character completely changed.

SECTION 22: FREEDOM OF EDUCATION

The family is an incomplete society in the sense that it cannot fulfil all of its functions or attain all of its objectives by its own means. Justice, protection, and the production of wealth are examples of such objectives, but the chief thing for which it needs outside help is education. That is why education is the main field in which family rights and interests can clash with state action. It is also the field where the ideologies that struggle for world supremacy are most active, because the easiest way to conquer minds is to capture them in their youth.

For centuries the churches provided the only system of public education and they did a reasonably good job of it. But they did not try to make it universal in the way that we now have universal compulsory schooling. The demand for that did not exist until the last century. Then it did become apparent that a stable modern democracy requires a reasonably well educated electorate. Moreover, it seemed contrary to the spirit of equality coming to be largely accepted as a political ideal, that any child should be denied an education because he was poor.

The fact that parents need state aid so that their children can learn enough to keep up with the rest of the world means that universal, free, public education fills a real need in which there is a strong vested interest. But many conceive that its main end is to educate for the public and only incidentally for the family. It should obviously be the other way up. The state has a legitimate interest in seeing that all schools turn out good and useful citizens but the school itself exists chiefly to help the parents do the job that is naturally theirs. The school is merely an indispensable auxiliary.

Education free of charge is commonly confused with freedom of education, although it is patent that they have no common meaning or content. Educational freedom means that parents, pupils, and teachers will be able to choose from a wide field and that there will be many different choices. This implies great variety in schools, curricula, and methods, as well as well-distributed control; but in the typical public school system, the schools, teachers, and methods show marked uniformity. Clearly, freedom is on the side of variety and a system that does not permit reasonable differences cannot be called free.

There are those who deny that anyone who pays for education outside of the public system is doing his fiscal duty adequately and should not be required to pay twice. This denial treats the state as if it were a real, concrete being, endowed with vast resources which it can rightfully use, however, only for strictly secular purposes. The taxpayer has no claim to benefit from his money once it goes into the public coffers. This is an almost superstitious idealization of the state. We need to come down to earth and see the commonwealth as a social construct through which men secure justice, safety, and other mutual help, including help in teaching their children.

The Preamble to the Articles asserts the primacy of the individual and that civil society exists for his benefit and not for its own. To use public funds to coerce people into the melting-pot of educational uniformity is to deny this principle. So is it also, to refuse to give to the truly free schools, the non-public schools, the benefit of the educational taxes of their constituents. We can see how harsh is this refusal when we consider in addition that parents who undertake the very large burden of putting a child through college have also to contribute to the general taxes for education. This is neither the equal protection of the laws, nor just administration of taxation, nor yet a suitable distribution of social functions.

The ideal school system would provide both legal and practical freedom of choice. That is, not only would it be lawful to choose what school you wished (within the limits of the criminal law) but this would be made financially possible. As we have remarked repeatedly, true freedom has two aspects: it requires not only the absence of legal restrictions but also the positive ability to do what we want.

The only valid objection to such a system on the grounds of liberty and equality is that too much dependence on public support would weaken the freedom of the now free schools. There is such a danger but it seems to have been overcome by the universities of Canada and the other schools that get grants in aid. It seems more likely that the proposal would encourage the founding of many more free elementary and secondary schools. The limitation in the section to twelve years means that the universities would be outside of the plan and fiscal aid to them would be arranged under the ordinary law.

Fortunately we do not have the traditional opposition, so dominant in the United States, to a public school system that allows for a variety of approaches to suit the groups, religious, linguistic, or the like, for which it exists. In that country the opposition is largely due to the constitutional bar of the First Amendment against the establishment of religion. This noble ideal has been reduced to an absurdity by an illiberal insistence on uniformity. There is no place for that in Canada.

Section 22 is essential to the plan of freedom in the Articles, which seek not only the liberty of the individual but also the independence of those associations of individuals that are entitled to claim it because of their fundamental nature and primacy.

SECTION 23: ENTRENCHED EDUCATIONAL RIGHTS

This is a further aspect of freedom of education, but it needs separate treatment in a section of its own because of its place in Canadian history and politics. There were bitter struggles before the compromise was agreed on in the two Canadas before Confederation. The talks leading to the union of 1867 threatened to reopen the matter, and in order to prevent this, which could well have shattered the plan, a confirmation of existing rights was inserted in Section 93 of the B.N.A. Act, 1867, and carried forward in the acts relating to the Prairie provinces.[20] An aggravated conflict over the dual school system in Manitoba in the 1890s[21] showed that the guarantees given by Section 93 could not be relied on. So, when Newfoundland joined the Confederation in 1949, that province insisted on writing its own terms in lieu of Section 93, terms that provide extremely equitable provision for all schools and colleges in the jurisdiction.[22] The terms form a true constitutional guarantee of human rights.[23]

Every practical project for the amendment of the constitution has treated the existing rights and privileges as sacrosanct and requiring the highest degree of agreement before any change might be made. This idea is incorporated in Section 23 and in Article 12, Section 1.

SECTION 24: INDEPENDENCE OF CHURCH AND STATE

The freedoms of assembly and expression are, at the core, political rights and do not justly apply to those not citizens. But religious practice cannot be limited to citizens in a free state. The workings of the average state constitute human conduct, which is, often enough, fit material for moral strictures. It is of the utmost importance for human freedom that the organized bodies most likely to give sound moral judgments should enjoy a true independence from the state.

This independence need not be absolute. To the extent that the churches traffic in civil matters, such as contracts, property, torts, and trade, there is no ground for independence. But they should be able to manage their own internal business without state intervention and without the need of it. That is, not only should the state have no right to nominate or veto bishops, moderators, parsons, and the like, no right to control the number of churches, dioceses, parishes, etc., no right to prescribe the number of candidates for the ministry or to regulate their education, no right to forbid religious costumes and symbols – and every one of these things is done by one or more governments – but the religious bodies should not have to seek authority to exercise corporate powers. It should not be necessary for the Anglican Bishop of Nova Scotia or the United Church of Canada or the Congregational Church at Bitter Brook to rely on an act of the legislature for his or its legal capacity to make contracts or hold land or for perpetual succession. Where declaratory legislation is necessary, as it may be, it should be expressed so as not to imply any subordination of the religious bodies to the legislature. It should operate on the principle of recognition of rights rather than on any notion that the religious bodies are the creations of the legislature.

Section 24 sets aside for the churches the rights they need to function effectively free of any political influence on their internal affairs and free also of governmental coercion. It does not make them immune from the ordinary law beyond the scope of these liberties. Some states recognize the churches as special associations. For example, in East Germany they are public-law corporations[24] and may levy taxes. This is not independence as we conceive it; the use of civil process to collect financial support is too close to an establishment of religion to suit us.

Some might object to the terms of Section 24 as too wide: after all, there are religions that preach and practise things we would find intolerable, such as ritual murder, prostitution, cannibalism, drug addiction, and other even more extreme deviations from the norm. Are we to protect and encourage such excesses by giving them independence and a home?

Here, once again, the word 'peaceable' has an important function in keeping the freedom in question within the limits of the criminal law. According to the present jurisprudence, these limits are wide but they effectually exclude from the cover of the freedom any real breach of a law that the legislatures have a right to make, considered without reference to religious liberty. It is quite certain that none of the above practices would be permitted.

The section carefully avoids anything that would prevent collaboration between the churches and the governments. There is no reason why they cannot and should not work together in those fields, such as education, charity, family counselling, where they are most likely to meet. Accordingly, it does not expressly ban an establishment of religion, for two reasons: this has been used in the United States to forbid civil and religious co-operation and any suggestion of such a prohibition should be avoided; if peaceable freedom is secured to all religions, the establishment of one is not an interference with freedom or an act of discrimination but a recognition of the special potential of that one to sum up the religious and moral spirit of the nation. Such is Anglicanism in England, Catholicism in Italy,[25] Islam in Pakistan, Judaism in Israel, Lutheranism in Norway, and Presbyterianism in Scotland. The establishment of religion is something of a red herring with respect to religious freedom. It can be very repressive or it can be quite insignificant.

But the importance of the independence of the churches cannot be exaggerated. They have been the most constant and vital bastions of the moral values without which freedom perishes. It is therefore essential that their independence be asserted in our primary statute.

The eight sections (17-24) of this chapter have a common theme, as has each of the prior groups of eight. The theme has had various names in history, the latest being the principle of subsidiarity. That is, a higher organization should not take over the functions that are suitable to a lower body. It thus appears that the principle is just one branch of the more general idea of suitability: that what is right is what is suitable to the nature and essence of a being. For example, freedom is right for human beings because, by their nature, they have the power of rational decision and free choice. This is an obvious echo of Plato's treatment of justice in *The Republic* although the modern development prefers Aristotle's formulations as more true to life and nature. But the equation of what is suitable to what is just was asserted as long ago as that, at the first real flowering of philosophy, and remains valid.

It is easy to see that by keeping organizations as small as is practically possible there is a real gain in freedom. Not only do the people in them take an actual part in more real decisions but they are not as powerful against the individual. This retention of freedom is in accord with the concept of justice (as we understand it) and of suitability.

The core of the sections of this Article might be summed up with the leading theme of each group of sections, thus:

None shall be denied the equal protection of the laws; nor shall anyone be deprived of life, liberty, or property without just process of law; and no individual or association shall arrogate to itself functions that naturally belong to other individuals or associations.

SECTION 25: SUSPENSION OF GUARANTEES

This section is a concession to the possibility of governmental ineptitude. In theory, the sanctity of human rights should be no obstacle to a proper and just defence of the commonwealth. Those rights that are absolute cannot and should not be infringed for any reason and those that are not absolute must yield on occasions when the common good demands it. Legislators should so enact, executive officers should so act, and judges should so read and apply the law that it would permit a licit defence of the public good. For example, it is never licit to cause the death of an innocent human being by a direct intentional act, or otherwise deliberately to destroy his integrity as a person. But the rights to security of person and property, to association, to free movement and expression, to work, are all relative and may rightly be overridden for the good of the individual or the nation. The rights of just process are a more debatable quantity. One cannot deny that in time of national peril the government should be able to act in the public interest on a *prima facie* view or even on a strong suspicion, but the human being who is the subject of this process should have some means of clearing himself.

The War Measures Act,[26] as amended by the Canadian Bill of Rights, provides that in time of real or apprehended war, invasion, or insurrection, the Governor General in Council (i.e. the federal cabinet) may do what he thinks advisable for Canada and this may include censorship, arbitrary arrest and detention, exclusion and deportation, control of ports, vessels, transport, and production, and seizure of property. This may be rescinded by parliament.

The existing law permits the use of arbitrary powers on the initiative of a single branch of government. The proposed section requires the executive branch to obtain the concurrence of the legislature or the judiciary. It is also limited to a one-year period. This does not seem unreasonable or unworkable.

The ancient name for the powers given by the War Measures Act was 'dictatorship'. Some of the greatest men of the Roman Republic exercised the office of dictator. It was an honour to bear the title but it was also an honour to lay it down, the state having been made secure, in the shortest time. The name and office have been defiled in this age of the world, in common with many other noble things, but the need for it remains even more pressing when total war threatens so constantly and abruptly.

Some such section as that proposed is necessary to avoid the pitfalls of statutory drafting and enactment, executive error, and judicial misinterpretation. In time of peace prepare for war. A useful preparation is to foresee what freedoms must be exempt from the upheaval of judgment and the lessening of guarantees so prevalent in wartime. The proposal is certainly not the last word and the whole subject needs further consideration to determine whether the emergency powers cannot safely be more narrowly hedged.

CHAPTER 27

Amendment and Transition

The history of constitutional amendment in Canada is interesting from the lawyer's point of view and exasperating from any other. In nothing is the Confederation more similar in principle to the constitution of the United Kingdom than in this, that the procedure for procuring these amendments is not settled by law in a plain, straightforward way, but is a hodge-podge of custom, convention, statute, and political in-fighting, all subject to the practical bounds that the current balance of political power puts on what can be done.

The struggle to find a more suitable and less one-sided way of amendment-making is also interesting and this time without limitation, because a study will show progress, very gradual it is true, from a complete impasse to a position of nearly complete agreement. There is no need to relate the story here: it is told elsewhere with great care and skill in several places.[1] But it should be remarked that the earlier difficulties arose from the adherence of Quebec and Ontario to the 'compact theory', the theory that Confederation is the implementation of a treaty, whence they drew the conclusion that any change in the compact should require the assent of all the parties. It is arguable, however, that this theory was advanced to protect a more radical position, that is, that certain provincial functions are so essential to a proper autonomy that they should be practically unalterable. The latest approach has found a solution to this difficulty. Before considering that approach we should state what the present position is.

Since the 1949 (No. 2) Amendment the legal powers of amendment are distributed as follows:

1. The provincial legislature may amend the constitution of the province, except as regards the office of lieutenant-governor.[2]

2. The parliament of Canada may amend the constitution of Canada, except as regards

    (a) matters coming within the classes of subjects assigned by the B.N.A. Act, 1867, exclusively to the legislatures of the provinces;

    (b) rights or privileges by the B.N.A. Act, 1867, or any other constitutional 'Act' granted or secured to the legislature or the government of a province or to any class of person with respect to schools;

    (c) the use of the English or the French language;

    (d) the requirements that there shall be a session of the parliament of Canada at least once in each year, and that no House of Commons shall continue for more than five years from the day of the return of the writs for choosing the House: provided, however, that a House of Commons may in time of real or apprehended war, invasion, or insurrection be continued by the parliament of Canada if such continuation is not opposed by the votes of more than one-third of the members of such House.[3]

3. The parliament at Westminster may amend anything in the constitutions of Canada and the provinces, including the exceptions in paragraphs 1 and 2.

We have already mentioned the ambiguity in clause (b) of paragraph 2: that is, whether 'with respect to schools' applies to the whole clause or only to classes of persons. And it is probable, but by no means certain, that the parliament of Canada can deal with the exception to provincial powers contained in paragraph 1. With respect to the exceptions in paragraphs 1 and 2 (which are now all that matter) the practical situation, as distinct from the legal, appears to be this. The British parliament has bound itself by the Statute of Westminster, 1931, and the conventions of the Commonwealth not to legislate with respect to Canada unless requested to do so by Canada. The only request from Canada that will be recognized, however, is one transmitted by the federal government. The British government and parliament will not act on provincial representations for amendment nor will they accede, officially at any rate,[4] to provincial objections to a proposed amendment. Whether objections supported by a majority of the provinces would fare better is a moot point. It has not arisen so far, and every federal request for an amendment has been eventually granted.

The last point is important as it casts doubt on the validity of the stand of those few who oppose repatriation of the constitution on the ground that the disinterested sense of fairness of the British parliament is a better guarantee of provincial and minority rights than any purely Canadian machinery that could be devised. The disinterest and sense of fairness undoubtedly exist, but the British have taken the position that their proper role is to act very much as the Queen herself acts, that is, on the advice of the responsible ministry. In this case, the responsible ministry is the Canadian government.

There are no legal controls on the action of the Canadian government in sending forward an amending act to the Imperial parliament, and some of the early amendments were made without submitting them to the Canadian parliament. In each such case, however, there was an act of the latter parliament that appeared to require to be validated,[5] and, since 1895, each request for an amending act has been based on a resolution of the Senate and House of Commons.

But where do the provinces fit in the picture? In only five of the fifteen cases where the Canadian government has sought an Imperial amending act has it consulted the provinces. These were in 1907, concerning the system of subsidies, in 1940 and 1951, concerning unemployment insurance and old-age pensions, and in 1960, concerning the retirement age for superior court judges, and in 1964 concerning survivor benefits. The central government has consistently taken the stand, in the other cases, that the interests affected were fully represented in the parliament of Canada. This book takes issue with that view. In practice, the sanctity of the Canadian constitution depends upon the prudence, the political sagacity, the restraint, or the daring of the Ottawa government. This conflicts with the federal idea.

Every amendment has had its own peculiar procedural history and there have been almost as many different approaches as there have been amendments. Why any particular approach was adopted in any individual case forms a ripe subject for discussion and speculation,[6] and in each instance we can see the federal government balancing and juggling a multitude of factors of opinion and policy. This occurs in every polity that is influenced by opinion, but it is characteristic of cabinet government in a unitary state, in the sense that there are no other limits or curbs. The objection to this in a federal state is that it delivers the means of control to one element of the federation, in contradiction of its essence.

This has proven bearable until now, because many of the amendments which were secured without consulting the provinces were not of a fundamental-law nature. They were the kind of thing that should not be put in a constitution. But others were fundamental, those of 1886, 1915, 1946, and 1949 (No. 2) in particular, and they should have been adopted by a process of amendment that recognized the federal nature of the state. They deal with the type of thing that belongs in a constitutional law.

The 1949 (No. 2) Amendment cleared the way for dealing with constitutional amendment on its merits. It gave the federal parliament the powers that the provinces already had over their own constitutions. But it must be remarked that there are many features of the federal structure that are of vital interest to the provinces, while, on the other hand, it is not true that the Confederation has a vital interest in all the like features of the provincial structures. It is not parity or fairness that matters, but what is suitable to the different levels of government.

In 1950, a Federal-Provincial Conference postulated six classes of matters and tried to allocate the subjects of Canadian government among them. The classes were:[7]

Class 1 – Provisions that concern the parliament of Canada only and that should be amendable by an act of that parliament.

Class 2 – Provisions that concern the provincial legislatures only and that should be amendable by an act of the legislature in question.

Class 3 – Provisions that concern the parliament of Canada and one or more but not all of the provincial legislatures. These should be amendable by concurrent acts of all the law-making bodies concerned.

Class 4 – Provisions that concern the parliament and all provincial legislatures. Here, amendment would be made by an act of parliament and acts of such majority of the legislatures and upon such additional conditions, if any, as might be agreed upon.

Class 5 – Provisions concerning fundamental rights (e.g., of education, language, administration of justice, solemnization of marriage, provincial property in lands, mines, and other natural resources) and the amendment of amending-procedure. Any change here would require the unanimous consent of the parliament of Canada and the provincial legislatures.

Class 6 – Provisions that should be repealed.

The 1950 conference and its legal committee made good progress in putting sections of the B.N.A. Acts in the above classes, but there remained many differences of opinion.[8] Little further progress was made in the next decade and then, all at once, at the end of 1961, it was announced that the committee of attorneys-general had agreed upon an acceptable scheme of amending procedures, the Fulton Formula, as the press promptly named it. Without detracting from the skill and leadership of Mr. Fulton, who was then minister of justice, it can be asserted that the replacement of Premier Duplessis by Premier Lesage was at least a condition precedent to this event. In fact, Mr. Lesage took the first steps leading to the apparent consensus.

The committee met in secret and its proceedings were not published. It is rumoured that the agreement was not complete, and that the federal representatives would not consider reopening the principles of the 1949 (No. 2) Amendment and refused even to discuss it. This may have inspired the Association of Canadian Law Teachers to call upon the conference to hold public hearings, where briefs and suggestions might be presented, and to publish the proposals that it had had under consideration.[9] This was before the Fulton Formula was announced.

The Fulton Formula is based on the continuation of mutually exclusive law-making powers, which we have found to be the main source of our constitutional ills. It also provides for delegation of powers between the governments, a suggestion of the 1950 conference that was probably inspired by an article of Raphael Tuck's in 1945.[10] Delegation requires a constitutional amendment because delegation of powers between the federal and provincial governments is contrary to law.[11] Under the Articles it would not be unlawful: on the other hand, it would be quite unnecessary. Each government would have full power within the whole field of legislation but, in any case of a clash, one would prevail over the other.

The Articles have been so drafted that each law-making body may make laws in the cases that concern it alone. This eliminates any need to deal with the Class 1 or Class 2 amendments above. What should be repealed has been left out and that disposes of Class 6 matters. Class 3 consists of subjects that are at least analogous to agreements and can be dealt with on that basis, as they are, in Section 2 of this Article. This leaves Class 4 and Class 5 amendments; Section 1 of the Article, therefore, has been drafted with those classes in mind. It follows the spirit of the Fulton Formula but spurns the letter – the text of the formula is neither clear, convincing, nor elegant.

SECTION 1: CONSTITUTIONAL AMENDMENT

At first thought, the straightforward approach to setting up a process of constitutional amendment would be the comparative one: see how they do it in other states and then adopt the best plan from among them. This has hardly figured in the Canadian history of the question and should not be passed over lightly. But when you get down to the meat of the matter, the chief advantages of the comparative method appear to be two: firstly, it may show up some things to avoid; secondly, it may provide some help in drafting, in the choice of language, after the method of amendment suitable to the particular case has been agreed upon. In other respects, the solutions accepted in other states do not help much, because a federal constitution is adopted to ensure a distinctive political balance and the method of amendment must be designed to preserve that balance while its elements persist. Accordingly, what is workable in one federation can easily go awry in another.

Any plan for amendment of the Canadian constitution must thus take into account the balances that exist or should exist between various groups in the nation. These groups are in several divisions:

(a) The language division, in which the major groups are English and French and the others tend to identify themselves in sentiment with one of these two, usually the English.

(b) The religious division, in which the major groups are Catholic and Protestant; here again, the others tend to sympathize on most political questions that touch on religion or morality, with one or the other major group, most usually the Protestant.[12]

(c) The regional division, consisting of the western provinces, Ontario, Quebec, and the Atlantic provinces as the four chief regions; but British Columbia is rather complementary to the Prairie provinces than part of them, and Newfoundland, while its interests are largely identical with the Maritimes, is quite distinct in history and outlook. Moreover, there are divisions and alliances of sympathy between individual provinces that transcend regional ties.

Our constitutional equilibrium depends upon keeping these divisions in balance. This is not to ignore smaller interest groups. The operative principle of the Articles is to protect minorities against the denial of their general human and civic rights rather than to give them special privileges. Indeed, it is profoundly repugnant to the spirit of the Articles to create special privileges. The problem is to ensure that a majority will not override such fundamental rights to the prejudice of some minority.

Jewish Canadians, for example, have an educational problem in Quebec because they are neither Catholic nor Protestant. Section 22 of Article 11 supplies a solution for this problem, not in terms of educational rights for Jews or Jehovah's Witnesses, but by declaring equal rights for all in such a way that each group can really get what it wants. Now, to preserve these rights in the constitution it would be neither practicable nor desirable to give the Jewish or the Catholic or the French-speaking group, as such, a curb on the amendment of the constitution. This would mean a classification of citizens for voting purposes by language or religion, which is contrary to the spirit of Article 2. Moreover it poses a threat of second-class citizenship. Accordingly, the sanctity of the constitution and of the rights embedded in it must depend on the political divisions. Fortunately, these are so constituted that each will tend to protect different non-political minorities and thus maintain the balance. Each political division, therefore, must be able to muster a veto if a proposed change is important enough to it.

There is a plan put forward by Dr. Gérin-Lajoie (now Minister of Education in the Quebec government) that meets the demands of the problem in all aspects in a very satisfactory way without requiring the consent of all the provinces.[13] In this plan, the consent of two-thirds (or three-quarters) of the provinces, representing three-quarters of the population of Canada, would be needed and would be enough to ratify an amendment. If two-thirds were the number chosen, the western provinces could combine to bar any change they found repugnant; so also could the Atlantic provinces or any other group of four provinces. This would happen only in extreme cases. If the number of provinces chosen were three-quarters, any three, such as the Maritimes or the Prairie provinces, could combine to veto an amendment. On the other hand, the population part of the plan ensures that Ontario and Quebec would each have a veto. This is not inconsistent with the constitutional background, especially those provisions of the B.N.A. Acts that give the four regions equal representation in the Senate (a scheme that was put out of shape with the entry of Newfoundland). In fact, each of the two major provinces needs this protection against possible combinations of the others against it. To put either of them completely in subjection to the will of the majority would foster dissension and separatism. It would also be quite unjust.

Either form of the Gérin-Lajoie plan would provide sufficient safeguards for the rights restated in the Articles without making constitutional amendment impossible. The Fulton Formula would require the accord of two-thirds of the provinces representing one-half of the population in ordinary cases, and (except in respect to education) the consent of all the provinces to change the following: the formula itself, the rule giving a province at least as many members in the Commons as it is entitled to senators, the provincial legislative powers, provincial legislative or governmental rights or privileges, the assets and property of a province, or the use of the English or French languages. The Fulton Formula suits the text of the B.N.A. Acts but the Articles have been drawn not only in more general but in more fundamental terms. They obviate the need to make many of the amendments that might be considered under the B.N.A. Acts and they establish our constitutional rights on a new and higher plane of law. In almost every instance there is a more urgent need to protect and entrench a provision of the Articles than its analogue, if any, in the B.N.A. Acts. Consequently, we have opted to include the less stringent of the Gérin-Lajoie plans. Either would suit well enough.

This, as we have noted, is probably sufficient, but almost every Canadian proposal for an amendment procedure has made the unanimous consent of the provinces the condition for some changes. If there are any parts of the Articles that are more fundamental than others, they are the first and the eleventh Articles, defining the principles of the union and establishing a bill of rights. Of necessity, the amendment procedure itself must belong to the basic class of amendable provisions, if it is to be capable of change at all. The Articles cited include the sections that protect linguistic, religious, and educational rights, but those Articles are all of a piece in this regard. Their remaining content is equally important.

Some constitutions provide for special devices to deal with amendments. Thus, in Australia, Section 128 of the Constitution contemplates referenda in all the states rather than acts of the state legislatures. To pass, an amendment needs a majority of those voting and a majority of those voting in a majority of states. Several constitutions, such as that of the United States, make constitutional conventions the method or an alternative method of proposing and ratifying amendments. The weakness of this feature in the United States Constitution is that it commands the Congress to call such a convention on the application of two-thirds of the states, a command that is neither self-enforcing nor enforceable in the courts. In that country, one could count on the national reverence for the constitution to bring about compliance. In Canada, it would probably prove futile to direct the houses of parliament to adopt an act or resolution in the like case. It might be practicable to have the Governor General summon a convention on the application of a certain number of the provinces, but the directions in the Articles would have to be rather elaborate.

The constitutional convention has two virtues. It allows for prolonged study and discussion by experts in the field and it can be used to by-pass a recalcitrant house of parliament that blocks change in its own vested interests. Parliament, although it contains many very able members, cannot be expected to provide all the time and talent that the task requires; but this is not decisive. A governmental conference of jurists and others can be called to work up the material, as is done in other cases of important general legislation, for presentation to the parliament. In this aspect, the parliament and a constitutional convention can be placed on an equal plane of virtue. In the other aspect, the electorate can always overrule the House of Commons in a general election and the House, by Section 8 of Article 3, can override the Senate. Accordingly, vested interests cannot block a desirable change forever.

Again, a constitutional convention might be used so that the provinces could overcome opposition of the parliament. On the pure 'compact theory', this is a rational and even desirable possibility, but it underlines a valid federal objection to provincial intervention in the amending process. We have disagreed with other objections but it is right to assert that the interests of the provinces are just that – provincial – even if they are not, as the federal partisans would contend, limited to provincial *governmental* interests. That is, the national, general interest is an essential part of the equilibrium that should be embodied in any amendment, and the federal government and parliament are designed to represent that interest best.

Is there anything in the Articles that should not be capable of amendment? No doubt an argument can be made for several provisions, such as the right of each province to equal representation in the Senate.[14] But the imperfections of language are such that it may be necessary to amend the most sacrosanct clause, if only to restate its intended meaning more clearly. It seems more prudent to allow every provision to be amended in some way.

It is apparent that Section 1 is absolutely essential to a viable and useful fundamental law.

SECTION 2: AMENDMENT OF PROVISIONS APPLICABLE TO SOME PROVINCES ONLY

In addition to the general elements of the Confederation that are restated in the Articles there are relations between the federal government and some particular provinces that have a constitutional quality. These arise from provisions that may, for constitutional purposes, be equated to the matters in Class 3 above: provisions that concern the parliament of Canada and one or more but not all of the provinces. These are contained in various enactments of different degrees of authority, but for the most part they are to be found in agreements between the Dominion and some other body that have been scheduled to an Imperial act of parliament or order in council. Thus they have a dual character, being partly contract and partly law, which gives them an ambiguous and elusive legal quality.

It would be impertinent to include these in the Articles, since they do not concern the nation as a whole or are transitory in nature. Yet they are too important to be left to the operation of the private law of contract (quite apart from the difficulty of finding the proper law). The Fulton Formula provides, by Section 3, that no change in this class of provisions is effectual unless the legislature of every province to which the provision refers concurs in the change. Certainly in such a case as a change in the Terms of Union of British Columbia, Prince Edward Island, or Newfoundland, or a change in the equivalent instruments relating to the Prairie provinces, no individual government should be able to carry it through by what amounts to a unilateral repudiation of the original agreement. In this instance the Fulton Formula makes sound constitutional sense.[15]

Indeed it would be better if all these relations could be restated in fresh treaties before the Articles came into force. This would do away with the uncertainty that prevails as to just what provisions of this class are executory (still in force), and which have been executed. It would also be valuable to have a coherent body of live law in this field. But in addition to these desirable codifications, there is a need for constitutional control of the amendment of these instruments.

There are drafting difficulties. The Fulton Formula defines the class as consisting of provisions of the 'constitution of Canada' that relate to one or more, but not all, of the provinces. This convenient device is not usable here: the Articles are intended to contain the complete constitution, known as such; hence these more particular enactments must find another name.

Again, shall the provisions be treated as contractual or statutory? Some of the intergovernmental agreements provide special rights for classes of persons.[16] If the provisions are merely contracts between governments, the persons in these classes would have no legal right to enforce claims under them, as they are not parties to the contract. It may be that the rule of *privity of contract* continues to apply to the agreements even when they are embodied in statutes; however, in general, when a statute declares that a person has a right, he is entitled to enforce it.

In this situation, it seems preferable to continue the existing law while incorporating a means of amending it by agreement of the law-making bodies involved in any particular case. That is the aim of Section 2, as drafted, but only live law is carried forward. The terms under which Ontario and Quebec came into the Confederation include rights and obligations between these provinces only, and the same is true of Alberta and Saskatchewan. The provisions in question, however, must have been long since executed,[17] so that it is morally certain that the remaining material in this class comprises rights and obligations of the federal government in relation to the provinces or to classes of persons in the provinces.

It is necessary to limit the surviving provisions of Class 3 to rights and obligations of this nature because, otherwise, vast masses of the old statutes, including the 1867 Act, might be held to be still operative. Our handsome new ship of state would be towing the battered wrecks of the B.N.A. Acts in its wake. This would frustrate one of our chief purposes in adopting the Articles – to rid ourselves of the ungainly body of legislation under which we function. Rather than this, it would be better to try to catalogue the material covered by this section and put it in Article 9, 'Relations between the Governments', at least by reference. The problem of amendment would remain, however, and thus we are brought back to the principles of Section 2. These appear adequate to deal with all the problems we have raised.

SECTION 3: THE CONTINUATION OF INSTITUTIONS

It is virtually impossible to foresee in detail all the problems that can arise in passing over to a new legal régime. An institution is the flexible solution to this predicament, a solution already adopted in Article 8, 'Fiscal Powers and Institutions'. It might be a continuing constitutional convention or a body specially constituted for the purpose. The parliament and legislatures, however, are able to speak and act with far more authority and political support than such a body; there is no reason why they should not be the appropriate institutions and every reason why they should. To continue the parliament and legislatures implies that the executive governments also continue, but it would appear desirable to make explicit mention of the courts, which otherwise might be created and staffed anew. This offers a great temptation to politicians.[18]

A similar temptation might arise in relation to the Senate; possibly some explicit plan for the change-over of that body should be included. But it is not absolutely necessary, as the Senate will have a voice in any change under the Articles.

SECTION 4: THE MANNER AND DATE OF ADOPTION

This section prescribes a procedure for the adoption of the Articles that is the same as that laid down for the most important class of amendments. This seems reasonable but it is not essential. What is essential is that the Articles should be considered and enacted in such a way that they will prove acceptable to the determining majority of the Canadian people in each of the chief regions of the country. The method outlined in the section would ensure this, but a lesser consensus could meet the test and may be the only practicable one.

How to achieve this end, despite the very great practical obstacles in the way of the degree of unanimity we desire, is the theme of the next part of this book.

CHAPTER 28

What shall we do now?

What practical prospect is there of having the Articles adopted? The reader, although convinced that they are needed, may well ask what hope there is of making them law. While not really revolutionary, they do contain some radical provisions – radical in the sense that they spring from the roots of human nature and politics. People are commonly wary of an appeal to fundamentals if it means disturbing settled habits. The Articles contain enough that is new, different, and startling to stir up very formidable opposition to them, should they ever appear likely to be enacted. But they must become known and accepted as desirable by a large part of the Canadian people even before they can evoke opposition, and this primary task seems grossly difficult.

The author finds his own inspiration and justification for the Articles in religious liberal democracy and, despite a determination to exclude all offensive or polemical material, this bias is not concealed. It may, at first blush, tend to put off those who cannot accept religion, or who distrust liberalism, or who find democracy inadequate. But men of good will will find that however narrow they consider the grounds upon which the Articles are put forward here, they can be supported, in themselves, on the most general grounds, on whatever is universal in human nature. No philosopher can claim a monopoly of the ideas that underlie them, nor are they aimed against anyone.

Details are much more likely to raise obstacles – things that people dislike as a matter of taste or distrust as a matter of prudence. The non-committal nature of the measures designed to preserve representative democracy, for example, may offend those who share Bagehot's appreciation of the British cabinet system as well as those who would have us switch to the American plan. Each group is numerous. The Articles, designed to leave the matter at large and give us that much more freedom, will hardly satisfy either extreme.

But this is no time to throw in the towel. There are forces in our favour. No doubt there is hardly anyone who will find nothing to dislike in the proposal but there is hardly anyone, also, who will not find in it something that stirs him favourably. One very good reason for this is that the deficiencies of the B.N.A. Acts are becoming more and more apparent and the need to repair them more and more acute. Thus, the number of those who seek a solution similar to that proposed in this book is already large and is growing.

Specifically, there is a body of opinion, which now has no significant opposition, that wants the constitution 'repatriated'. And there is a somewhat smaller but quite formidable body of opinion that wants the constitution reformed, if only to give it a definite shape. There is, thirdly, a strong body of opinion in favour of an entrenched bill of rights. There is an almost universal opinion that the constitution should be distinctly and independently Canadian.

There is a feeling of expectancy in the air, a sense of impending changes, the advance of forces that have surged and receded in the past three decades but have come nearer to bringing these ideas to fulfilment each time. With the influence of such forces, any plan that is complete and concrete is likely to be caught up by the current and impelled towards its destination. But if the plan is trimmed to the winds that prevail, its chances are the better for it. Still, to get the Articles into the current will require promotion and discussion by an active nation-wide group. This is not a project for lobbying but for acquainting the Canadian people with the proposal and seeking their backing. This will have to be done in both English and French.

So, if enough people are interested, it is proposed to incorporate a non-profit society, to be called the Constitutional Association, to promote the reformation of the Canadian constitution, so that it will contain:

(a) all fundamental law governing the Confederation in a single document;

(b) provision for provincial autonomy in a federal union comprising a national partnership of English-speaking and French-speaking Canadians;

(c) definitions of the citizenship and citizens' rights, especially freedom of speech and assembly;

(d) provision for the equal representation of each province in the Senate by senators elected or appointed by the provincial electorate or some provincial body;

(e) safeguards that representative democracy shall prevail in the parliament and in the provincial legislatures;

(f) a measure of mutual independence for the legislatures, the executives, and the judiciary;

(g) entrenched conditions of tenure for superior court judges;

(h) full parliamentary powers, subject only to the constitution, for all legislatures, with rules to determine which body shall prevail in case of conflict, in place of the present exclusive powers;

(i) full powers of taxation for all the legislatures, subject to interprovincial free trade and subject also to allocation of the tax sources among the governments by a constitutional institution;

(j) provision for national grants to the provinces to bring provincial services to the national average;

(k) means to regulate the relations between the governments;

(l) limitations on the governments for the protection of human rights and liberties, including the right to the equal protection of the laws, to just process of law, and to the natural and proper liberty of individuals to associate, especially in marriage, in education, and in religious confessions, without undue public intervention;

(m) a method whereby Canadians may, by processes wholly

Canadian, amend the laws that govern them (the repatriation of the constitution).

The chief ideas of the Articles are summed up in these objects: why not put in the Articles themselves? It would seem simpler and less liable to error in interpretation to do so. But the Articles are not the last word: they are, rather, a first draft, or to be more accurate, a fifth or sixth draft. Although they have been worked over and over for a long time with care and diligence, a committee of experts might do much to better them, if only by cutting out any traps they may contain. Constructive criticism is one job such a committee can do well. It is reasonable to believe that the Articles would be improved by such a process.

And the author has addressed too many judges and juries with adverse results to feel any confidence that the Articles will gain uncontested and universal approval. He is even inclined to doubt that they are the perfect expression of what he has in mind or that they are best suited to give Canada what it needs. Something like them is wanted, but the precise form and content of the constitution should, no doubt, be the product of discussion and criticism by a representative group. The Articles would serve as a useful framework for the discussion.

This suggests the next step that the proposed association should take after it has begun to inform the public. That is, it should try to promote something in the nature of a constitutional convention. This topic has been considered above in relation to the process of amendment, but here it would be of a somewhat different nature. The function of the convention would be to represent and advise the governments and people of Canada in putting together the proposal to be submitted for enactment. That is to say, it would *draft the bill*. For this there is the remarkable precedent of the convention that drew up the Constitution of the United States.

What form should such a convention take? The answer is ready to hand. Any government in Canada, when it wants the answer to a problem and wants that answer to be brought before the public in such a way that it will be accepted as non-partisan and definitive, appoints a royal commission. It is the obvious and complete mechanism to suit the situation.

The commission itself, however, would have to be a little out of the ordinary to deal with the matter in an acceptable way. It would, of course, be established by the federal government but it would have to include a representative of each province. The plan of the Federal Council, as in Article 8, or something like it, would suit. It is important that it should be small enough to work for an extended period and without assuming parliamentary habits of debate and opposition. This suggests that it should not have more than fifteen members. It would have to keep the governments informed of progress and the members would have to undertake to persuade their own principals, as well as the commission, so that the final report would be capable of enactment on the scale contemplated for amendments.

It would be like a Federal-Provincial Conference but unlike it in that ministers would not take part and its work would be sustained over a much longer period. Part of this work would be the receipt of briefs and suggestions from non-governmental bodies and individuals. This would certainly be necessary before the commissioners sat down to draw up the document.

The temptation would be to appoint senior civil servants to such a commission because of the time involved, but it would be preferable to have the commissioners appointed on the principles that are usually applied. That is, a commissioner should be a person with a broad grasp of Canadian affairs or an expert in the field under scrutiny. Or both. In the field of constitutional law and policy it is possible to get people with both qualifications.

The drafting should go hand in hand with continuous consultation of the governments so that a measure acceptable to all of them can be produced. If this can be done, and this is the major uncertainty in the proposal, it should be feasible to have the reported solution enacted as law.

There is not much danger of a political party trying to take over the idea, but it is evident that party sponsorship or opposition could be very dangerous, if only because it is unlikely that all governments in Canada will follow the same political banner. But aside from this, regionalism and particularism are more likely to prove obstacles. Even these can be overcome by the determination and good will of the people. In the result, there is a good fighting chance that the final draft will be adopted by the parliament of Canada and ratified by the provincial legislatures. When this has been accomplished, it will still be legally necessary for the United Kingdom parliament to enact something like the following:

1. The Articles of Confederation enacted by the Parliament of Canada and ratified by the Legislatures of the Provinces of Canada shall come into force upon a day to be fixed by the parliament of Canada and shall be the supreme law of Canada.

2. When the Articles of Confederation come into force the following Acts shall stand repealed: ...

Here would follow the British North America Acts and the other acts that the British would want off their statute book. The act would conclude with a short title, such as:

3. This Act may be cited as *The Canadian Constitution Act, 1967*.

Every book should come to a decent conclusion. The usual conclusion, if this were a legal argument, would be a summary of the points made. But it is not a legal argument, however much the law has intruded. It is a political appeal for a needed reformation of our fundamental institutions and it follows that the final note must be part of that appeal – an invitation to the reader, and to those to whom he will carry the appeal, to join with the author and those of like mind in giving to Canada a just, a generous, and a notable first law, fit for the government of a free people. It is a task worthy of a true patriotism.

Notes

M.P.R.	Maritime Provinces Reports
N.E.	North Eastern Reporter (U.S.A.)
N.S.C.A., Ont. C.A., etc.	Nova Scotia Court of Appeal, Ontario Court of Appeal, etc.
O.L.R.	Ontario Law Reports
O.R.	Ontario Reports
O.W.N.	Ontario Weekly Notes
Q.B.	Law Reports, Queen's Bench, 1865-75, 1891 onwards
Q.B.D.	Law Reports, Queen's Bench Division, 1876-90
Que. K.B. or Q.B.	Rapports Judiciaires de Québec, Cour du Banc du Roi
Que. S.C.	Rapports Judiciaires de Québec, Cour Supérieure
R. & R.	Russell & Ryan's Crown Cases Reserved, 1799-1823
R.S.B.C., R.S.C. R.S.M., etc.	Revised Statutes of British Columbia, of Canada, of Manitoba, etc.
R. L.	Revue Légale
S.C.R.	Canada Supreme Court Reports
S. Ct.	Supreme Court Reporter (U.S.A.)
Stats. Can.	Statutes of Canada
T.L.R.	Times Law Reports
U.S.	United States Supreme Court Reports
W.W.R.	Western Weekly Reports

INTRODUCTION

1. Resolution introduced by Hon. A. W. Roebuck requesting the government to submit to the forthcoming Dominion-Provincial Conference a draft Amendment to the British North America Act, to be known as the Canadian Bill of Human Rights and Fundamental Freedoms.
2. The British North America (No. 2) Act, 1949, 13 Geo. VI (Imp.) ch. 81.
3. *Ibid.,* Section 92, Class 1.
4. House of Commons Bill C-60, 1st Session, 24th Parliament; House of Commons Bill C-79, 3rd Session, 24th Parliament.
5. An Act for the Recognition and Protection of Human Rights and Fundamental Freedoms, Stats. Can. 1960, ch. 44.
6. *R.* v. *Gonzales* (1961) 35 C.R. 155 (Pool, P.M.). *R.* v. *Steeves* [1964] 1 C.C.C. 266, 42 D.L.R. (2d) 335 (N.S.C.A.).
7. *Dominion-Provincial Conference, 1960* (Ottawa: Queen's Printer, Z2-1960/1), pp. 25-34.
8. The British North America Act, 1867, Section 91, Class 26.
9. *Debates of the Senate,* 3rd Session, 24th Parliament, vol. 108, No. 70, p. 1020.
10. *Confederation Debates: Parliamentary Debates on the Subject of*

Confederation (Ottawa: Queen's Printer, 1951), p. 33, col. 2. The speech is interesting as a study in human fallibility. Did Sir John A. believe that conflict could be thus avoided?

11. *Labour Conventions Reference, Attorney General for Canada* v. *Attorney General for Ontario* [1937] A.C. 326, per Lord Atkin at p. 354.
12. The *Nova Scotia Delegation Case*: *A.G. Nova Scotia* v. *A.G. Canada* [1951] S.C.R. 31, [1950] 4 D.L.R. 369. The decision could just as easily have gone the other way. Cf. judgment of Doull J. in (1948-9) 22 M.P.R. 83.

Chapter 1

1. By the Parliament Act, 1911, 1 & 2 Geo. V (Imp.) ch. 13.
2. D. A. MacRae, *Constitutional Law* (Toronto: Osgoode Hall casebook, mimeographed, 1946), ch. I.

Chapter 2

1. 30-31 Vic. (Imp.) ch. 3.
2. O'Connor Report: *Report Pursuant to Resolution of the Senate to the Honourable the Speaker by the Parliamentary Counsel* (Ottawa: King's Printer, 1939, reprinted 1961, Y9-139).
3. *Ibid.*, p. 29, and Annex 4, pp. 37-49.
4. Rupert's Land Act, 1868, 31-32 Vic. (Imp.) ch. 105.
5. North-West Territories Act (1869), 32-33 Vic. (Can.) ch. 2.
6. British North America Act, 1871, 34-35 Vic. (Imp.) ch. 28.
7. British North America Act, 1886, 49-50 Vic. (Imp.) ch. 35.
8. British North America Act, 1907, 7 Edw. VII (Imp.) ch. 11.
9. British North America Act, 1915, 5-6 Geo. V (Imp.) ch. 45.
10. British North America Act, 1916, 6-7 Geo. V (Imp.) ch. 19.
11. British North America Act, 1930, 20-21 Geo. V (Imp.) ch. 26.
12. Statute of Westminster, 1931, 22 Geo. V (Imp.) ch. 4.
13. British North America Act, 1940, 3-4 Geo. VI (Imp.) ch. 38.
14. Unemployment and Social Insurance Act, Stats. Can. 1935, ch. 38.
15. British North America Act, 1943, 7 Geo. VI (Imp.) ch. 30.
16. British North America Act, 1946, 10 Geo. VI (Imp.) ch. 63.
17. See 'The Latest Amendment to the British North America Act', (1946) 24 Can. Bar Rev. 609.
18. British North America Act, 1949, 12-13 Geo. VI (Imp.) ch. 22.
19. British North America (No. 2) Act, 1949, 13 Geo. VI (Imp.) ch. 81.
20. British North America Act, 1951, 14-15 Geo. VI (Imp.) ch. 32.
21. Stats. Can. 1952, ch. 13; R.S.C. 1952, ch. 304.
22. 9 Eliz. II (Imp.) ch. 2.
23. British North America Act, 1964, given Royal assent July 31, 1964.
24. There are others that might be included, e.g., The Parliament of Canada Act, 1875, 38-39 Vic. (Imp.) ch. 38; The Canadian Speaker

(Appointment of Deputy) Act, 1895, 59 Vic. (Imp.) ch. 3; and the various Statute Law Revision Acts of 1891, 1927, and 1950. For a survey of the difficulties in deciding what is included, see William S. Livingston, *Federalism and Constitutional Change* (London: Oxford, 1956), ch. 2.

Chapter 3

1. But see *Liversidge* v. *Anderson* [1942] A.C. 206, for an example of a House of Lords decision obviously affected by wartime bias. This is sometimes referred to as the *Humpty-Dumpty Case.*
2. The fate of the Canadian New Deal was decided in a series of Privy Council cases reported in [1937] A.C. 326, 355, 368, 377, 391, and 405. Five out of eight statutes were held *ultra vires* of the parliament of Canada.
3. Cf. 'The Amendment of the Constitution' by R. F. McWilliams in (1938) 16 Can. Bar Rev. 466.
4. *Ibid.,* pp. 469 ff.
5. Cf. *Confederation Debates,* T. D'Arcy McGee, p. 146: 'We hope, by having that Charter, that can only be amended by the authority that made it, that we will lay the basis of permanency for our future government.'

Chapter 4

1. Cf. Introduction, note 11.
2. *Inclusio unius est exclusio alterius.* This is generally blamed on Chief Justice Coke, than whom there could be no more suitable culprit.
3. Written previous to the 1960 Amendment. Let it stand!
4. *Ad proximum antecedens fiat relatio nisi impediatur sententia.* See 154 E.R. 580.
5. In the Canada Evidence Act, R.S.C. 1952, ch. 307, Section 5.
6. Cf. *Bank of Toronto* v. *Lambe* (1887) 12 App. Cas. 575, at p. 588.
7. But see *A.G. Ontario* v. *Barfried Enterprises Ltd.* (1964) 43 D.L.R. (2d) 137 (Can. Sup. Ct.).

Chapter 5

1. Cf. *Bank of Toronto* v. *Lambe* (Chapter 4, note 6), at p. 579. Also *Edwards* v. *A.G. Canada* [1930] A.C. 124, at pp. 136-7.
2. *Edwards* v. *A.G. Canada,* at p. 136.
3. Cf. Chapter 2.
4. There is a passing reference in the *Edwards Case* (note 2) at p. 136. W. F. O'Connor holds that the Privy Council were unaware of the London Resolutions (O'Connor Report, Annex 4, pp. 30-1). Cf. also *John Deere Plow Co.* v. *Wharton* [1915] A.C. 303.
5. Contrast D. A. MacRae, *Constitutional Law,* p. 89, and the O'Connor

Report, Annex 1, pp. 13 ff.
6. See the speech of Prime Minister St. Laurent at Queen's University, October 21, 1951, as reported by Canadian Press.
7. Cf. *Confederation Debates,* p. 91, col. 2, for the views of Sir John A. Macdonald. The other promoters spoke in like vein.
8. The name has one unfortunate reference – the unworkable first constitution of the United States of America. In that case, the central body had no autonomy and no direct relations with the citizens. Cf. Alexander Hamilton in *The Federalist,* nos. 15 and 16.

Chapter 7

1. *Re Eskimos* [1939] S.C.R. 104, [1939] 2 D.L.R. 417. *In re Regulation and Control of Radio Communication in Canada* [1932] A.C. 304.
2. There may, of course, be details of fundamental importance. Harrington, in his *Oceana* (London: 1656), attaches great importance to details of procedure in his legislature. The details of representation in the House of Commons can be of vast importance.
3. Cf. Chapter 5, note 2.
4. *The Social Contract,* Book I, ch. 6 (trans. G.D.H. Cole. London: Dent, Everyman's Library, 1935).

Chapter 8

1. Cf. *The Social Contract,* Book III, ch. 1. Surprisingly enough, there are probably few real differences here between Rousseau and Leo XIII, although verbal differences aplenty. Compare Rousseau in extreme form (Book III, ch. 18) with *Libertas Humana.*
2. This seems to be a fundamental element of law. Compare a fragment of the Twelve Tables of Rome (Table IX, fragment 1, *Privilegia ne inroganto*: 'laws respecting individuals are not to be proposed') with Leviticus 19, verse 15.
3. The Constitution for the United States of America, Section 1 of Articles I, II, and III.
4. 'In the Government of this Commonwealth the legislative department shall never exercise the executive and judicial powers, or either of them. The executive shall never exercise the legislative and judicial powers, or either of them. The judicial shall never exercise the legislative and executive powers, or either of them. To the end it may be a Government of laws and not of men.' Massachusetts Declaration of Rights, 1780.
5. Montesquieu, *Esprit des lois,* Book XI, ch. VI.
6. *Politics,* Book IV, ch. XIV.
7. This avoids such consequences as followed from *A.L.A. Schechter Poultry Corp.* v. *United States* (1935) 295 U.S. 495, where the National Industrial Recovery Act of the United States was held *ultra*

vires of the Congress because it delegated too much legislative power to the President.

Chapter 9

1. Sir John A. Macdonald favoured 'Kingdom of Canada' as a title, but the British thought it would stir up feeling in the U.S.A. The name appeared in some drafts. For controversy see letters of Dr. Eugene Forsey, Dean F. R. Scott, Mr. R. B. Cantlie, and Prof. G. D. Kennedy in (1954) 32 Can. Bar Rev. 1062, 1063, and 1188, and in (1955) 33 Can. Bar Rev. 253.

2. William Rand, a hardy old Nova Scotia secessionist, used to insist that 'Canada' was derived from the Spanish note on a map, *haca nada,* meaning 'nothing here'.

3. E.g., see 'The End of Dominion Status' by F. R. Scott (1945) 23 Can. Bar Rev. 725. See also letters in note 1.

4. *Bank of Toronto* v. *Lambe* (Chapter 4, note 6), at p. 587. *A.G. Australia* v. *Colonial Sugar Refining Company* [1914] A.C. 247.

5. O'Connor Report, pp. 25 ff. For a different view see letter of R.F. McWilliams in (1940) 18 Can. Bar Rev. 516.

6. Hon. W.H.P. Clement, *The Law of the Canadian Constitution,* 3rd ed. (Toronto: Carswell; London: Sweet & Maxwell, 1916), ch. XXII, p. 452.

7. In contrast, the Australian States are continuing bodies that still have some direct links with the United Kingdom government. Here, certain undesirable features have also evolved, the chief being that the High Court of Australia is not the last appeal court for certain questions. See H. S. Nicholas, *The Australian Constitution,* 2nd ed. (Sydney: Angus, 1952), pp. 367 ff.

8. Cf. *Hodge* v. *The Queen* (1883) 9 App. Cas. 117, at p. 132.

9. See Chapter 13 for a fuller discussion.

10. See Chapter 4, note 2.

11. The Manitoba Act, Section 23, has a similar provision which has, however, long been repudiated by the Manitoba Legislature; cf. (1890) 53 Vic. (Man.) ch. 14, and R.S.M. 1954, ch. 187.

Chapter 10

1. But see Clement, p. 166.

2. The Canadian Citizenship Act, R.S.C. 1952, ch. 33.

3. Part I deals with native citizens of Canada. For a comment on the act see (1947) 25 Can. Bar Rev. 364.

4. Clement, p. 171.

5. International acceptance of a régime of naturalization is a product of the nineteenth century. Before that, many states, including Great Britain, while themselves commonly naturalizing aliens, claimed a right of perpetual allegiance from their own nationals. See *Halleck's*

International Law, 4th ed. (London: Kegan Paul, 1908), ch. XII.

6. *Ibid*. Note the case of Garry Davis, who tore up his United States passport and renounced that citizenship to become a One World citizen. In May 1962, the British government granted this stateless individual leave to live in the United Kingdom and issued him a certificate of identity.

7. E.g., Nova Scotia Labor Act, 1953 N.S. Laws, ch. 10.

8. *Reference re Alberta Legislation* [1938] S.C.R. 100, [1938] 2 D.L.R. 81.

9. *Reference re Alberta Legislation* [1939] A.C. 117.

10. [1938] S.C.R., at p. 132.

11. *Ibid.*, at p. 133.

12. *Ibid.*, at p. 146.

13. *Ibid.*, at p. 134.

14. *Ibid.*, at p. 146.

15. The Second Amendment: 'A well regulated Militia being necessary to the Security of a free State, the Right of the People to keep and bear Arms shall not be infringed.' This is a States' right, not an individual one.

Chapter 11

1. *Confederation Debates,* p. 34, col. 2.

2. *Ibid*. The whole speech is well worth reading both with respect to the points validly made and proved by the sequel and also for the un-fulfilled and erroneous expectations.

3. *Ibid.*

4. Cf. R. A. MacKay, *The Unreformed Senate of Canada* (London: Oxford, 1926. Revised reprint, Toronto: McClelland, 1963).

5. *Confederation Debates,* p. 24, col. 1.

6. It became a little strident in April 1964, when Senator Grattan O'Leary refused to permit quick passage of a supply measure; but Mr. Stanley Knowles's Bill C-88, to abolish the Senate, was talked out on April 7. Vol. 109, No. 16, of the House of Commons Debates has a good discussion on both sides. Both Mr. Pearson's and Mr. Diefenbaker's ministries have proposed to make 75 the age limit.

7. See *Confederation Debates* for the argument: Hon. Alexander Campbell, pp. 20-4; Hon. John A. Macdonald, pp. 35-8.

8. *Loc. cit.*

9. See the revealing question asked by the Hon. Alexander Vidal in *Confederation Debates,* p. 24; Quebec Resolutions, No. 14; London Resolutions, No. 15; also 'The Canadian Revolution' by D. J. Goodspeed, *Queen's Quarterly,* Vol. 64, p. 521.

10. Comparison of largest and smallest units:

Canada   United States

Population

$$1870 \; \frac{\text{Ontario}}{\text{P.E.I.}} = \frac{1{,}620{,}851}{94{,}021} = 17.24 \qquad 1790 \; \frac{\text{Virginia}}{\text{Delaware}} = \frac{747{,}610}{59{,}096} = 12.6\text{?}$$

$$1960 \; \frac{\text{Ontario}}{\text{P.E.I.}} = \frac{6{,}089{,}000}{103{,}000} = 59. \qquad 1960 \; \frac{\text{New York}}{\text{Alaska}} = \frac{16{,}782{,}304}{226{,}167} = 74.$$

Area

$$1870 \; \frac{\text{Quebec}}{\text{P.E.I.}} = \frac{201{,}986}{2{,}184} = 92.5 \qquad 1790 \; \frac{\text{Virginia}}{\text{Rhode Is.}} = \frac{104{,}048}{1{,}058} = 98.$$

$$1960 \; \frac{\text{Ontario}}{\text{P.E.I.}} = \frac{412{,}582}{2{,}184} = 189. \qquad 1960 \; \frac{\text{Alaska}}{\text{Rhode Is.}} = \frac{571{,}065}{1{,}058} = 540.$$

11. It is becoming difficult to find a true federation in our times. The following states have basically equal state representation in their second chambers: Argentina, Australia, Brazil, Chile, Mexico, and Switzerland. The West German Bundesrat has a basic three votes for each state, but gives four to states with more than 2,000,000, and five to those with more than 6,000,000 population.

12. As an added feature, six senators plus the minimum two Commons members would give P.E.I. the equivalent of its present minimum parliamentary representation of eight.

13. Sir Alan Herbert is the one that most readily comes to mind.

Chapter 12

1. In the 1958 election, every province except Newfoundland had a ratio greater than 2 to 1 between its most and least populous divisions: Ontario, 5.3; Quebec, 10.8; N.S., 3.68; N.B., 3.77; P.E.I., 2.43; Manitoba, 2.42; B.C., 3.2; Saskatchewan, 2.12; Alberta, 2.35; Newfoundland, 1.54. For all Canada, the ratio was 14.4. The federal Redistribution Act would make the maximum ratio 1.5 to 1.

2. Plato was very concerned with such questions both in *The Republic* and in *The Laws*. Prof. C. Northcote Parkinson in *Parkinson's Law* (Boston: Houghton, 1957) in ch. 4, 'Directors and Councils or Coefficient of Inefficiency', uses suave satire to display shrewd observation of human foibles.

3. Membership in the Canadian Legislative Assemblies in 1964 (*Canadian Almanac & Directory, 1964*): Alta., 63; B.C., 52; Man., 57; N.B., 52; Nfld., 42; N.S., 43; Ont., 108; P.E.I., 30; Que., 95; Sask., 55.

4. Cf. *Bank of Toronto* v. *Lambe* (Chapter 4, note 6); also *Edwards* v. *A.G. Canada* (Chapter 5, note 1).

5. Charles Dickens, *American Notes,* ch. II.

6. Plato, *The Laws,* Book VI, 756B, favours three hundred and sixty

as the number of his state council, but on purely mathematical grounds of divisibility; only thirty of these were to function for any one month. He conceived this figure to be midway between the monarchical constitution and the democratic.

7. *Baker* v. *Carr* (1962) 82 S. Ct. 691 decided that the failure of the legislature of Tennessee to apportion divisions on a rational basis *could* found a cause of action, under the Equal Protection clause of the Fourteenth Amendment, capable of being litigated in federal courts.

8. R.S.C. 1952, ch. 304.

9. Plato, *The Laws*, Book IV, 722B, argues that laws should try to persuade obedience as much as to coerce it. We need not go that far to uphold the proposition in the text: even fear is a moral force.

10. Cf. A. P. Herbert, *Uncommon Law* (London: Methuen, 1935) No. 65, 'Rex vs Haddock', for an amusing but basically accurate account of the legal tangles possible when the courts and the houses of Parliament become involved in each other's business. It is based on *R.* v. *Graham-Campbell et al.* [1935] 1 K. B. 594 (instigated by Mr. Herbert). An even more fantastic case is *Stockdale* v. *Hansard, In re Sheriff of Middlesex* (1840) 113 E.R. 405, 411. The Court of Queen's Bench held that a resolution of the House of Commons could not justify the publication of a libel, and Stockdale got judgment against Hansard and issued execution. But the Commons resolved that the execution was a contempt and the sheriffs were imprisoned on a Speaker's warrant when they levied under it. Stockdale then got an attachment against the sheriffs from the Court for non-payment of the levy. The sheriffs asked the Court, on *habeas corpus,* to declare the imprisonment under the Speaker's warrant illegal, but the Court held that it was legal. In the result, the sheriffs would be imprisoned whatever they did! See also *Burdett* v. *Abbot* (1811) 14 East 1, and *Bradlaugh* v. *Gossett* (1884) 12 Q.B.D. 271.

11. In 1947, the government imposed a 25 per cent excise tax because of the very grave imbalance of payments with the United States, and this was ratified at the next session of parliament. In the summer of 1962, the government (of a different political party) imposed surcharges on imports for similar reasons.

12. A favourite of the federal departments is the Writ of Extent, under which the Crown takes judgment for the debt first, *ex parte,* and the trial follows later if one should prove necessary. Shades of Alice in Wonderland!

13. Article I, Section 7, Clause 1.

14. The Constitution of Australia, Sections 53, 54, 55.

15. The B.N.A. Act, 1867, Section 54; The Constitution of Australia, Section 56.

16. Hon. John A. Macdonald, in *Confederation Debates,* p. 36, col. 2: ' . . . but it will never set itself in opposition against the deliberate and understood wishes of the people'.

17. Cf. Nicholas, *The Australian Constitution,* ch. VII; and J.D.B. Miller, *Australian Government and Politics,* 2nd ed. (London: Duckworth, 1959), p. 97.

18. The Imperial Conference of 1930 approved the results of a Conference on Dominion Affairs and Shipping of 1929, which recognized that the power to reserve for the Crown or to disallow, contrary to the advice of the Dominion ministry, was obsolete. In an article, 'The Last Vestige of Disallowance', (1934) 12 Can. Bar Rev. 579, Thomas H. LeDuc notes that the Imperial government had once demanded an acknowledgment of the right to disallow a Dominion act affecting stocks listed as trustee securities in the United Kingdom.

19. Article I, Section 7, Clause 2.

Chapter 13

1. Some Commonwealth countries have abandoned this principle: e.g., Pakistan, India, Ghana.

2. This is thought to have been settled in Canada by the Byng-King dispute and the subsequent election of 1926; but R. MacGregor Dawson, in *The Government of Canada,* 3rd ed. (University of Toronto Press, 1957), pp. 189-90, takes a different view. The problem is mentioned in 'The Office of Governor General in Canada' by W. P. M. Kennedy (1953) 31 Can. Bar Rev., at p. 996, and discussed in 'The Governor General and the Head of State Functions' by Thomas Franck (1954) 32 Can. Bar Rev., at p. 1094; these two articles led to a series of letters by Dr. Eugene Forsey, Prof. Edward McWhinney, and Prof. J. R. Mallory in (1955) 33 Can. Bar Rev. 252 and 505, and in (1957) 35 Can. Bar Rev. 242, 368, 369.

3. Walter Bagehot, *The English Constitution* (1867), No. 3 (page 67 of World's Classics Edition, 1961).

4. See *King George V, A Personal Memoir* by John Gore (London and Toronto: Murray, 1941), p. 374.

5. Bagehot, *op. cit.,* p. 9, had some inklings of what was to come, but he would surely be astonished at the feebleness of parliament today.

6. Clement, pp. 1 and 2, gives the pre-1949 view.

7. O'Connor Report, Annex 1, p. 157.

8. *Bonanza Creek Gold Mining Co. Ltd.* v. *The King* [1916] 1 A.C. 566. On the implications of the title 'viceroy', with respect, for example, to personal immunities from action, see the article by Thomas Franck (note 2), at p. 1096.

9. The convention may be law on a certain construction of the Preamble and of Section 12 and 13 of the 1867 Act.

10. A. V. Dicey, *Introduction to the Study of the Law of the Constitution* (London: Macmillan, 7th ed., 1908), p. 420.
11. O. Hood Phillips, *The Principles of English Law and the Constitution* (London: Sweet & Maxwell, 1939), p. 235.

Chapter 14

1. See *The Lion and the Throne* by Catherine Drinker Bowen (New York: Little, Brown, 1957), ch. 28, for the story of this. Judges did not hold office during good behaviour until the Act of Settlement, 12 & 13 William III ch. 2, which provided that a judge could be removed only on a joint address of the houses of parliament.
2. Bank of Canada Act, R.S.C. 1952, ch. 133, Section 6(3)(a).
3. Bora Laskin, *Canadian Constitutional Law,* 2nd ed. (Toronto: Carswell, 1960), pp. 192. The statement to the contrary in *Vaillancourt* v. *Hull* (1949) Que. K.B. 680 may be due to some peculiarity of Quebec practice or law, possibly a strained interpretation of Section 6 of the Magistrates Privileges Act, R.S.Q. 1941, ch. 18. Some other cases followed this uncritically. The Irish constitution, Article 34, Section 3, Clause 2°, explicitly limits this jurisdiction to the superior courts.
4. The British North America Act, 1960, 9 Eliz. II (Imp.) ch. 2.
5. A constitutional guarantee did exist, in theory, by Section 99 of the B.N.A. Act, 1867, which provides for the removal of superior court judges only on a joint address of the houses of Parliament. This was characterized by Lord Atkinson in *Scott* v. *A. G. Canada* 40 T.L.R. 6, [1923] 4 D.L.R. 647, in these words:

    > This section provides for the well-known and historical protection of Judges against the unjust and oppressive or arbitrary action by the Executive of a state or province. But it is obvious that it has no application whatsoever to the legislative action of such a state or province.

    Since the 1949 (No. 2) Amendment there seems to be no reason why Section 99 cannot be altered by an ordinary act of parliament unless, perhaps, the length of judicial tenure could be construed as falling within Class 14 of Section 92 of the 1867 Act. It is hardly conceivable that the provinces could so legislate. This implies that the federal parliament can. See *In re Boucher* (1879) Cassels S.C. 327 (Henry J.); and Clement, p. 521.
6. See *Scott* v. *A.G. Canada* (note 5).
7. Sir Alan Herbert scores again here. *Uncommon Law* No. 43, 'What is a Judge?', gives the essentials of the argument in an amusingly far-fetched way. In 1933, the Canadian House of Commons passed, by 54 votes, a bill to cut the salary of a judge, when he became 75,

to the amount he would receive as a pension. The bill did not become law.

8. ' . . . justice should not only be done but should manifestly and undoubtedly be seen to be done.' *R.* v. *Sussex JJ. ex parte McCarthy* [1924] 1 K.B. 257, per Lord Hewart C.J. at p. 259. This is frequently employed to excuse a gross absurdity in the law resulting from its application on a pedantic or technical construction.

9. Article I, Section 2, Clause 5, and Section 3, Clause 6; and Article II, Section 4. The first two conditions of judicial tenure are those specified for the judges of the United States Supreme Court and the federal courts by Article III, Section 1. The third condition, provided by Article I, Section 4, removability only on impeachment, is similar in expression to Section 99 of the B.N.A. Act but very different in effect.

10. Cf. 9 Halsbury 346:

> In the case of courts not expressly declared to be courts of record, the answer to the question whether a court is a court of record seems to depend in general upon whether it has power to fine or imprison (that is, to imprison by way of punishment and not merely for safe custody), by statute or otherwise, for contempt of itself or other substantive offences; if it has such power, it seems that it is a court of record.

Conversely, a court of record has power to penalize for contempt: *Griesley's Case* (1588) 8 Co. Rep. 38, 77 E.R. 530. But inferior courts have no power to punish for contempt committed out of court: *R.* v. *Lefroy* (1873) L.R. 8 Q.B. 134. See also *R.* v. *Harry Rose* [1964] 1 C.C.C. 25 (Ont. High Ct.).

11. The proposition in the text is implied by two statements of Duff C.J. in *Reference re Adoption Act etc.* [1938] S.C.R. 398:

> I agree with the view expressed by Mr. Justice Drake, in his judgment in *Re Small Debts Act,* that it is inadvisable to attempt to draw an abstract line for the purpose of classifying courts as falling within section 96 or otherwise.

And also:

> Looking at the question in controversy from the point of view most favourable to the attack, the question one must ask oneself is this: does the jurisdiction conferred upon magistrates under these statutes broadly conform to the type of jurisdiction generally exercised by courts of summary jurisdiction rather than the jurisdiction exercised by courts within the purview of s. 96?

12. See note 10.

13. To avert the possibility of packing the Court, in derogation of provincial interests, it is better to fix the number of judges, although it cannot be pretended that this is essential. The provision concern-

ing salaries is broadly in accord with the scales now in force. Compare the Judges Act, R.S.C. 1952, ch. 159, as amended by Stats. Can. 1963, ch. 8, with the Salaries Act, R.S.C. 1952, ch. 243, as amended by Stats. Can. 1963, ch. 3; and with the Senate and House of Commons Act, R.S.C. 1952, ch. 249, Sections 33 and 44 (4), as amended by Stats. Can. 1963, ch. 14.

14. B.N.A. Act, 1867, Section 101.
15. A number of Quebec legal and political voices have proposed that English and French Canada have equal representation on the Court, which would thus become a treaty tribunal.
16. *Lunenburg (Town)* v. *Lunenburg (Municipality)* [1957] S.C.R. 400. Either the town or the municipality had to maintain the child.
17. *In re Board of Commerce Act, 1919, and Combines and Fair Prices Act, 1919* [1922] 1 A.C. 191; and *R.* v. *Hume* [1930] S.C.R. 531; also Laskin, p. 803.
18. *A.G. Ontario* v. *A.G. Canada and A.G. Quebec* [1947] A.C. 127.
19. Laskin, p. 804.
20. *R.* v. *St. Louis* (1897) 1 C.C.C. 141 (Wurtele J.).
21. See, for example, *The Blind Eye of History* by Charles Reith (London: Faber, 1952), ch. 10, for an historical summation of the reasons for such local control in the case of the police.
22. Nicholas, *The Australian Constitution,* ch. XXIV.
23. Clement, p. 531; *Valin* v. *Langlois* (1879) 3 S.C.R. 1, 5 App. Cas. 115 (leave to appeal refused); *A.G. Canada* v. *Sam Chak* (1909) 44 N.S.R. 19.
24. Anyone interested should look at 'Section 96 of the British North America Act' by Prof. John Willis, in (1940) 18 Can. Bar Rev. 517 (his usual lucid style), and 'Section 96 of the British North America Act Re-Examined', by Dr. Morris C. Shumiatcher, in (1949) 27 Can. Bar Rev. 131.
25. See, for example, *Scott* v. *A.G. Canada* [1923] 3 W.W.R. 929, 40 T.L.R. 6.
26. Cf. note 24, and *Polson Iron Works* v. *Munns* (1915) 9 W.W.R. 231; *French* v. *McKendrick* (1931) 66 O.L.R. 306; and *Roskiwich* v. *Roskiwich* [1931] 3 W.W.R. 614.
27. It is difficult to be accurate. Beamish Murdoch's *History of Nova Scotia* (3 vols. Halifax: 1865-7), vol. 3, p. 302, gives an instance of local appointment in the case of Mr. Justice Hutchinson. R.S.N.S. 3rd Series (1864) provides for local appointment subject to being supplanted by a London appointee. R.S.N.B. 1854 seems not to deal with the appointment of judges. Governor Cornwallis was given power in his commission to set up courts and appoint judges: see *Scotia,* ed. T. B. Akins (Halifax: 1869), p. 501. See also the *Durham Selections from the Public Documents of the Province of Nova*

Report (London: Methuen, 1905), pp. 20, 248.

28. It is rumoured that Mr. St. Laurent and Mr. Duplessis were able finally to achieve a rare degree of agreement on the appointment of ten judges under an act of the Quebec legislature which was not, however, proclaimed until some such agreement was reached. This is denied by persons in a position to know.

29. See, for example, *Public Accounts of the Province of Ontario for the Fiscal Year Ended 31st March, 1960* (Toronto: Queen's Printer, 1960), Department of the Attorney General, p. B15. Parliament has since changed the Judges Act.

30. Laskin, p. 777, gives material on this.

31. The existing law on this is doubtful. There are cases each way. Contrast *Re North Perth* 21 O.R. 538, and *A.G. Canada* v. *Flint* 15 N.S.R. 453 (reversed on other grounds in 16 S.C.R. 707). See also *Re Bell Telephone Co.* 7 O.R. 605, 4 Cart. 618, 9 O.R. 339.

Chapter 15

1. *Confederation Debates*, p. 29, col. 1. Cf. the article by W.P.M. Kennedy in *Constitutional Issues in Canada 1900-1931,* ed. R. MacG. Dawson (London: Oxford, 1933), p. 51.

2. This was the pre-Confederation concept subsequent to the acceptance of the principles of the Durham Report and the yielding of responsible government. See W.P.M. Kennedy, *The Constitution of Canada* (London, New York, Toronto: Oxford, 1922), pp. 178-80; *The Speeches and Public Letters of Joseph Howe,* ed. J. A. Chisholm (2 vols. Halifax: 1909), vol. 1, pp. 221, 231, 243, and 251; 'The Office of Governor General of Canada' by W.P.M. Kennedy (1953) 31 Can. Bar Rev. 994; and letters of Dr. Forsey and Prof. McWhinney in (1955) 33 Can. Bar Rev. 252, 505.

3. There seems to be no instance of disallowance or reservation of Dominion legislation, but the Imperial government threatened to use these powers to secure changes in Canadian legislative proposals that did not suit it. For example, when the Supreme Court of Canada was first established, a clause cutting off appeals to the Privy Council was deleted in parliament by the Canadian ministry under threat of disallowance: see Kennedy, *The Constitution of Canada,* p. 341. See also 'The Last Vestige of Disallowance' by Thomas H. LeDuc (1934) 12 Can. Bar Rev. 579.

4. Kennedy, *The Constitution of Canada,* p. 342. In 1879 the instructions to reserve classes of legislation were deleted at the instance of Edward Blake, then Minister of Justice. In 1954 the power of disallowance was considered 'deceased' by T. Franck in 'The Governor General and the Head of State Functions' (1954) 32 Can. Bar Rev.

1084. See also the letters noted in note 2, Chapter 13.
5. One draft of the B.N.A. Act actually used this title for the office. See Appendix to Sir Joseph Pope's *Confederation Documents* (Toronto: 1895).
6. John T. Saywell, *The Office of Lieutenant Governor* (University of Toronto Press, 1957), pp. 112 ff.
7. G. V. LaForest, *Disallowance and Reservation of Provincial Legislation* (Ottawa: Department of Justice, 1955), Appendix; and Saywell, p. 221.
8. Saywell, *loc. cit.*
9. In 1945, the lieutenant-governor of P.E.I. vetoed a bill to liberalize the liquor laws. He had addressed a temperance meeting the day before. In 1961, Lieutenant-Governor Bastedo reserved a bill to renegotiate two thousand Saskatchewan mineral leases. The bill was promptly approved by the federal government.
10. G. V. LaForest, *op. cit.*, Appendix A.
11. See, for example, J. M. Beck, *The Government of Nova Scotia* (University of Toronto Press, 1957), p. 185.
12. Cf. W.P.M. Kennedy, 'Law and Custom in the Canadian Constitution', reprinted in *Constitutional Issues in Canada 1900-1931* (ed. Dawson), pp. 59, 60.
13. Saywell, p. 191.
14. This is the usage in Ontario and some other provinces, although at variance with the plain intendment of Sections 90 and 55 of the B.N.A. Act, 1867.
15. Article IV, Section 4.

Chapter 16

1. *Hodge* v. *The Queen* (1883) 9 App. Cas. 117 (Lord FitzGerald at p. 130); see also Laskin, pp. 76-83.
2. *O'Grady* v. *Sparling* [1960] S.C.R. 804.
3. Prof. J.Ll.J. Edwards suggests that this argument could be applied to invalidate speeding laws. This would follow inevitably, if the powers were truly exclusive, but they are construed so as to avoid, if possible, the more impractical consequences of the doctrine.
4. Cf. Hon. V.C. MacDonald, *Constitutional Law: Validity of Provincial Legislation* (Halifax: 1951), p. 3: 'The Method of Inquiry'. See also Laskin, p. 71.
5. *Union Colliery Co.* v. *Bryden* [1899] A.C. 580, at p. 588.
6. For a variety of approaches to this test see the several judgments in the *Margarine Case*, i.e., *Reference re Validity of Section 5 (a) of the Dairy Industry Act* [1949] S.C.R. 1.
7. *Confederation Debates*, p. 33, col. 2.

Chapter 17

1. Clement, p. 829.
2. The cases deal with such things as game laws, liquor control, professional associations, shop closing hours, etc., etc.
3. Clement, pp. 448, 473; O'Connor Report, Annex 1, p. 25.
4. This appears from Laskin, pp. 221-4 and 430-1, although Laskin is not sympathetic to the view. The Supreme Court of Canada has tended to veer to the O'Connor Report approach since appeals to the Privy Council were done away with in 1949. See also Clement, chs. XLI and XLII, especially p. 829.
5. *In re Board of Commerce Act, 1919, and Combines and Fair Prices Act, 1919* [1922] 1 A.C. 191.
6. O'Connor Report, Annex 1, p. 53. See also *Riel* v. *R.* (1885) 10 App. Cas. 675.
7. I have been unable to find any discussion of why this interesting version of the paramountcy principle was not used as a general rule in the B.N.A. Act, instead of being restricted to Section 95.
8. Cf. O'Connor Report, Annex 1, pp. 21, 25, 27, 59-61.

Chapter 18

1. See 12 Corpus Juris 825-9 for the possible questions as they have arisen in the United States. There does not seem much cause to fear unreasonable results, because even in states such as Massachusetts, where the division between legislature and judiciary is strict, according to the state constitution (Chapter 8, note 4), the legislature may regulate procedure as long as it does not inhibit the inherent jurisdiction of the courts.
2. There is an account of the historical development in the *Canada Year Book, 1961,* with an interesting series of maps opposite p. 50.
3. *Re Eskimos* [1939] S.C.R. 104.
4. The phrase is used to give a similar power to the Australian parliament in Section 51, placitum (xxix), of the Constitution of Australia.
5. *Labour Conventions Reference, A.G. Canada* v. *A.G. Ontario* [1937] A.C. 326. In this case, Lord Atkin used the following metaphor:
   > While the ship of state now sails on larger ventures and into foreign waters she still retains the watertight compartments which are an essential part of the original structure. . . .
   See also *Re Aeronautics* [1932] A.C. 54; *Radio Communication, In re* [1932] A.C. 304; and *Re Hours of Labour* [1925] S.C.R. 505.
6. E.g., the *Margarine Case* (Chapter 16, note 6); and *A.G. Ontario* v. *Reciprocal Insurers* [1924] A.C. 328.
7. See *Toronto Electric Commissioners* v. *Snider* [1925] A.C. 396, per Viscount Haldane, at p. 406:

The Dominion Parliament has, under the initial words of s. 91, a general power to make laws for Canada. But these laws are not to relate to the classes of subjects assigned to the Provinces by s. 92, unless their enactment falls under heads specifically assigned to the Dominion Parliament by the enumeration in s. 91.

O'Connor dissents vigorously (O'Connor Report, Annex 1, pp. 52 ff.); but see *Insurance Act, 1910, Reference: A. G. Canada* v. *A. G. Alberta* [1916] 1 A.C. 588.

8. See *Russell* v. *The Queen* (1882) 7 App. Cas. 829; *In re Board of Commerce Act* (1960) 60 S.C.R. 456; *Fort Frances Pulp & Paper Co. Ltd.* v. *Manitoba Free Press Co. Ltd.* [1923] A.C. 695; *Toronto Electric Commissioners* v. *Snider* (note 7); *Distillers' and Brewers' Case* [1896] A.C. 348; *Re Wartime Leasehold Regulations* [1950] S.C.R. 124.

9. *Standard Sausage Co.* v. *Lee* [1934] 1 W.W.R. 81.

10. By Class 2A of Section 91 of the B.N.A. Act, 1867, added by the B.N.A. Act, 1940, 3-4 Geo. VI (Imp.) ch. 36.

11. By Section 94A of the B.N.A. Act, 1867, added by the B.N.A. Act, 1951, 14-15 Geo. VI (Imp.) ch. 32.

12. *Canada Year Book, 1961*, pp. 267-85, gives a survey of the field with details of the financial participation of the central government and the provinces.

13. *Ibid.*, pp. 267-71. The Canada Pension Plan was the product of diplomacy rather than dictation.

14. Cf. *Radio Communication, In re* (note 5).

15. Clement, p. 801.

16. *Reference re Alberta Legislation* [1938] S.C.R. 100, [1939] A.C. 117.

17. See *Canada Year Book, 1961*, p. 1112.

18. 11 Halsbury 190 notes the following characteristics of the law merchant:

> A usage of the law merchant has therefore two characteristics – it must in the first place amount to *jus gentium,* that is to say, it must be in vogue beyond the limits of this country and its notoriety must be cosmopolitan rather than national; and in the second place it must be of such a nature that it will receive judicial notice in our courts.

19. Cf. O'Connor Report, Annex 1, p. 120.

20. For the problems involved in the present legal control of insurance, see Dean V. C. MacDonald, 'The Regulation of Insurance in Canada' (1946) 24 Can. Bar Rev. 257; V. Evan Gray, 'More on the Regulation of Insurance' (1946) 24 Can. Bar Rev. 481; Bora Laskin, letter (1946) 24 Can. Bar Rev. 843.

21. *Citizens' Insurance Co.* v. *Parsons* (1881) 7 App. Cas. 95, at p. 112.

22. *Ibid.*, at p. 113; *Good Humor Corporation of America* v. *Good*

Humor Food Products Ltd. and Bradley [1937] Ex. C.R. 61; *A.G. Ontario* v. *A.G. Canada (Reference re Dominion Trade and Industry Commission Act, 1935)* [1937] A.C. 405.

23. *John Deere Plow Co.* v. *Wharton* [1915] A.C. 330.
24. Cf. *In re Board of Commerce Act, 1919, and Combines and Fair Prices Act, 1919* [1922] 1 A.C. 191; and *Proprietory Articles Trade Ass'n* v. *A.G. Canada (In re Combines Investigation Act and Section 498 of the Criminal Code)* [1931] A.C. 310.
25. *Citizens' Insurance Co.* v. *Parsons* (note 21), at p. 113. See also *Toronto Electric Commissioners* v. *Snider* (note 7); *A.G. Canada* v. *A.G. Alberta (Insurance Reference)* [1916] 1 A.C. 588; and *R.* v. *Eastern Terminal Elevator Co.* [1925] S.C.R. 434.
26. See Nicholas, ch. XXI, for the Australian situation. The 'inter-state free trade' clause is the most litigated in the Australian constitution.
27. *Johannesson* v. *West St. Paul* [1952] 1 S.C.R. 292. In the *Aeronautics Case* [1932] A.C. 54, the Dominion power was found to rest on a treaty coming under Section 132.
28. *Canada Year Book, 1961,* p. 599.
29. But only in a minimal way since the establishment of a Parliamentary Divorce Commissioner in 1963.

Chapter 19

1. O'Connor Report, pp. 12, 13.
2. Cf. *In re Initiative and Referendum Act* [1919] A.C. 935; *Hodge* v. *The Queen* (1883) 9 App. Cas. 117; *R.* v. *Ulmer* (1923) 38 C.C.C. 207; and *A.G. Nova Scotia* v. *Legislative Council of Nova Scotia* [1928] A.C. 107.
3. See Chapter 15, note 5.
4. For the fuss about salutes, see Saywell, pp. 14-17.
5. Cf. W.P.M. Kennedy, *The Constitution of Canada,* p. 381; and *In re Initiative and Referendum Act* (note 2).
6. *R.* v. *St. Louis* (1897) 1 C.C.C. 141, per Wurtele J., a most knowledgeable judge in criminal law.
7. There are some immaterial exceptions.
8. *R.* v. *Nat Bell Liquors Ltd.* [1922] 2 A.C. 128; *R.* v. *Gardner* (1892) 25 N.S.R. 48.
9. *Confederation Debates,* Hon. John A. Macdonald, p. 33, col. 2.
10. O'Connor Report, Annex 1, p. 110.
11. *Ibid.,* pp. 110-11.
12. *Ibid.,* p. 114.
13. *Ibid.,* p. 115.
14. See 36 Corpus Juris 967. 'Private law' is not a term of art in Anglo-American law and it is not indexed in the second edition of *Halsbury's Laws of England,* in *Bouvier's Law Dictionary,* in *Words and Phrases,*

or even in Cheshire's *Private International Law* or Dicey's text of
the same name. Cheshire uses the phrase. For the rationale of the
English attitude, see 7 Halsbury (3rd ed.) 187.

15. As O'Connor shows, the phrase 'property and civil rights' has a continuous history, in the meaning 'private law', from the British con-
quest of Quebec, through the Quebec Act of 1774 (Section 8), the
Acts of Upper Canada of 1792, the B.N.A. Act, 1867, and even
afterwards. See O'Connor Report, Annex 1, pp. 113-15.

16. See *Confederation Debates*: Langevin, pp. 388-9, 575, 579, 781;
Cauchon, pp. 577-8; Dorion, pp. 690-1; Geoffrion, pp. 775-81.
O'Connor's comment (Report, Annex 1, p. 120) that 'not a dozen
lines relate to this now tremendous power' over civil rights is therefore quite misleading.

Chapter 20

1. Rowell-Sirois Report, i.e., *Report of the Royal Commission on
Dominion-Provincial Relations* (Ottawa: King's Printer, 1940), Book
I, pp. 41, 43; Book II, p. 274. Also Dawson, *The Government of
Canada,* pp. 116-17.

2. The basic allotment:

Provincial Population		Grant to Province
Under	150,000	$100,000
150,000	200,000	150,000
200,000	400,000	180,000
400,000	800,000	190,000
800,000	1,500,000	220,000
1,500,000 and over		240,000

In addition, a grant of 80 cents a head up to a population of 2,500,000,
and 60 cents a head for population in excess of that. There were
special provisions for British Columbia and Prince Edward Island.

3. Rowell-Sirois Report, Book II, pp. 270-1.

4. *Ibid.,* 269 ff.

5. *Ibid.,* p. 271. Emphasis added.

6. *Ibid.,* p. 272. Here 'normal' means 'average'. Cf. p. 272, col. 1:
'It is not the service which each province is at present providing,
but the average Canadian standard of services, that a province must
be put in a position to finance.'

7. By the British North America Act, 1940, 3-4 Geo. VI (Imp.) ch. 36.
House of Commons Address moved and agreed to June 25, 1940.
Bill passed by Imperial parliament, July 10, 1940. Invitation to the
Conference from federal government, November 2, 1940. The period
is summarized in Dawson, *The Government of Canada,* pp. 126-9.

8. *Dominion-Provincial Conference, Tuesday, January 14, 1941, and*

Wednesday, January 15, 1941 (Ottawa: King's Printer, Z2-1941/2.1),
pp. 12-15, 79-80.

9. *Ibid.*, pp. 57-9.

10. *Ibid.*, pp. 38-9.

11. *Canada Year Book, 1945*, p. 951.

12. Confirmed by the Dominion-Provincial Taxation Agreement Act,
1942, 6 Geo. VI ch. 13, in force March 15, 1942.

13. The methods of compensation are outlined in the *Canada Year Book,
1942*, p. 748.

14. Conference proceedings, p. 74. Mr. Ilsley is now the Right Honourable, the Chief Justice of Nova Scotia.

15. *Dominion-Provincial Conference on Reconstruction, 1945-1946*
(Ottawa: King's Printer, Z2-1945/1.1), p. 113.

16. *Loc. cit.*, Hon. J. L. Ilsley.

17. *Dominion-Provincial Conference, 1960,* Ottawa, July 25, 26, and
27, 1960 (Ottawa: Queen's Printer Z2-1960/1), pp. 10-11.

18. *Ibid.*, pp. 17, 24-5.

19. *Ibid.*, pp. 27-9, translated at pp. 126-8.

20. *Ibid.*, pp. 32-4, translated at pp. 131-3.

21. The proceedings have not been printed for the public at the date of
writing, May 1964.

22. The proposals are summarized in the *Canada Year Book, 1961,*
p. 1069.

23. The quotations are from Canadian Press reports.

Chapter 21

1. *Dominion-Provincial Conference on Reconstruction, 1945-1946,*
p. 601.

2. *Ibid.*, p. 595.

3. *Ibid.*, p. 161.

4. *Ibid.*, p. 162. The Manitoba brief is very comprehensive, lucid, and
persuasive.

5. Cf. Dawson, *The Government of Canada,* pp. 116-17.

6. Rowell-Sirois Report, Book I, pp. 40, 64.

7. *The Canada Year Book, 1961,* p. 1035, is the source of the figures
for 1958.

8. Provincial access to the indirect sales tax has been mooted for years
and Mr. St. Laurent apparently agreed to it in 1955. See *Proceedings
of the Federal-Provincial Conference, 1955, Ottawa, October 3rd,
1955* (Ottawa: Queen's Printer, Z2-1955/2), p. 14.

9. All provinces, including Quebec and Ontario, seem to want annual
federal-provincial conferences with a permanent secretariat. See, for
example, Messrs. Drew and Duplessis in the proceedings of the 1945-
1946 Conference, p. 366. And see *Correspondence since the Budget*

of 1946 (Ottawa: King's Printer, Z2-1947/2), letters of Mr. Drew and Mr. King; the latter would not be so trapped (*ibid.*, p. 35).

10. Rowell-Sirois Report, Book I, p. 60.
11. Compare the figures in the Rowell-Sirois Report, Book I, p. 40 (Table 4), and p. 45 (Table 7). These do not agree with Table 6, p. 44, but if customs and excise are deducted from Table 6, the proportions of the remainder are much the same.
12. *Ibid.*, p. 41 (Table 5). This omits municipal expenditure, which was not on a comparable basis and did not affect the chief problems after 1867.
13. This has been accepted in study after study. The most lucid presentation of the case is that of Norman McL. Rogers on behalf of the Province of Nova Scotia to a Royal Commission established by that province in 1934. See p. 198 of his brief, *Royal Commission, Provincial Economic Inquiry, 1934* (Nova Scotia), 'A Submission on Dominion-Provincial Relations'. See also Dawson, *The Government of Canada*, p. 126.
14. The Rogers brief, *loc. cit.*
15. Cf. proceedings of the 1945-1946 Conference, pp. 242-3.
16. *Proceedings,* October 1955 Conference, p. 39.
17. *Proceedings of the Conference of Federal and Provincial Governments, December 4-7, 1950* (Ottawa: Queen's Printer, 1953. Z2-1950 /3), p. 54. (Note the change in the conference name, part of the movement to outgrow 'Dominion'. This usage started with the January 1950 conference.)
18. *Proceedings,* October 1955 Conference, p. 92.
19. Cf. proceedings 1945-1946, pp. 418-20; *Federal-Provincial Conference, 1955, Preliminary Meeting, Ottawa, April 26th, 1955* (Ottawa: Queen's Printer, Z2-1955/1), p. 26; *Dominion-Provincial Conference, 1957, Ottawa, November 25th and 26th, 1957* (Ottawa: Queen's Printer, 1958. Z2-1957/1), pp. 29-31. (Note the regression to 'Dominion').
20. For a choice example see *A.G. Nova Scotia* v. *Delamar* (1921) 54 N.S.R. 497, in which it was held that the province could not tax a transfer of shares in a Nova Scotia company because they were registered in New York. This case is good cause for omitting the expression 'within the Province'.
21. Nicholas, ch. XXI, p. 250.
22. (1819) 4 Wheaton 316, 4 L. Ed. 579.
23. See, for example, *Graves* v. *New York ex rel O'Keefe* (1939) 59 S. Ct. 595. See also Nicholas, pp. 7, 336.
24. Premier Macdonald at the 1945-1946 Conference called for a finance commission, similar to the one that operates in Australia, to calculate the necessary grants. See proceedings 1945-1946, pp. 418-20.

Chapter 22

1. Article I, Section 10, Clause 3. See, for example, *Virginia* v. *Tennessee* (1893) 13 S. Ct. 728.
2. The six are: (Ontario) The Dominion Courts Act, R.S.O. 1950, ch. 108; (Saskatchewan) The Dominion Courts Act, R.S.S. 1953, ch. 71; (New Brunswick) The Federal Courts Jurisdiction Act, R.S.N.B. 1952, ch. 83. British Columbia, Manitoba, and Newfoundland also use the latter title for their statutes in R.S.B.C. 1960, ch. 141; R.S.M. 1954, ch. 51; and 1954 Nfld. St. No. 13, respectively. The federal law is Section 30 of the Exchequer Court Act, R.S.C. 1952, ch. 98.
3. Lord Loreburn L.C. at p. 645, [1910] A.C. In the Supreme Court of Canada it was argued, and accepted by Iddington J., that the proper law was *lex loci* because the problem involved a contract respecting land in Ontario. This was hardly an accurate description of the claim, which was either quasi-contractual or an equitable claim arising out of improvements to land.
4. See, for example, *Beauharnois Light, Heat & Power Co.* v. *Ontario Hydro-Electric Power Commission* [1937] O.R. 796 and 847, holding that a province has no power to abrogate its contracts in derogation of civil rights outside the province. This abridges the external scope of its sovereignty decisively.

Chapter 23

1. The Constitution of the United States, Article I, Section 3, Clause 7.
2. The main differences are conveniently summed up in the *Encyclopaedia Britannica* under 'Impeachment'. Or see 9 Halsbury 360-1.

Chapter 24

1. 63 & 64 Vic. (Imp.) ch. 12.
2. Article VI, Clause 2.
3. Cf. the Criminal Code, Section 19; Justinian's Digest, 22, title 6, law 4.
4. See *R.* v. *Bailey* (1810) R. & R. 1, where a mariner was convicted of an offence against an act of parliament enacted while he was at sea. The offence was committed before the news of the enactment could reach him.
5. Bracton, folio 5b, as translated in 7 Halsbury 190, note f.
6. See *Fergus* v. *Marks* (1926) 152 N.E. 537. This is not really contrary to *Baker* v. *Carr* (1962) 82 S. Ct. 691, which makes no suggestion as to procedure. *U.S. News and World Report,* May 21, 1962, has a story on the then pending suits at p. 52. *Newsweek,* April 9, 1962, has an excellent article on *Baker* v. *Carr.*

7. *Stockdale v. Hansard* (1839) 9 Ad. & El. 1; (1840) 113 E.R. 405, 411. See Chapter 12, note 10, for the story.
8. Visiting Forces (British Commonwealth) Act, R.S.C. 1952, ch. 283; Visiting Forces (North Atlantic Treaty) Act, R.S.C. 1952, ch. 284; Visiting Forces (United States of America) Act, R.S.C. 1952, ch. 285. The last has been merged in the second.
9. Criminal Code, Section 12.
10. The phrase 'the rule of law' was made popular by Dicey. See A. V. Dicey, *Introduction to the Study of the Law of the Constitution* (London: 1885), Part II: 'The Rule of Law'.
11. E.g., *Plessy v. Ferguson* (1896) 163 U.S. 537, where the United States Supreme Court held that if the civil and political rights of both races are equal, that is sufficient. The Constitution did not aim at social equality, and separate public conveyances were not unreasonable.
12. *Sweatt v. Painter* (1950) 70 S. Ct. 848; and *McLaurin v. Oklahoma State Regents* (1950) 70 S. Ct. 851.
13. (1954) 74 S. Ct. 686.
14. *State Board of Tax Commissioners of Indiana v. Jackson* (1931) 283 U.S. 527.
15. *Kotch v. Board of River Port Pilots Commissioners for the Port of New Orleans* (1947) 67 S. Ct. 910.
16. *Terrace v. Thompson* (1923) 263 U.S. 197 (in which alienage was held to be a reasonable basis for barring a person from owning land); *Plessy v. Ferguson* (note 11); *State Board of Tax Commissioners v. Jackson* (note 14); *Kotch v. Board of River Port etc.* (note 15); *Baker v. Carr* (note 6).
17. E.g., France, Germany, Japan, U.S.A.
18. E.g., East Germany, Ireland, Italy, Switzerland, U.S.S.R.
19. The text of the Declaration will be found in (1949) 27 Can. Bar Rev. 203. Article 7 reads:
    > All are equal before the law and are entitled without any discrimination to equal protection of the law. All are entitled to equal protection against any discrimination in violation of this Declaration and against any incitement to such discrimination.

    The first sentence became Article 5 of Senator Roebuck's project to add a bill of rights to the B.N.A. Act. The Canadian Bill of Rights recognizes and declares 'the right of the individual to equality before the law and the protection of the law'. The statement that this right has existed is not altogether true and the matters in Section 1 of this bill are also so generally stated as to be of dubious worth.
20. The history is given by D. J. Goodspeed in 'The Canadian Revolution', *Queen's Quarterly*, vol. 64, p. 521. Mr. J. B. McGeachy argues for the revival of knighthoods (but not of hereditary titles) in 'Will

Knighthood Flower Again?', *The Financial Post,* November 30, 1957, p. 7.

21. E.g., Quebec Civil Code, Articles 326, 349, 351.

22. Article 15 of Senator Roebuck's bill of rights is identical. The Canadian Bill of Rights states only that 'freedom of religion' has existed and will continue to exist and no law shall be construed or applied to abridge it. The Supreme Court of Canada achieved a more concrete result in *Saumur* v. *Quebec* [1953] S.C.R. 299 without the help of the act.

23. *Marsh* v. *State of Alabama* (1946) 66 S. Ct. 276.

24. *R.* v. *Hicklin* (1868) L.R. 3 Q.B. 360.

25. Roman Catholics may not be Lord Chancellor, or High Commissioner of the Church of Scotland. Protestant dissenters may, and (possibly) Jews. Cf. 7 Halsbury 367, and 13 Halsbury 520 ff.

26. Article 13 (Italy); Article 12 (Germany); Article 18 (Japan). It is a fairly direct carry-over of the United States Thirteenth Amendment.

27. *Bailey* v. *Alabama* (1911) 219 U.S. 219. An Alabama statute made failure to carry out a work contract *prima facie* evidence of intent to defraud. The U.S. Supreme Court held this was an unconstitutional device used to force fulfilment of the contract by threat of criminal sanctions.

Chapter 25

1. Probably ch. XXIX, *Nullus liber homo capiatur . . . nisi per legale judicium parium suorum vel per legem terre.* Ruffhead, *Statutes at Large,* Runnington Edition (London, 1786), p. 7.

2. 28 Edw. III ch. 3 (1354): *Item qe nul homme de quel estate ou condition qil soit ne soit oste de terre ne de tenement ne pris nemptisone ne desherite ne mis a la mort saunz etre mesne en respons par due proces de lei.* Ruffhead, p. 277. (Is *nemptisone* a misprint for *nemprisone?*)

3. The Canadian Bill of Rights, Section 2 (e).

4. As used in the Canadian Bill of Rights, Section 1 (a): 'the right not to be deprived thereof except by due process of law'.

5. The Constitution of Australia, Section 80.

6. (*Dred*) *Scott* v. *Sandford* (1857) 19 Howard 393. This was the case that upset the Missouri Compromise. Scott, a slave, was taken to a free state, then back to Missouri. His claim that he had been freed by the status laws of the free state was disallowed. Contrast *Somerset* v. *Stewart* (1772) 98 E.R. 499, in which Mansfield C. J. held that any

slave who came to England was *ipso facto* free. See also *Smith* v.
Brown (1705) 91 E.R. 566.

7. *A.G. Canada* v. *Bégin* [1955] S.C.R. 593, 112 C.C.C. 209; *R.* v.
McNamara (1951) 99 C.C.C. 107; *Kuruma* v. *R.* [1955] A.C. 197.

8. See 15 Halsbury 260.

9. Compare *Kennedy* v. *Tomlinson* (1959) 20 D.L.R. (2d) 273, and
Langlais v. *R.* [1960] Que. S.C. 644.

10. E.g., Criminal Code, Sections 221, 222, 223, 225 (3). An arrest may
be justifiable although it is illegal, but the way this result is arrived at
in the Code encourages escapes, rescues, and breaches of the peace.

11. Criminal Code, Section 435, as amended by Stats. Can. 1961, ch. 43,
Section 14.

12. *West Virginia State Board of Education* v. *Barnette* (1943) 63 S. Ct.
1178. Jackson J. used the expression in holding that 'no official, high
or petty, can prescribe what shall be orthodox in politics'.

13. Income Tax Act, R.S.C. 1952, ch. 148, Section 126.

14. Criminal Code, Section 29 (2).

15. Canadian Bill of Rights, Section 2 (c) (i).

16. Criminal Code, Section 438 (2).

17. Canadian Bill of Rights, Sections 2 (c) (ii) and 2 (f).

18. In *Re Somervill's Prohibition Application* (1962) 38 W.W.R. 344,
Disbery J. said, 'Every citizen in custody has the right to make an
application for bail at any time,' but he cites no authority for this
proposition. It does not clearly follow from either the Criminal Code
or the Canadian Bill of Rights.

19. Sir James Fitzjames Stephen, *History of the Criminal Law of England*
(London: Macmillan, 1883), vol. 1, pp. 221-230, 497.

20. Compare *R.* v. *Carroll* (1960) 31 C.R. 315, and *R.* v. *Patrick* [1960]
O.W.N. 206, with *Hinchcliffe* v. *Sheldon* [1955] 3 All E.R. 406, and
R. v. *L.* (1922) 51 O.L.R. 575.

21. One Nova Scotia judge died leaving cases over eight years old unde-
cided. The Nova Scotia Judicature Act, Section 42 (4), gives a judge
sixty days to make up his mind, but it does not state what happens if
he fails to.

22. Juvenile Delinquents Act, Section 12; Criminal Code, Section 427.

23. Criminal Code, Section 428.

24. In the Sixth Amendment of the U.S. Constitution: 'In all criminal
prosecutions the accused shall enjoy the right to a speedy and public
trial . . . . ' See also 16 Corpus Juris 807, Section 1052, regarding
publicity of trial, and cases there cited.

25. E.g., Quebec Code of Civil Procedure, Articles 237 to 250.

26. Cf. *R.* v. *Milledge* (1879) 4 Q.B.D. 332; *R.* v. *Woodroof* (1912) 20 C.C.C. 17; *R.* v. *Sussex JJ. ex parte McCarthy* [1924] 1 K.B. 256.
27. *Powell* v. *Alabama* (1932) 287 U.S. 45.
28. Section 1 (a).
29. Cf. cases cited in the practice texts under Order II, Rule 1, and Order XVIIIA (now long repealed) of the English Rules of the Supreme Court, 1883. The English rules are the bases of most Canadian ones.
30. *R.* v. *Simmons* [1923] 3 W.W.R. 749; *Kelley* v. *R.* (1917) 54 S.C.R. 220; *R.* v. *Sylvester* (1912) 45 N.S.R. 525; *R.* v. *Canny* (1945) 30 C.A.R. 143; *R.* v. *Kingston* (1948) 32 C.A.R. 183.
31. Compare *R.* v. *Picariello and Lassandro* (1923) 39 C.C.C. 229, and *Woolmington* v. *D.P.P.* [1935] A.C. 462; *D.P.P.* v. *Beard* [1920] A.C. 479; and Section 16 (4) of the Criminal Code.
32. Listed in the Criminal Code, Section 467.
33. Cf. opinion of Wurtele J. in 1898 noted in *Tremeear's Criminal Code,* 5th ed., at p. 1092, and in *Verroneau* v. *R.* (1916) 54 S.C.R. 7.
34. Wigmore, vol. VIII (*McNaughton Revision, 1961*), Sections 2250, 2251, gives an exhaustive review of the privilege and of the policies usually proposed in its favour.
35. Canada Evidence Act, Section 4 (5).
36. Cf., for example, *Buck* v. *Bell* (1927) 274 U.S. 200.
37. Vehicles Act, 1957 Sask. Laws, ch. 93, Section 92 (4).
38. *Reference re Vehicles Act s. 92 (4)* [1958] S.C.R. 608.
39. The Constitution of the Federal Republic of Germany, Article 104 (1).
40. The Constitution of the Italian Republic, Article 13.
41. *Ibid.,* Article 27.
42. The Constitution of Japan, Article 36.
43. Cf. Catherine Drinker Bowen, *The Lion and the Throne,* pp. 91-2.
44. In *Calder* v. *Bull* (1798) 3 Dallas 386, per Chase J.
45. Cf. Salmond, *The Law of Torts* (9th ed. London: Sweet, 1936), pp. 17 ff.
46. The Exchequer Court Act, R.S.C. 1952, ch. 98, especially Sections 18 and 46-8; The Expropriation Act, R.S.C. 1952, ch. 106, especially Sections 8 and 16.
47. *Woods Mfg. Co.* v. *R.* [1951] S.C.R. 504, per Kerwin J. (later C.J. Can.).
48. F. O. Arnold, *The Law of Damages and Compensation* (London: Butterworth, 1913), pp. 1, 7, 8.
49. *Parkinson's Law,* ch. 6.

Chapter 26

1. Compare the description of 'Socialization' in *Mater et Magistra,* Encyclical Letter of His Holiness, Pope John XXIII, May 15, 1961,

Section 59. English translation by William J. Gibbons, S.J. (New York: The Paulist Press, 1961).

2. 2 Thessalonians 3, verse 10.

3. For example, Constitution of the French Republic, 1946, preamble; Constitution of the Italian Republic, Article 40. See also Constitution of the German Democratic Republic (East Germany), Article 14.

4. Constitution of the U.S.S.R. (1936), Articles 1 and 4.

5. *Ibid.,* Article 9.

6. For example: U.S.A., Amendments IV, V; France, Declaration of Rights, 1789, Articles 2, 17; Germany, Article 14 (1); East Germany, Article 22; Italy, Article 42; Japan, Article 29; U.S.S.R., Article 10.

7. Article 27 (2) of the Universal Declaration of Human Rights protects copyright and the like.

8. Table VIII, fragment 27.

9. Gaius, libro IV. ad L. XII Tab. fr. 4. D. de collegiis (47, 22).

10. Identical with Article 17 of Senator Roebuck's bill.

11. The similar provision in the First Amendment to the United States Constitution is a privilege of citizens. See *Hague* v. *C.I.O.* (1939) 307 U.S. 496.

12. *Schenck* v. *United States* (1919) 249 U.S. 47; *Dennis* v. *United States* (1951) 71 S. Ct. 857.

13. *Boucher* v. *R.* [1951] S.C.R. 265.

14. *Ibid.,* per Cartwright J.

15. Universal Declaration of Human Rights, Article 16 (2); Roebuck bill, Article 12 (2).

16. For a discussion see the articles 'Marriage', 'Polyandry', and 'Polygyny' in the *Encyclopaedia Britannica.*

17. *Quadragesimo Anno,* Encyclical Letter of His Holiness, Pope Pius XI, May 15, 1931, Section 79 of the English translation in *Five Great Encyclicals* (New York: The Paulist Press, 1939). This book contains also a different translation of *Rerum Novarum* from that in Etienne Gilson, ed., *The Church Speaks to the Modern World* (New York: Doubleday Image Books, 1954), pp. 206-7.

18. It is implicit in several passages of *Rerum Novarum*: cf. Sections 4, 7, 14, 35-6, 45, 51, and 55 in the translation in *The Church Speaks to the Modern World*. See also *Mater et Magistra,* note 1.

19. Child Welfare Act, R.S.N.S. 1954, ch. 30, Section 1 (h). Other provinces have similar legislation.

20. Manitoba Act, 33 Vic. (Can.) ch. 3, Section 22, confirmed by the British North America Act, 1871; The Alberta Act, 4-5 Edw. VII (Can.) ch. 3, Section 17; The Saskatchewan Act, 4-5 Edw. VII (Can.) ch. 42, Section 17.

21. The story is given in *Manitoba: A History,* by W. L. Morton (University of Toronto Press, 1957).

22. The British North America Act, 1949, 12-13 Geo. VI (Imp.) ch. 22, Term 17.
23. There are only two such in the B.N.A. Act; the other is that respecting the English and French languages in Section 133.
24. Constitution of the German Democratic Republic, Article 43.
25. Although Catholicism might be said to be the established religion of Italy, Article 7 of the Constitution of the Italian Republic asserts: 'The state and the Catholic Church are, each in its own order, independent and sovereign', and Article 8 extends a similar independence to other religious confessions.
26. R.S.C. 1952, ch. 288, as amended by 1960, ch. 44, Section 6.

Chapter 27

1. Cf. Dawson, *The Government of Canada,* ch. VII; *Constitutional Amendment in Canada* by Paul Gérin-Lajoie (University of Toronto Press, 1950); 'Du pouvoir d'amendement constitutionel au Canada' by Paul Gérin-Lajoie (1951) 29 Can. Bar Rev. 1136 (a summary in French of some points in the book); *Federalism and Constitutional Change* by William S. Livingston, ch. 2; there are several earlier articles in the *Canadian Bar Review.*
2. B.N.A. Act, 1867, Section 92, Class 1.
3. B.N.A. Act, 1867, Section 91, Class 1, as enacted by the B.N.A. (No. 2) Act, 1949.
4. A phrase in the 1907 Amendment, as proposed, was deleted in Great Britain, ostensibly because it purported to bind future parliaments but probably because the sentiments of the Imperial government agreed with those expressed by Premier McBride of British Columbia about the phrase. For a different view, see Livingston, pp. 56-8 and 78.
5. Thus the 1871 Amendment confirmed the North-West Territories Act and the Manitoba Act; the Parliament of Canada Act, 1871, confirmed the Oaths of Allegiance Act; and the Canadian Speaker (Appointment of Deputy) Act confirmed Dominion legislation appointing a Deputy Speaker.
6. Dr. Livingston (at p. 60) was evidently bemused by a characteristic Mackenzie King statement concerning the 1940 Amendment. The prime minister argued that the government had avoided any concession to the 'compact theory' by getting the consent of all the provinces to the change.
7. *Proceedings of the Constitutional Conference of Federal and Provincial Governments, January 10-12, 1950* (Ottawa: King's Printer, 1950), p. 117.
8. *Proceedings of the Constitutional Conference of Federal and Provincial Governments (Second Session), Quebec, September 25-28,*

1950 (Ottawa: King's Printer, 1950), Appendix III (appendices I to IV thereto), pp. 79-86, and Appendix IV, pp. 86-130.

9. 4 *Canadian Bar Journal* 330, August 1961.

10. 'Delegation – A Way over the Constitutional Hurdle' by Raphael Tuck (1945) 23 Can. Bar Rev. 79.

11. *A.G. Nova Scotia* v. *A.G. Canada* [1951] S.C.R. 31.

12. With all due respect to the views of Anglo-Catholics, in constitutional law and practical politics they are Protestants. On the other hand, Jehovah's Witnesses are probably not Protestants. For differing views, see *Chabot* v. *Commissaires d'Ecoles de Lamorandière* [1958] R.L. 204, reversed [1957] Que. Q.B. 707. Jews are not Protestants: see *Hirsch* v. *Protestant Board of School Commissioners* [1928] A.C. 200.

13. Cf. the text and the article of Gérin-Lajoie cited in note 1.

14. The equivalent provision in the Constitution of the United States cannot, it is considered, be amended.

15. The Fulton Formula withdraws education from the Class 3 provisions and puts it in a special category. In this, Newfoundland is in splendid isolation. It is submitted that it is better to treat the entrenched rights in education as a national question (because it is truly a matter of basic human rights) while preserving the historic development in the different provinces. That was the purpose of putting education in our Article 11.

16. E.g., the Ontario and Quebec Boundaries Extension Acts of 1912 provide that Indians are to have certain rights. The Terms of Union with Newfoundland scheduled to the British North America Act, 1949, provide that Newfoundland war veterans are to have the same rights as Canadian war veterans.

17. The author has not searched the sources for an answer to the implied question, as it did not seem worth while. The governments concerned could, no doubt, provide the answers if the question became important.

18. Cf. *Scott* v. *A.G. Canada* [1923] 4 D.L.R. 647, reversing 64 S.C.R. 135. The Alberta legislature split its Supreme Court into appellate and trial divisions and the Dominion government appointed a new chief justice over the head of the former chief justice of Alberta, who was named chief justice of the trial division. This is the kind of skulduggery that goes without challenge in a 'responsible goverment' polity because the wrong done to the former chief justice was not of a nature to rouse much public sympathy or reaction. The absoluteness of the cabinet system can only be checked by a strong tradition or a very powerful public revulsion.

Index

Where a number is followed by a bracketed number, the latter is the text page.

318